Do They Miss Me at Home?

DO THEY MISS ME AT HOME?

The Civil War Letters of William McKnight,

Seventh Ohio Volunteer Cavalry

Edited by

Donald C. Maness
and H. Jason Combs

OHIO UNIVERSITY PRESS ◆ ATHENS

Ohio University Press, Athens, Ohio 45701
www.ohioswallow.com
© 2010 by Ohio University Press
All rights reserved

To obtain permission to quote, reprint, or otherwise reproduce or distribute material from Ohio University Press publications, please contact our rights and permissions department at (740) 593-1154 or (740) 593-4536 (fax).

Printed in the United States of America
Ohio University Press books are printed on acid-free paper ♾ ™

First paperback printing in 2012
ISBN 978-0-8214-2008-9

HARDCOVER 18 17 16 15 14 13 12 11 10   5 4 3 2 1
PAPERBACK 20 19 18 17 16 15 14 13 12   5 4 3 2 1

Library of Congress Cataloging-in-Publication Data

McKnight, William, 1832–1864.
  Do they miss me at home? : the Civil War letters of William McKnight, Seventh Ohio Volunteer Cavalry / edited by Donald C. Maness and H. Jason Combs.
      p. cm.
  Includes bibliographical references and index.
  ISBN 978-0-8214-1914-4 (hardcover : alk. paper)
 1. McKnight, William, 1832–1864—Correspondence. 2. Soldiers—Ohio—Correspondence. 3. United States. Army. Ohio Cavalry Regiment, 7th (1862–1865) 4. Ohio—History—Civil War, 1861–1865—Personal narratives. 5. United States—History—Civil War, 1861–1865—Personal narratives. 6. Ohio—History—Civil War, 1861–1865—Regimental histories. 7. United States—History—Civil War, 1861–1865—Regimental histories. 8. Langsville (Ohio)—Biography. I. Maness, Donald C., 1942– II. Combs, H. Jason, 1970– III. Title.
  E525.67th .M35 2010
  973.7'471—dc22
                          2009046151

We dedicate this book to our wonderful wives, Connie and Gayle,

who have provided love, support,

and understanding, which allowed us the opportunity

to present the untold story of

William McKnight

Contents

	List of Illustrations	ix
	Preface	xi
	Acknowledgments	xiii
	Editorial Comments	xv
	Introduction	1
Chapter 1.	Preparing for War (September 1862–January 1, 1863)	18
Chapter 2.	Life as a Soldier and Divided Kentucky (January 8, 1863–July 8, 1863)	35
Chapter 3.	The Fourth of July Presents and John Hunt Morgan's Raid (July 11, 1863–August 20, 1863)	107
Chapter 4.	Going for Dixie (August 25, 1863–March 28, 1864)	121
Chapter 5.	The Final Months (April 1, 1864–June 21, 1864)	167
	Epilogue	190
Appendix A.	Ohio Civil War Troop Statistics	195
Appendix B.	List of Officers, Seventh Regiment Ohio Volunteer Cavalry	197
Appendix C.	Major Engagements Listed for the Seventh Ohio Volunteer Cavalry	200

Appendix D.	Official Roster, Company K, Seventh Ohio Volunteer Cavalry	201
Appendix E.	William McKnight's Poem to Samaria, April 4, 1852	209
	Notes	211
	References	259
	Index	267

Illustrations

Figures

Envelopes addressed to Samaria McKnight	xi
Envelopes addressed to Samaria McKnight and Lieutenant William McKnight	xii
William McKnight	2
Samaria McKnight	3
Martin Entsminger	7
Addison Braley	7
Alexander Braley	7
The Braley sisters	7
William McKnight's original commission papers	13
William McKnight's poem to Samaria Braley, April 4, 1852	15
William McKnight's letter to Samaria, November 14, 1862	21
William McKnight's letter to Samaria, November 18, 1862	22
Civil War stationery symbol	23
William McKnight's letter to Samaria, November 25, 1862	24
Lettie McKnight	41
Leila McKnight	41
Mary Lucy McKnight	41
Thomas McKnight	83
Martha and Myrtha McKnight	111
Mattie (Martha) McKnight	111
Letter from William to Samaria written on paper from railroad ledger book	131
Tombstone receipt for Levi Little and Warren Coulter of the 7th OVC	133

Private William Lemon Johnson	141
Colonel Santmyer's orders used by McKnight for a letter to Samaria	149
Lock of William McKnight's hair sent to Samaria	185
Samaria and the McKnight girls	192
Flood of Langsville, Ohio, 1908	194

Maps

Meigs County, Ohio	12
Important Civil War locations in Kentucky, Ohio, and West Virginia	38
Important Civil War locations in Alabama, Georgia, Mississippi, and Tennessee	123

Preface

A letter dated September 14, 1863, from William McKnight to his wife, Samaria, describes General Ambrose Burnside's operations in eastern Tennessee and the Union action around the Cumberland Gap. Reading the letter, I was intrigued about the possibility of additional letters in the family's possession. Matt Hauger provided the September 14, 1863, letter and indicated that his family had additional correspondence, approximately thirty to forty more letters.[1] Further inquiry elicited that there are well over one hundred letters in the McKnight collection. The letters were in two locations: some were in the possession of Terry Hauger (Matt's father); the others were with an aunt in Ohio (one additional letter was added to the collection by Ruth Hayth of Wellston, Ohio).[2] A few short months later, the collection was in one site, and I was provided the opportunity to review,

Envelopes addressed to Samaria McKnight. *Courtesy of Terry Hauger.*

copy, and transcribe the letters with the family's blessing. Most of the letters are written on fibrous paper and folded in the original envelopes, approximately three by five inches in size.

As the project was developing, I invited Jason Combs to join me as co-editor. His scholarship and writing skills have been great additions to the research and editing of the letters. We have worked well together, as our abilities complement each other. Working with William McKnight's descendants throughout this project has been worthwhile both personally and professionally, and we thank them for their generosity and goodwill.

Envelopes addressed to Samaria McKnight and Lieutenant William McKnight. *Courtesy of Terry Hauger.*

Acknowledgments

The authors would like to personally thank McKnight family members Matt Hauger, Terry Hauger, Susan Hayes, Ruth Hayth, Mary Johnston, and Lois Mohler.[1] Matt Hauger provided us the majority of the letters, while Susan Hayes, Ruth Hayth, and Mary Johnston contributed valuable family history, copies of the diaries, and photos. The staff at the Meigs County Historical Society and the Meigs County Public Library deserve recognition as well—Margaret Parker and Robin Parker from the Meigs County Historical Society and Wanda Ashley at the public library were invaluable sources of information and material. Additionally, Linda Keller (interlibrary loan supervisor at Arkansas State University), Sheryl Heidenreich (interlibrary loan coordinator at the University of Nebraska–Kearney), and Ruby Rogers (director of the Cincinnati Historical Society Library) deserve recognition for retrieving and recommending dozens of books and articles in a most professional manner. Furthermore, Keith Ashley, who is a noted Civil War historian from Meigs County; Donald Johnson, who is William Lemon Johnson's great-grandson; and Brian Johnson (Donald Johnson's son) provided information about Morgan's Raid and the Seventh Ohio Volunteer Cavalry. A special thanks goes to Mary Maness for her transcription and word processing skills and abilities. Without her assistance, the project would have been considerably delayed. The editors appreciate the advice and counsel provided by Dr. Steven Woodworth, a prolific Civil War scholar and professor at Texas Christian University. We would also like to thank Gillian Berchowitz, senior editor at Ohio University Press; Nancy Basmajian, managing editor; the staff members at Ohio University Press; and the anonymous reviewers for their insights, constructive comments, and professionalism. Finally, to everyone previously noted and a host of friends, we say thank you for your encouragement and support.

Editorial Comments

The collection was transcribed in McKnight's words. For instance, misspelled words were not corrected, and capitalized words within sentences remained as such, although the first word of each sentence was capitalized. Slight punctuation, however, was required to maintain consistent flow. Periods were sparingly used to allow more accuracy and convenience in reading. When a period was inserted, the word starting the following sentence was capitalized. Furthermore, each letter's heading was standardized for date (all dates were spelled out) and location. Additionally, ellipsis points were used in place of illegible words and phrases. The editors take full responsibility for any transcription errors.

Introduction

During the Civil War, letters were among the few connections to home that soldiers had; their importance increased as the war advanced and troops found themselves farther from family and friends.[1] Soldiers constantly complained of not receiving "enough letters," and one soldier wrote, "You can have no idea what a blessing letters from home are to the men in camp. They make us better men, better soldiers."[2] Today, such correspondence offers "authentic, unfiltered glimpses of the realities of war," and with "careful editing, collected letters provide fascinating sources of information about the people and the times of the Civil War."[3]

Thwarting loneliness and homesickness, Civil War letters were mailed in large numbers. On the "Union side, 45,000 were sent daily via Washington to members of the Eastern armies and an equal number went off from soldiers to those at home. Ninety thousand more passed daily via Louisville for and from soldiers in the Western armies."[4]

Several accounts indicate that "ordinary soldiers were perhaps the most prolific writers."[5] Most "soldiers spent their free time writing letters home, detailing their reactions to their new surroundings, politics, and emotions."[6] Indeed, numberless soldiers filled their "journals, their letters home, and their memoirs with the moral values they knew to be at issue in the conflict between North and South: manliness, godliness, duty, [and] honor."[7]

INTRODUCTION

The McKnight Collection of Civil War Letters

William McKnight of Langsville, Ohio, was one such common soldier who contributed to the thousands of letters sent daily. McKnight was a member of the Seventh Ohio Volunteer Cavalry (OVC) from September 1862 until

William McKnight of the Seventh Ohio Volunteer Cavalry. *Courtesy of Ruth Hayth.*

his death in June 1864. During his time in the service, McKnight penned dozens of letters, primarily to his wife, Samaria. McKnight's writings reveal his viewpoints, emotions, and thoughts—the human side of the Civil War.[8]

In total, there are 108 letters in the collection. The vast majority are from William to Samaria, whom he also refers to as "Mary" and "Molly."[9] The letters are extremely accurate.[10] McKnight mentions dozens of battles, dates, people, and places, and his letters closely follow the official record (OR) and the accounts that deal specifically with Ohio and the Seventh—Whitlaw Reid's two-volume *Ohio in the War* (1895a; 1895b) and R. C. Rankin's *History of the Seventh Ohio Volunteer Cavalry* (1881). The remaining correspondence is primarily from Samaria to William and from other family members to William (see appendix A).[11]

The pervasiveness of loneliness, suffered by thousands of soldiers, is documented in histories by Civil War scholars such as Gary Gallagher (Gallagher et al. 2003), Gerald Linderman (1987), and Steven Woodworth (1996). In one of his first letters home, McKnight confesses, "I had to get up and leave the table to hide my tears warm tears of love for you and the little ones at home."[12] On November 26, 1862, McKnight remarks that his "mind is constantly turning homewards."[13] In one of the last letters before he is killed in action, McKnight expresses his homesickness and notes, "if I owned this whole State I would give it to be with you and this war at an end so that we might never more be separated."[14]

Coupled with McKnight's loneliness is his desire to receive a "likeness." Historian Andrew Carroll states that "what makes the letters so powerful is not only the history they record but also the common humanity they reveal"; part of this humanity is reflected in the "homesickness felt by Civil War soldiers who thanked their sweethearts for sending them 'likenesses.'"[15] On January 9, 1863, McKnight writes to Samaria, "I keep your likeness in my Pocket al the time and it is great comfort to look at your sweet face.

Samaria McKnight, Rutland Township, Meigs County, Ohio. *Courtesy of Ruth Hayth.*

Although it dont speak it seems so near & dear to me."[16] A few days later, McKnight states, "Your likeness is a great Comfort to me" and later adds, "I wish I could get the childrens likenesses."[17] In an undated letter to his son, Thomas McKnight describes William's likeness and shares "oh how Dear it looks to me."[18]

In addition to loneliness and family matters, McKnight writes of his patriotic beliefs, a sense of duty and honor and commitment to his country.[19] Early in the war, McKnight shares that "I like Soldering foral the hardships I go with a wil. I think it my Duty and Calling" and that he perseveres for the "sake of [his] family and Country."[20] In hearing the good news from Vicksburg, Mississippi, McKnight pens that the "news of the success of our arms is cheering to evry Union loveing heart and to none more so than the soldier who has left home and evrything thing near and dear to him and Perils his life for his Countries sake."[21] Finally, McKnight frequently reveals his desire for the war's end: "when peace spread her majestic wings ore this crushed & heart bleeding Country & the Clash of arms shal be nomore."[22]

Believing duty and honor to be essential parts of a soldier's character and responsibility, McKnight was deeply troubled by comrades who deserted.[23] McKnight writes, "Rather would I have my Dear little children . . . say that Pa was killed in War . . . than have it thrown up to them that [their] father was a *Deserter.*"[24] A few months later, McKnight identifies several men who deserted: "R. T. Andrews and Wm Burns has Deserted yes and Harry Spires and E. Andrews the[y] have reached home. They have disgraced themselves by their conduct."[25]

A devout Christian, McKnight displays an untenuous faith, which was common for Civil War soldiers and was "another buttress of the war's moral framework for both soldiers and civilians."[26] McKnight, for instance, frequently closes his letters with a prayer for his family and asks them to do the same for him. McKnight encourages Samaria, "Put your trust in him who is able and willing to save and who has always showered Blessings on our heads. Surely goodness and mercy has followed us al the days of our lives."[27] McKnight closes another letter with a similar sentiment: "All the Consolation is that God in his infinite Mercy doeth all things wel. His wil be done."[28] McKnight also relies on his faith to cope with the hardships of war. In May 1863, McKnight confesses, "I had rather a narrow escape. . . . As it is I feel thankful to the kind Providence for his mercies shown," and then on June 2, 1863, in regard to Isaac Meaner's death, McKnight writes, "but he that giveth and he that can take away gave him an everlasting one. One that we are all shure of sooner or later."²⁹ Finally, McKnight provides Samaria with godly advice for their children: "Bring them up in they way that they should go and you never wil have cause to regret it," and "Teach them to love the *Savior* for he says in the *Holy Book* to Suffer little *Children* to *come unto me & forbid them* not for of *such* is the *Kingdom* of *heaven*."³⁰

McKnight's writings reveal great respect and admiration for one of his commanding officers—Captain Joel Higley.³¹ McKnight often speaks of Higley and describes him as the "best and truest friend that I had this side of the great water."³² McKnight also states, "He [Higley] and I are like true Brothers. He sticks to me all the time."³³ McKnight adds, "I wish this world contained more men of Captain Higleys qualities."³⁴

Captain Higley's death profoundly affected McKnight.³⁵ Higley was killed in action at the battle of Blue Springs on October 10, 1863.³⁶ McKnight describes Higley's death to Samaria: "I discover to my Horror our Brave & Noble Capt laying upon his Face upon the Ground. Hastening to him & speaking kindly to him receiving no answer I seen he was mortaly wounded. He never spoke."³⁷ Higley was later described as a "most valuable officer, who was commanding a battalion and was killed in the thickest of the fight while encouraging and leading his men."³⁸ An entry in McKnight's diary comes to a similar conclusion: "Capt. Higley was instantly killed at the head of his Comd."³⁹ Approximately five months after Higley's death, while visiting his grave, McKnight writes, "But alas he is laid in the Cold Cold ground on the silent Breeses of the suny South lighs a requiem over his unwept and untimely Grave. I have visited his grave thre times since we came here. The last time placed with my own hands a Decent tomb Stone to mark the resting place of him we all loved."⁴⁰

Finally, McKnight was deeply concerned about Samaria's well-being and her ability to support herself and the children. McKnight frequently questioned whether folks from Meigs County had paid their debts for the blacksmith services he provided before leaving for the war. On August 4, 1863, McKnight writes, "I would like to know whether you have money enough and how you get along." Nearly a year later, on May 10, 1864, McKnight pens, "I want to send you plenty of money to live on so if you are deprived of my Company you wil not suffer bodily nor those dear little ones come to want as I hope they never may" and "I am going to send my over coat home and some money enough to by the little ones and yourself some summer ware. I felt as though I had not done enough for my family but I have been in such circumstances that I could not help it."

After the war, much of the burden of caring for soldiers and their families shifted to the government. Historian Megan McClintock states that this had a tremendous impact on the federal budget. By 1890, the annual budget "for the Bureau of Pensions was $106 million, and the federal government had paid over $1 billion for Civil War pensions alone."[41] Moreover, in 1893, "over 40 percent of the federal budget went to support widows, orphans, the elderly and invalid soldiers."[42] Samaria McKnight was one of the many widows who received a government pension. Initially, the stipend was two dollars per month per child; according to Samaria's pension records in 1874, that amount increased to fifteen dollars per month, which she received until her death in 1905.[43]

The McKnight Family

William McKnight's parents were Thomas McKnight and Jane McMaster. Both were born in Dumfrieshire, Scotland—Thomas on January 12, 1803; Jane on February 5, 1805.[44] Thomas and Jane McKnight left Scotland in 1830 with two children (Susan, born in 1826, and Jeanett, born in 1828) and arrived in Napan, New Brunswick, the same year with two children: although Jeanett died at sea, Samuel was born at sea. After spending six years in Canada, where they had three more children—Jeanett II (born in 1831), William (born in 1832), and John (born in 1835)—the McKnight family settled in Pomeroy, Meigs County, Ohio, in 1836. In 1840, they moved across the county to Langsville and proceeded to have six more children: James (born in 1837), Mary (born in 1837), James II (born in 1838), Mary Jane (born in 1843), Elizabeth (born in 1846), and Samuel (born in 1847). Both of McKnight's parents died in Meigs County, but they outlived their son. Thomas died in 1873, followed by Jane in 1875.

William McKnight, who had eleven siblings, was born on July 2, 1832, in New Brunswick, Canada, and married Samaria Braley (born October 31, 1837, in Meigs County, Ohio) on March 8, 1855.[45] Samaria was one of nine children born to Ruel Braley (born in Maine on January 17, 1810) and Cynthia Rathburn (born May 9, 1812, in Rutland, Ohio).[46] The Braleys, "of Mayflower descent," were among the earliest Meigs County settlers, arriving from Maine around 1816.[47] William was a blacksmith by trade. At the Civil War's onset, William and Samaria had four children—Leila (born July 26, 1855), Thomas (born January 14, 1857), Lettie (born December 24, 1859), and Mary (born March 29, 1861).[48] Two more children joined the family

Martin Entsminger, William and Samaria McKnight's brother-in-law. *Courtesy of Lois Mohler.*

Addison Braley, Samaria McKnight's brother. *Courtesy of Lois Mohler.*

Alexander Braley, Samaria McKnight's brother. *Courtesy of Lois Mohler.*

Three of the Braley sisters. *Left to right:* Emma Jane Entsminger, Samaria McKnight, and Ellen Sidenstricker. *Courtesy of Lois Mohler.*

on July 4, 1863. McKnight's first response to the news that he was father to twins was "it surprises me so to hear that you have two little girls."[49] He then inquires about their names and writes, "you must let me know what you are going to call those little fourth of July Presents."[50] McKnight was able to take two furloughs home: the first, from April 16, 1863, until May 2, 1863; the second, from April 25, 1864, until May 6, 1864. Martha and Myrtha would have been nearly nine months old before William first saw them, just weeks before his death at Cynthiana, Kentucky, in June 1864.

William McKnight's letters also make reference to several other family members, of whom many fought in the Civil War. McKnight mentions five cousins by name who served: Will Halliday, James Johnson, William and Lenox McMaster, and Marion Rathburn. Halliday (Company K), Johnson (Company A), and Rathburn (Company I) were members of the Seventh Ohio Volunteer Cavalry.

Ohio in the War

The Ohio Valley played an essential role in the eventual Union victory.[51] At the beginning of the war, Ohio had the third largest state population (2,339,511) and also ranked third in wealth. In the 1850s and 1860s, Ohio also contained many of the nation's largest cities—Cincinnati, Cleveland, Columbus, and Dayton were all in the top fifty largest cities in 1860.[52] Geographically, the state was in the center of the country, connected to the Ohio and Mississippi rivers and the Great Lakes, and Ohio led the nation in railroad track mileage.[53]

Ohio contributed a substantial number of men to the Union cause and initially responded to the war with great excitement. Following Fort Sumter's surrender, President Abraham Lincoln issued a call for seventy-five thousand troops—Ohio's quota was thirteen thousand. Without hesitation and before the War Department had officially established Ohio's quota, Governor Dennison (who stated, "Ohio must lead") wired Lincoln and asked, "What portion of the 75,000 militia . . . do you give Ohio? We will furnish the largest number you will receive." Governor Dennison went even further after learning of Kentucky's refusal to supply troops: "If Kentucky will not fill her quota, Ohio will fill it for her."[54]

Thousands of Ohioans responded to the call. Columbus at the time was a city of less than twenty thousand and was quickly overwhelmed by some thirty thousand troops.[55] Volunteers stayed in hotels and private residences; few had uniforms, weapons, or any other essentials.[56] However, Ohio's patriotic fervor and "lingering images of a brief and glorious war were shattered" at the battle of Shiloh in early April 1862.[57] The Union victory came with approximately ten thousand casualties—a number that "shocked Northerners." In Ohio, "residents' responses to the new reality of a lengthy and costly war ranged from active mobilization of relief efforts to scathing criticisms of the troops in the field."[58]

In April 1861, Governor Dennison was turning away thousands of potential Ohio troops, but a year later it "became necessary to coerce and bribe men into service."[59] Although few Ohio troops were ever drafted—a total of 12,251 were drafted and of that number only 2,400 served—it was an effective tool to stimulate enlistment.[60] Those who were drafted instead of volunteering carried a "terrible stigma," for "military service was something of a patriotic duty in which all should take pride. To be *compelled* to serve, therefore, made one appear unpatriotic."[61]

A total of 313,180 Ohioans served in 198 infantry regiments and 13 cavalry regiments, in addition to several artillery regiments and various independent units (see appendix B).[62] Ohio "probably led the northern states in the percentage of its eligible men serving in the military forces" and was outranked in total numbers enrolled only by New York (448,850) and Pennsylvania (337,936).[63] A significant number of high-ranking officers were also from Ohio. During the war, ninety-nine Ohioans achieved the rank of general—including major general, brevet major general, brigadier general, and brevet brigadier general—and exercised "commands in accordance with the rank."[64] Additionally, five Ohio-born Union officers later became presidents of the United States: Ulysses S. Grant, Rutherford B. Hayes, James Garfield, Benjamin Harrison, and William McKinley.

Buckeye volunteers participated in nearly every major battle, including Shiloh (April 1862), Antietam (September 1862), Fredericksburg (December 1862), Murfreesboro (December 1862), Chancellorsville (May 1863), Gettysburg (July 1863), Vicksburg (July 1863), Chickamauga (September 1863), Missionary Ridge (November 1863), and Nashville (December 1864). Moreover, more than fourteen thousand Ohio troops accompanied General Sherman on his march to the sea—Atlanta to Savannah—in late 1864, and an Ohio regiment was present at Lee's surrender at Appomattox on April 9, 1865.[65] Even though Ohio troops fought in most major battles, the majority saw action only in the western theater; only "one-fourth of the Ohio troops served in the eastern theater of the war." Most served in the western theater in central Kentucky and Tennessee.[66]

Not only did Ohio provide a significant number of soldiers, but also its farms and factories played important roles in the eventual Union victory. In the 1850s and 1860s, Ohio was one of the leading agricultural states in the country—over half the state was being cultivated, and the majority of adult males were farmers. In 1860, the state exported "nearly two million barrels of flour, over two and a half million bushels of wheat, three million bushels of other grains, [and] half a million barrels of pork."[67] During the war, Ohio's farms supplied a great number of draft animals, in addition to cattle, fruit, and wheat.[68] In regard to manufacturing, Ohio was home to several of the nation's leading industrial cities—Cincinnati was the third largest manufacturing center in the country and by population the largest city west of the Appalachians—and contained 11,123 manufacturing establishments in 1860.[69] Carl Becker describes Cincinnati as the "entrepot of the Ohio and the Mississippi valleys" and the "industrial showcase of the West."[70] Factories in Cincinnati produced a wide variety of goods, ranging from candles and caskets to shirts, shoes, and trusses. The war initially caused a sharp recession in Cincinnati; however, factories quickly turned to new markets and the manufacturing of war materials. For example, John Van, a "fledgling manufacturer," in 1863 patented the #5 Army Range, which was the "first all-steel portable stove used in the field for hot rations; in a modified form, it is still used by the Army."[71] Additionally, Holenshade, Morris, and Company in Cincinnati had approximately six hundred employees and manufactured as "many as 6,000 army wagons a year during the war, as well as thousands of camp kettles, mess pans, tin cups, and bolts."[72]

The Seventh Ohio Volunteer Cavalry, Company K, and Meigs County

One of the military units from Ohio was the Seventh Regiment of the Ohio Volunteer Cavalry (for a list of officers, see appendix C). The "Seventh Ohio Volunteer Cavalry was recruited on an order emanating from the War Department, that Gov. Todd of Ohio, would raise one Regiment of Cavalry, for 'Border Service,' the Ohio River then being the boundary."[73] The Seventh, also known as the "River Regiment," had a total of thirteen companies (A–M) and 1,204 men.[74] Soldiers in the Seventh were mustered into service from September 12, 1862, through November 8, 1862, at "Columbus, Camp Ripley, Athens, Pomeroy, and Gallipolis, Ohio," and came from Adams, Athens, Brown, Clermont, Gallia, Hamilton, Lawrence, Meigs, Monroe, Scioto, and Washington counties.[75] According to the Roster Commission (1891), 840 men mustered out of the Seventh on July 4, 1865, at Nashville, Tennessee.

Although the Seventh fought primarily in Kentucky and Tennessee, members of the regiment had traveled throughout the southern United States by the war's end. McKnight's letters provide descriptive accounts of several battles and the landscapes and terrain that he encountered. Many of the battles and skirmishes McKnight describes are listed by the Roster Commission (1891) as major engagements (see appendix D). McKnight's letters also discuss many of the cavalry's daily activities. Typical cavalry duties included "conducting reconnaissance, establishing and maintaining contact with the enemy forces, screening the movement of friendly forces and raiding against enemy lines of communication."[76]

McKnight was a member of the Seventh Ohio's Company K. The official roster lists 110 men in Company K (see appendix E). Of that number, 13 were killed in action or died of illness or disease.[77] Company K's casualty rate of approximately 11.8 percent is slightly higher than Ohio's statewide average of 11.3 percent.[78]

McKnight was proud of the Seventh and frequently mentions the regiment's accomplishments and boasts of the men's fighting reputation. On one occasion, McKnight quotes Rebel prisoners: "They think that 7 OVC must be 3 or 4,000 thousand strong for they say they cant go any place but the d—d seventh is after them."[79] McKnight further states that the enemy thought that the Seventh "must be old soldiers," because of their fighting prowess and experience.[80] McKnight contends that Union military leadership also recognized the Seventh as a fine outfit. McKnight writes to Samaria that when General "Burnside passed our column he said that ours was the best regiment in the state."[81] McKnight adds that General Quincy Gilmore called them "the best in the field"—"that is the best Regmt in Ky."[82] Finally, McKnight boasts to Samaria, "Co K is a crack Co I tell you."[83]

McKnight, like several other members of Company K, was from Meigs County, which is located in extreme southeastern Ohio.[84] Meigs County, founded in 1819, was named after Return J. Meigs, an early Ohio governor.[85] Meigs County's population just before the war, in 1860, stood at 26,534.[86] When the Civil War broke out, Meigs County "was well settled and populated . . . and the industries related to timber, cooperage, hoop holes, logging, and the coal mines began to give employment to a large number of persons."[87] Other important industries prior to and through the Civil War included salt, bromine, and coal mining.[88]

INTRODUCTION

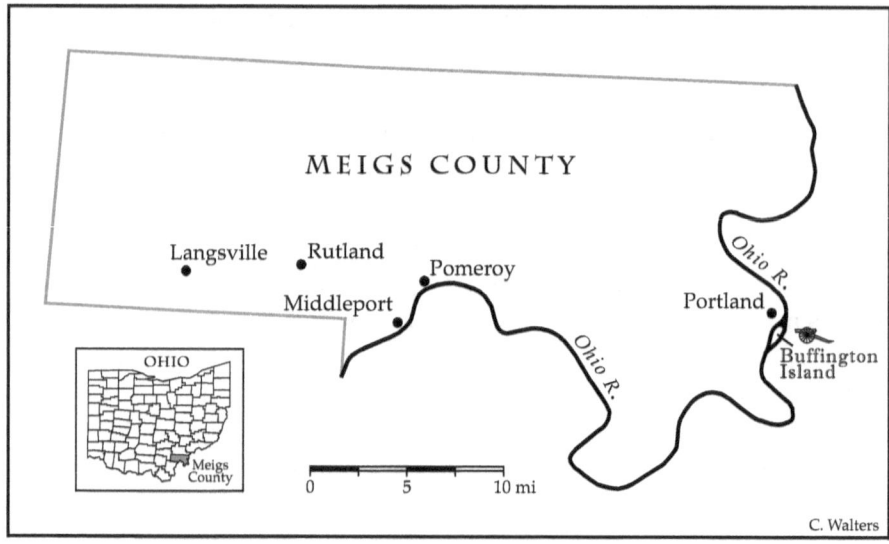

Meigs County, Ohio. *Map by Claudia K. Walters.*

The "Civil War dealt a great blow to the population of Meigs County. Nearly every family in the county was involved."[89] From the war's beginning until October 1862, Meigs County contributed 4,736 volunteers.[90] Meigs County lost a total of 505 men during the war. Their names are memorialized on a Civil War monument in Pomeroy, Ohio—the county seat.[91] In 1905, an attempt was made to determine how many Civil War veterans still lived in Ohio. Twenty men from the Seventh Ohio's Company K were still residing in Meigs County at the time.[92]

McKnight the Soldier

By many accounts, William McKnight was not a typical Civil War soldier. The typical soldier was "unmarried, white, native born, Protestant and between 18 [and] 24 years old."[93] McKnight was foreign born and joined Company K of the Seventh when he was twenty-nine years old and married with four children. According to the official roster, McKnight entered the service on September 12, 1862, and was appointed as first sergeant of Company K of the Seventh Ohio Volunteer Cavalry on November 8, 1862.[94] McKnight was later promoted to second lieutenant on April 19, 1864, shortly before his death on June 12, 1864; however, he was killed in action before being commissioned at that rank. Moreover, although the official

General Head Quarters, State of Ohio,
ADJUTANT GENERAL'S OFFICE,

Columbus, April 19th, 1864.

Sir:

His Excellency, the Governor of Ohio, has commissioned you 2d Lieutenant in the Seventh Regiment of Cavalry Volunteers, and your Commission was this day forwarded to the commanding officer of your Regiment, at Nicholasville, Ky. Immediately on receipt of your Commission, you will notify this Department of the acceptance or non-acceptance of the same.

Very respectfully, your obedient servant,

B. R. COWEN,
Adjutant General of Ohio.

William McKnight
Nicholasville
Kentucky.

OFFICIAL:

Assistant Adjutant General of Ohio.

P.S. Give your Post Office address when at home.

William McKnight's original commission papers. *Courtesy of Ruth Hayth.*

roster does not show McKnight as having been elevated to captain, Lester Horwitz contends that McKnight attained that rank,[95] and McKnight noted in his diary on November 3, 1863, that he had been appointed captain, even signing several letters as "Capt Co K."

McKnight was killed in action at Cynthiana, Kentucky, in June 1864. The battle's outcome was in doubt until the last day, when a Union victory was finally gained. After a "third charge," the enemy was routed: "mounting their horses they moved down the rail road through Cynthiana, hotly pursued by our troops, driving them through the streets and into the river, killing, wounding and drowning many."[96] Brigadier-General Stephen G. Burbridge describes the action in the official record and adds, "I attacked Morgan at Cynthiana . . . [and] completely routed him, killing 300, wounding as many, and capturing nearly 400. . . . Morgan's scattered forces are flying in all directions; many have thrown away arms; [they] are out of ammunition and wholly demoralized."[97]

In this fight, McKnight lost his life. Captain R. C. Rankin of the Seventh notes, "In this affair our loss did not exceed fifty in killed and wounded. Among the killed was Lt. McKnight, a brave and gallant officer."[98] William Hartley, a family friend and sergeant in the Seventh, provides a more detailed account of McKnight's death in a letter he wrote to Samaria: "Your Husband is Mortly Wounded . . . he is wounded in the Right Lung."[99] Hartley's assertion that McKnight had been wounded in the chest supports the family's claim that McKnight's now-bloodstained poem to his wife was folded in his vest pocket at the time of his death. The poem, dated April 4, 1852, was written to Samaria by William prior to their marriage in 1855 (see appendix F).

McKnight's death remains somewhat controversial. The official pension records make no mention of foul play.[100] However, Mary Johnston and Ruth Hayth (William's great-great-granddaughters) told us in October 2003 that foul play was involved and that McKnight was shot by one of his own men. Newspaper accounts support the family's argument. In the 1930s, a reporter for the *Daily Sentinel* of Pomeroy, Ohio, described "Captain McKnight" as "Langville's village blacksmith, who won his position by wonderful bravery and loyal service to the Union cause."[101] The newspaper article continues:

> The slaying of Captain Billy McKnight at Cynthiana by one of his own men . . . was one of the foulest and most treacherous crimes that ever disgraced the annals of modern warfare. This was revealed by an examination when they brought him home which showed that the bullet had entered his back and come out his breast and was further corroborated in a statement of the soldier made in confidence to a comrade who later imparted it to a writer that he shot Captain McKnight because he was brave to the point of rashness and likely to lead them into places that were not necessary, all of which was a virtual confession that he was too cowardly to follow where the Captain dared to lead.[102]

A later newspaper article further perpetuates the theory that McKnight was shot in the back by a fellow Union soldier: "The sight of a Civil War uniform

William McKnight's poem to Samaria Braley, April 4, 1852. *Courtesy of Terry Hauger.*

with a hole in the back made by the bullet which killed her great-great grandfather [sic], Capt. William McKnight of Langsville, remains vivid in the memories from the childhood of Mrs. Donna Tuckerman Russell."[103]

Whether McKnight was killed by his own men or by Confederate forces, the fact remains that Samaria, who never remarried, was widowed with six young children. Years later, Samaria was still grieving the loss of her husband. In her diary, on May 2, 1886, she recalls that "twenty too years [ago] to day was the last time that my dear husband was home."

John Hunt Morgan and William McKnight

July 1863 was a difficult month for the Confederacy. Robert E. Lee's loss at Gettysburg and Grant's success at Vicksburg turned the tide of the war. Also during this time, Confederate general John Hunt Morgan unsuccessfully raided through southern Indiana and Ohio. Much has been written about Morgan, the "Rebel Raider," and several of the accounts make a connection between William McKnight and John Hunt Morgan.

Morgan's raid through southeastern Ohio went directly through Meigs County and McKnight's hometown of Langsville. An earlier account notes that "not only was the princip[al] engagement fought on her soil, but while other counties got the 'once over' he crossed Meigs twice, first from west to east and then from north to south."[104] The McKnights feature in this incident: "Langsville has a story of Morgan's consideration for women and children. A Mrs. McKnight, wife of a Union soldier in the field, has twin babies two weeks old. It is said that Morgan kept a guard at each outer door of the house during his stay at the village."[105] One account states that "upon entering Langsville [Morgan] found the town deserted, except for Mrs. McKnight and her twin, two-week-old daughters who were frightened and seeking sanctuary in their little house with a lean-to back."[106] This version of the story places William McKnight in Ohio at the time: "Unknown to General Morgan, her husband, Captain William McKnight was part of the Union force pursuing him. True to his chivalrous code, the General posted guards around Mrs. McKnight's home so she would not be disturbed or endangered. In fact, he made himself a guest of Mrs. McKnight while he waited for the bridge to be built."[107]

Family history also supports the notion that Morgan stayed in the McKnight home and that McKnight was part of the Union detachment chasing Morgan.[108] McKnight's great-great-granddaughter Ruth Hayth notes that Samaria "with her newborn daughters remained in her home and newspaper accounts relate that she was forced to cook for General Morgan's Raiders, but was told she would not be harmed. During this time Mrs. McKnight's husband, Capt. William McKnight was following General Morgan, hoping to capture him and his troops."[109] Mary Johnston, also one of McKnight's great-great-granddaughters, relates a similar story: "Captain William McKnight was chasing Morgan's Raiders when they stopped at [McKnight's] home in Langsville, Ohio and spent the night."[110]

There is little doubt that Morgan passed through Meigs County and most likely spent time at McKnight's home; however, despite what some family and historical accounts assert, letters clearly indicate that McKnight was in Kentucky at the time. McKnight first writes, "The Capt [Captain Higley] is with the Regmt reported to be in Indiana after Morgan."[111] Less than two weeks later, McKnight acknowledges, "I would have given any thing that I possessed to have been at home when Morgan was there. . . . I would liked to have been with the Capt and would have been had I been permitted to do so. It seems to me a very unfortunate circumstance to have been obliged to remain with the camp when there was work at home." He would have offered a different welcome to Morgan: "one thing sertain if I had thought you were going to accomodate Rebs in my House I would have been there to accomodate him to a dose of lead the infamous thieving hounds of h—l." McKnight continues, "It makes my Blood boil to think that they were mean enough to impose their dirty Pictures on a poor defenceless helpless Family and what hurts me the worst is that for all we were goten up expresty for the Protection of our Homes we were absent and our homes disgraced and Country overund and destruction spread far and wide. Well its all come right I hope yet I should have been there had I been permitted to come but its al for the better I hope."[112] Without a doubt, then, McKnight was in Kentucky while other members of the Seventh were chasing Morgan through Ohio.

The final connection between McKnight and Morgan came in June 1864 at the battle of Cynthiana, Kentucky. On June 6, McKnight notes in his diary that "John Morgan [was] reported in the State." Four days later, McKnight writes, "Started 8 A.M. for Lex. Cannon heard in that direction. Rebels Reported in the Town arrived at Lex. 3 P.M. Rebels had gone we were 5 ms behind Halted and Fed and got Dinner. Slept 2 hours started out after Morgan in the direction of Paris took the George Town Road had an exciting chase." Finally, on June 12, Morgan was leading his troops into battle at Cynthiana against Union forces that included William McKnight of the Seventh Ohio Volunteer Cavalry.[113] The battle was a Union victory, although McKnight lost his life.[114] This occurred a month after his writing to Samaria, "I am just as firm [as ever] in the faith that I wil be spared to come home."[115]

Preparing for War

(September 1862–January 1, 1863)

Most of McKnight's early letters discuss routine issues that many soldiers faced during the war. For example, a letter dated December 9, 1862, describes in detail the first half of a typical day in camp: "I have to detail every day at day light I have the Roll to cal. Then we al have to feed our Horses then water. After water then Breakfast at 7 then Officers drill at 8 then Guard mount at 9 then Squad on Company drill then feed Horses grain then dinner at 12." McKnight also talks about having a "good Bed to sleep in" and for the most part seldom complains about the quality or quantity of food. McKnight often writes that they have "plenty to eat" and on December 15, 1862, pens, "I smel fresh meat Cooking."

Two common themes in these letters persist throughout the entire collection. McKnight repeatedly speaks of loneliness, and coupled with that is a desire to receive letters from home. On December 17, 1862, McKnight states, "I am wearying for a letter I have written one about every other day. I have received no answer to any that I have written."

Most of Company K's early training was conducted in camps located in Middleport and Gallipolis, Ohio. By December 1862, Company K had moved to Camp Ripley in Ripley, Ohio, and McKnight realizes that his unit is preparing to leave Ohio. In a letter dated January 1, 1863, McKnight writes that he will soon leave "our beloved state" and closes with "Good bye dear wife dear children Dear friends Dear old state."

These early letters also reveal two personal situations that McKnight confronted before leaving Ohio. Samaria's early letters do not exist, but she evidently informed McKnight of her pregnancy in the fall of 1862 (the twins would be born on July 4, 1863). McKnight's initial response is curious: "O I am so grieved to think of your affliction. It almost unmans me the anguish and Heart rending of Parting only seems Doubled at the news. . . . I know I am to blame for it al and cant help it." Soon after McKnight learned of Samaria's "affliction," he was apparently accused of being unfaithful. McKnight referred to the accusations as "slanderous lies" and stated that the mere suggestion of unfaithfulness had "inflicted a severe wound in [his] Heart."

September 1862[1]
Camp Midleport
Meigs Co Ohio

Dear Wife,

I seat myself to let you know how we are getting along in the first place. I am enjoying good health at present and we have sent for our clothing today they are at Athens.[2] We are to get Our clothing and be Mustered in and receive a part of our Money and it may be all of it and then we wil be permitted to come home once more to . . . see you all then we are to March to Athens thence to Cincinattia by Rail thence to Ripley Ohio fifty Miles above Cincinattia where there is Seven Companies of our Regiment.[3] There is a Mustering Officer on his way here we expect him here on Sunday and then you may look for me home.[4] My Horses is getting Better, when I was home last I tried to think and did not think that I was for all the Better and now there is Better Prospect for me than there ever has been seince I came into the company for useing a Horse of my own it would surprise you to know for it did me I dare not tell you now but wil when I get home. I was ordered out to drill the Men yesterday and the officer said it was the Best drill they had had for a

Week. I am still acting as Orderly, and the boys seem wel Pleased so far with me. Our Colonel was here day before yesterday to see us and it . . . through him that the change is to be made it is by no effort of my own that theree is a Better Prospect for me. I Believe I have nomore to . . . tel you worth telling—do nomore at Present. From your unfaithful Husband.

William McKnight to Samaria McKnight

P.S. tel James ther is a chance for him. Brunker wants to see him before long.[5]

W.M.

October 16, 1862
Camp Middleport Ohio

Dear Wife,

You have nodout heard before this line that we have received Order to report when we are ready to move which may alarm you and make you tremble for fear that we may have to go far away but fear Not if we do go it wil only be to Camp Denison to organize the Regiment.[6] I think which we Could not do any other way the Captain thinks that when we get our horses and get organized that we wil be sent back here again. Our clothing is at Athens we expect to get them Before we leave but it is very uncertain we may Stay here all Winter. War matters are so uncertain the Boys are making a Buz about dinner and I wil have to go to dinner. I have had plenty of Dinner plenty of Pork and beans and some Bread and Butter & shugar to top of . . . If you may gess how it makes me feel to think of leaving you But there is a smile in my dour above that. I Depend on . . . to Protect us and I hope you wil put your trust in him who is able and willing to save. I hope you wil Pray for me . . . feel that God is stil as he has ever been a father and friend and is abiding. Kiss the children for me Come & se me if you can. Bring the children if the weather is good, bought me a carpet sack yesterday so I can take care of what I have we have received more rations today from Galliopolis.[7] The Rebels left Canwha.[8] Nomore at present but pray the God of love guide and protect u is my Pray.

From your ever loving husband.
Wm. McKnight to Samaria

William McKnight's letter to Samaria, November 14, 1862. *Courtesy of Terry Hauger.*

November 14, 1862
Galiopolis

Dear Wife,

I seat myself to drop you a few lines to let you know our where abouts. We arrived here yesterday onboard the Lovel we are tolerably wel quarterd here and expect to remain here until the Colonel comes we expect to lay here until we get our Horses—and then we go through by land the horses are ready here and good ones. There is 2 Companies here belonging to this Reg and another the Athens Company expected today we expect to lay here about a week and mabe longer. I am geting Stripes put on my Jackcoat and pants and feathers in my hat which I Bought yesterday for two Dollars the hat and feathers and sabers letter and figure cost me $2.25, & when I get fixt out I am going to get some Pictures and send them home I hope you wil give yourself as little trouble about me possible for the Capt says I have to Stay with him all the time I got supper last Night at the American Hotel the firs meals vituals I have eaten since I left home but I like Soldering foral the hardships I go with a wil.[9] I

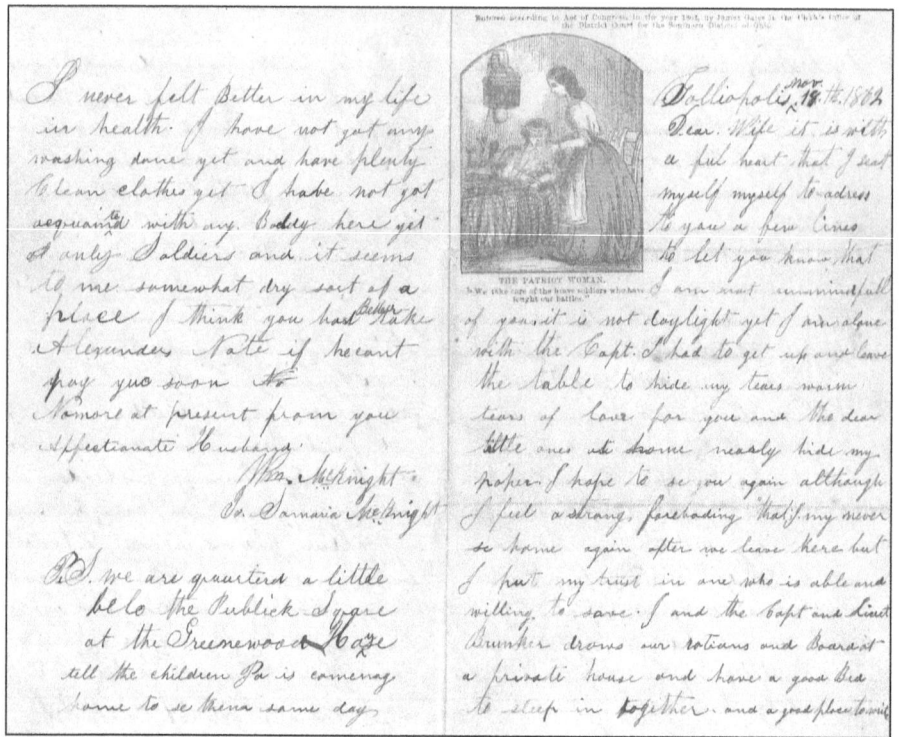

William McKnight's letter to Samaria, November 18, 1862. *Courtesy of Terry Hauger.*

think it my Duty and Calling write to me here send you letters to Rutland or Pomeroy to be Mailed as they may come sooner.[10] You had better hire some one to cut that wood for you whil the weather is good and have it put in the dry. Nomore at present but I wil write often if I cant write much so goodby God bless you and the children is my Prayer.

From Wm to Samaria McKnight

November 18, 1862
Galliopolis

Dear Wife,

It is with a ful heart that I seat myself myself to adress to you a few lines to let you know that I am not unmindfull of you. It is not daylight yet I am alone with the Capt. I had to get up and leave the table to hide my tears warm tears of love for you and the little ones at home nearly hide my paper. I hope to se you again although I feel a strong foreboding that I my never

September 1862–January 1, 1863

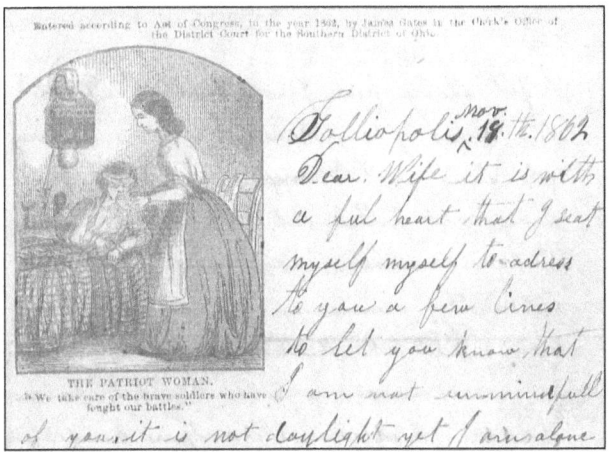

Civil War stationery symbol. *Courtesy of Terry Hauger.*

se home again after we leave here but I put my trust in one who is able and willing to save. I and the Capt and Lieut Brunker draws our rations and Board at a private house and have a good Bed to sleep in together and a good place to write. I never felt Better in my life in health. I have not got any washing done yet and have plenty Clean cloths yet I have not got acquainted with any Boddy here yet only Soldiers and it seems to me somewhat dry sort of a place. I think you had Better take Alexanders Note if he cant pay you soon. Nomore at present from your Affectianate Husband.

Wm. McKnight

To Samaria McKnight

P.S. We are quartered a little belo the Publick Square at the Greenwood House. Tell the children Pa is comeing home to se them some day.

November 25, 1862
Galliopolis

Dear Wife,

I landed here safe last Night and find that we are to leave tomorrow morrow morning for Ripley by land. I expect the orderly of Geyers Company got shot yesterday by a Negro in a drunken scrape.[11] He is better this morning. Direct your letters to Camp Ripley Brown Co Ohio.

Nomore from your loving Husband write as soon as you think that we get to camp. Good by dear ones. Good by.

From Wm to Samaria McKnight.

In margin:
In hast.

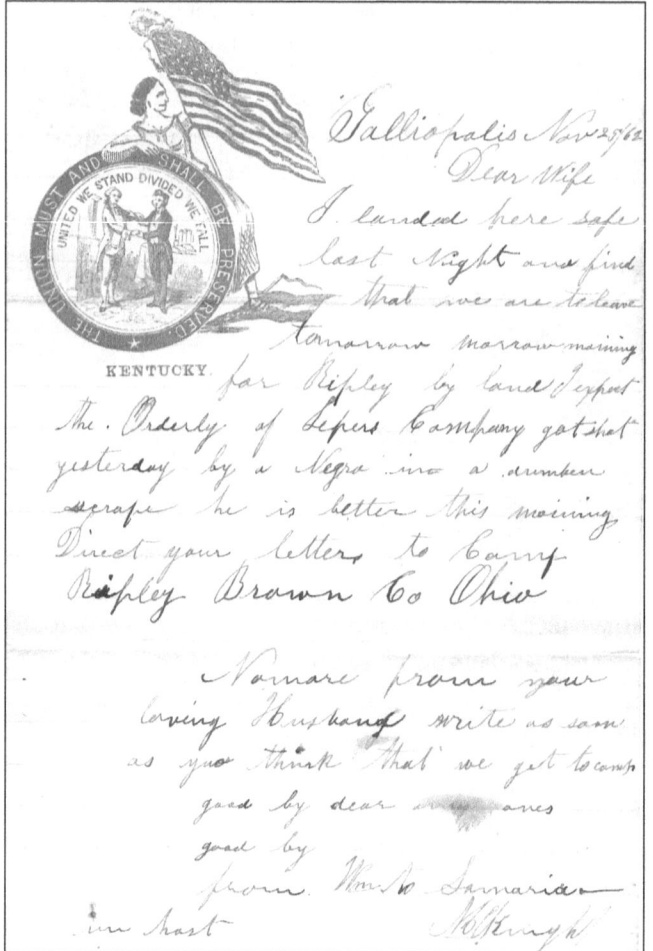

William McKnight's letter to Samaria, November 25, 1862. *Courtesy of Terry Hauger.*

November 26, 1862
Galliopolis, Ohio

Dearest wife,

I again take the oportunity of again adressing to you a few lines to let you know that I never forgit home and family. My mind is constantly turning homewards. I have just finished detailing the gards to gard our horses which we have drawn today.[12] I got my choice of the hole lot and got a very fine horse I think. We cant leave before the day after tomorrow I am glad I came back when I did for we have had a great deal to do today. We have 30 more Horses to draw in the morning. Our horses Color is dark browns and blacks and a very good lot of horses. They make a fine appearance. We drew our saddle and horse blankets today every thing except Revolvers we drew knives and forks and pans and Bought a Cooking stove so we get along very wel. We drew heavy Revolvers one for each man six shooters splendid weapons for fighting. I get along very well with the drill I can Beat either of Lieutenants. It is now near midnight and all the rest are in Bed and the old stove smokes and the night is getting cold and I am somewhat tire so I guess I had Better quit for the night. So good night Dearest. Good Night goodby little ones. The tears Blind me so I cant se to write any longer although I have felt livelier to Night than common. I cant tell any thing about comeing home yet But I think there wil be a chance. Write soon. Give my love to all my folks and keep it al for yourself and the children.

Old Frank was a relation of the Cap. The rest of the men were quartered around in town. The 3rd Night we stayed in Piketon and Fared very wel.[13] The 4th night at Locust grove fared prety hard.[14] 5th Night at North Liberty where we fared splendid put up early shaved and put on a clean shirt. Next morning we left 2 horses and proceeded. Arrived here about 3 o'clock with thre Horses less than we started with. Prety sore about where the horses tail sprouts. The trip cost me nothing. I never had my Purse out the whole way. The Peopl treated us with great kindness on our rout apples Pies sigars milk and cider plenty. Since I came here I have had twice as much to do as I had in Middleport.[15] I am quartered with the Captain Lieutenants and Sargeants by our selves and Hary Spires cooks for us.[16]

Again seat myself to finish my letter. We intended to start today But we have been busy al day and are hardly ready yet. We are to start tomorrow the 27th. We are to go by Centerville Jackson and Piketon and so on to Ripley.[17] When we get there you wil hear from me as soon as we get straightened out as I can find time. We have had a good deal of fun today riding bad horses. Several got unhorsed though none hurt. I have as much as I can attend to. I hardly get time eat. Our company has 50 horses to take for another Company. I hope you wil not be the least uneasy about me and I hope that you wil feel Better against these lines reaches you

Write me a great long letter when you rite again. Tel the children that I expect to surprise them again some Morning. Tel them to be good children and good to one another. Go to School if the weather is fit to go. Dear . . Dear . Wife and children can it be possible that I am destined to see you nomore in this World. Certainly not I hop not I think not. I feel assured that after Passing thrue many hardship I wil be permited to return to the Bosom of my family to enjoy home again. So may it be good night dear ones good night half past ten. Good night. Write as soon as you get this no more from your ever loving Husband.

William McKnight
To Samaria McKnight

December 6, 1862
Camp Ripley

Dear Wife and little ones,

I again seat myself to write you a few lines to let you know that I have not forgotten you. I received your letter of the 1st inst and it did me an awful site of good.[18] I was Proud of it. It was so well composed. Wel we left Galliopolis Nov 27th 11½ oclock am and marched to centervile that Night arived there after dark and had a pretty hard night of it. The men slept on an open Field had our suports get after feeding and taking care of horses our company led throug 50 Horses for an other Company. The thre companies led throught 200 Horses and we made a string about ½ mile long.

Oh I just wish you could have seen us. The 2nd Night we stayed at Jacson and they treated us like Brothers. The Cap and I stayed at the Widow Smiths. Old Frank smiths Widow. I received theops letter.[19] As soon as I get time I wil answer it if I had time. I want to write to Mother and Mary and Willie and Janet and Elliott Mart Emy Jane Elens folks Aunt Sallies folks and al the rest of our folks but they need not wait for I knew the real value of a letter before. Eleven o clock good night my own dear Wife good night. Tel the children that I wil try and bring them some Christmas Presents. Kiss them once for yourself and once for papa. Do the best you can. God bless you.

From William McKnight
to Samaria McKnight

December 9, 1862
Camp Ripley

Dear Wife,

I take this oportunity to inform you that I am wel at present sincerely hope these few lines may find you & our Dear little ones enjoying the same inestimable blessing. The camp has become quiet the men are al in bed except the guards. There is 12 men 3 Corporals & 1 Sargeant on

Horse Guards around our own Horses every Night and ten on Camp duty every day. Each relieved every twenty-four hours & sometimes 8 or 10 on fatigue duty around the Camp which makes 35 men. I have to detail every day at day light I have the Roll to cal. Then we al have to feed our Horses then water. After water then Breakfast at 7 then Officers drill at 8 then Guard mount at 9 then Squad on Company drill then feed Horses grain then dinner at 12 then Orderly call at 1 when I have to go to Headquarters and get the morning report Book where I have to keep an account of the number of men and horses fit for Duty unfit sick Commisioned and non Commissioned Officers present and absent at 2. Battalion drill at half past 3 water and feed Horses Hay super at 5 gard to put on Duty Roll call at half Past 8 at Eight forty five the taps. Al this done to the sound of the Bugle and so on to the end.[20] I am so busy that I do not get much time to study or to Play. I have not been in Town but 4 times since we came here. If there was any place here for woman I would like to have come to camp and se us but I cant say to yo come for I know the little ones wants to me and then I wil come and see you if there is any Possibl chance. I have no idea how long we wil stay here Probably some time. It is a very nice Place above town. It has been fitted for a fair ground the nicest kind. The boys are al wel in our Company except some thing not very serious. I am hearty and Contented with my fate but Oh for you and the Dear little ones is my great trouble. But know that God wil protect you an them. If you cant write very much write often. Tel children Papa say he would like to se them awful wel but Cant tonight.

We are considerable crowded here 4 shanties about 12x15 2 stories is al the room we have. The Furniture in our shanty consists of one table one Bench one stool 2 trunks one Barrel 2 Boxes stove and some Pots knives forks Pans and spoons for the mess and any amount of hors equipments sabers revolvers and Blankets. Oh yes we have a Broom and Plenty of towels. So nomore at present. Write soon Dearest and often to if you can find time. Good night deares ones good night.

> Do you mis me at home do you miss me
> Twould be an assurance most dear
> to know that at this time some loved one
> Is saying I wish he were here.[21]

From Wm McKnight to his Wife and family Samaria God Bless you good night.

December 13, 1862
Camp Ripley, Ohio

Dear Wife and children,

    It is under Painfuly tryings circumstances that I seat myself to let you know that I am well at Present. Hopeing and trusting that these lines may find you enjoying the same Blessing. I received your letter and likeness the joy of receiving was soon overcome by the contents of the letter it cast a damper over my soul that I cannot shake of. O my dear Wife what shal I do what shal I say what can I do for my Dear Wife. Here I am and Cant help myself. I hardly expect that any of us wil get a furlow from here the Probability is that wele not remain here long where we go I cant tel. O I wish I could se you again but if we never meet in this world I hope we wil in the next where Parting is nomore. O I am so grieved to think of your affliction. It almost unmans me the anguish and Heart rending of Parting only seems Doubled at the news. My dear Wife be Patient reconcile your self as wel as you can. Be assured of one thing you have my tenderest affections my deepest solicitude. I cant express my feelings. O I am so sorry that I hardly know what to do. If I could only be with you it would not seem so hard to bear. It is hard I know and you may cast reflections on me. I know I am to blame for it al and cant help it. I want you to writ all about it all about every thing concerning our family how you get along whether the children is shod and clothed or not O train them up in the way they should go. May God Bles them you and them are all the world to me. You may think I have neglected you but if you could se me while I write and see me turn my head away to keep from spoiling the Paper you would at least know that I had not forgotten you. O my dear Wife O my dear children. O if I could be with you to night it would be the happiest Hour in al my life Not because I am tired soldiering but because I love you better than any thing. God has blessed me with and you are mine and I am yours. I cant think of any thing else. But Gods wil be done. We have been drilling on horse today for the firs and did splendidly although I could Not take command of my Plattoon on account of horseness. I looked on and seen the movements and I tel you it is a splendid sight to se somany horseman with glittering sabers and Prancing Horses. There is 8 companies they cover several acres of ground in their movements. I can go through as wel as any of them in the company. I have Been asked if I had not been in the service. It getting late dear Wife and I have some other writing to do so I must close. I got another Pair of Pants since I came here and got Patrick McCans Wife to sew on the stripes.[22] They are different from the first ones nearly as Broad as your 2 fingers. I have never put them on yet. I think I shal save them until I come home. We received company teams today 26 Mule teams. We got some straw today to put in our Bunks. The Cap and I sleeps down stairs together the rest upstairs. We have plenty of every nesesary. Nomore write soon I have written 5 or 6 letters and received 2. O yes and your likenes. God bles you good night Dearest. Give my respects to and a thousand Kisses to the Children. O can I say good night.

From William McKnight to his Wife and family.

December 15, 1862
Camp Ripley

Dear Wife,

I again seat myself to write you a few lines to let you know that I am wel as usual. We have had fine weather for drilling although it has been rather Cold for sleeping comfortable but we get along very wel here. Every morning at 5'-45" oclock I have Roll to Call at 6 watter call & at 7 Breakfast at 8 sick cal. Al the sick have to report to the surgeon. Officers drill at 8 fatigue at 8 when I have to report men for duty. At 9 gard mount when I have to bring out 8 and 10 men for Camp guards then squad drill 2 hours, dinner at 12 then at 1 Orderly Call when I have to go to head quarter to get my morning report Book where I have to report al the sick men wel men sick horses wel horses number of men absent and present and a number of things not enumerated. But I get through them al very wel for the sake of my family and Country. I can goe through it all and more. But O dear Wife the hardest fate is to leave you and goe far away from you. Since I commenced writing the Captain tels me that we are to leave here in a few days 6 days at the farthest and we leave for Lexington Kentucky.[23] 4 companies of our Regiment goes tomorrow or next day then ours goes 4 day later. It is sealed. I goe far away without seing you. O may God help us to bear up under it and O may he watch over you and your littl flock and Dearest Wife put your trust in him who is able and willing to save. I would to God that it were otherwise but I am rezined to my fate. God's wil be done.

I would like to have some money but there is no chance now. I can get along some way. We do not expect to be Paid very soon I have a little money yet. I have been very saving of what I had. I have not gotten any washing done since I came here and I have 2 clean hankerchiefs and 2 Pair of socks yet. I pressed 2 Pair at Galliopolis gave one to the Captain and kept the others. They are the best socks I ever had home made and comes to the tops of my Boots. The Boys killed al the Hogs in Camp today had a great time of it and seems to me that I smel fresh meat Cooking. We have changed our mess. The Captain 2 Lietenants 2 sargeants 2 Buglers and the Orderly. I get very little else here. I doo wish some of my folks could come and se me. You can come to me but I cant come to you. I sent a letter to you yesterday. I intend to write you often whether I write to any one else or not. So nomore at present. Write soon Dear wife. Tel Willie to write to me I would like to know how he gets along. Letters that has any thing in it particular kep it to yourself. Good by dear Wife and Dear little ones good night.

From William McKnight to his Wife.

December 17, 1862
Camp Ripley

Dear Wife,

Again I seat myself to talk to you again throug the mails again. I am wel at present. There is some sickness in the Camp. I reported 4 this morning not bad. I am wearying for a letter I have written one about every other day. I have received no answer to any that I have written since I came here. The weather has changed and is very disagreable. The Horses stand out all tied on one line and eat their feed of the Ground. In the firs place there is posts set in the ground then Bored and a rope put through and al the Horses tied to it about 2 feet apart on each side alike. We dril thre times a day at half past 9 then at 2 oclock this afternoon we was out and I had Command of the first Plattoon. I dont like to Brag but I get along as wel as any of them. The Boys sid today Orderly you going out today if you are we go if not we dont. The Boys stick to me and have from the first. They think a great deal of our Captain. We all like him for al the Bad reports about him. If we stay here this winter we wil get to come home if not it wil be some time before you se me again. I would like to have the childrens likenesses if it was not so far of. If you have any more trouble let me know it. I do hope and pray that what you wrote to me is not so for I thought you would not have that to wory about. It has always been a source of trouble to you and I but blame me for it al for it is my fault I know But I know you will forgive for it. O dear it makes my heart acke for you it makes me sad but I cant help it now.

The Cap and I have got a very good Bunk to sleep in now. He is turned in and I am tired and feel like turning in to so good night sweet ones. O my heart wels up Bitter tears and my lip quivers and my breath groes hard when I close my letters to you. I can hardly se to write. So good night dear ones. I hope to see you al again. May God sustain us in this our severest troubles. O my dear Wife and children if I Could be with you again it would be the greatest Comfort of my life. Give my respects to al you know to be my friends for my sake. The fact of the case is there has been more slanderous lies told about the men of the company than I ever new about any thing this world. I think the folks at home must have very little to do and you dear Wife inflicted a severe wound in my Heart when you intimated that I had been unfaithful to you God bless. You are all the world to me. When I sit down to write I cant think to write to any body else but you. If you knew how much I mis you would never entertain the doubts to cause you trouble. If you never go any farther than I have it wil al be right. If you have any douts about me I wish you would write and let me know for if you do I want to know it for I am not aware that I have ever swerved from my duty to you or my children I hope not and with the help of God I never wil I hope. The Company that was to leave here to day has not gone but are getting ready as fast as possible. They wil possibly goe tomorrow. Tel the children to be good. I would like to bring them home some Christmas Presents and se their dear little faces again but alas that is denied me now but I hope it wil not be long for I think there is some Prospect of Peace.

Remember me to the Children and to Willie Saunders.[24] I know you wil Remember me for my meannes if nothing else. You must look over my poor compositions for the house has been crowded of night again. I bid you good night dear wife. Nomore good night.

From William McKnight
To his Dear Wife and children
Write soon.
Direct your letters Camp Ripley
7th OVC Co K Care Capt Higley

December 22, 1862
Camp Ripley

Dear Beloved Wife and children,

    I again seat myself to converse with you once more through the Mails. O if I could just see you or know how you was it would relieve me of an awful load of grief. I have written nearly every other Day to you and have only received 2 letters from you and none from any one else since I have been here. I have wrote to John Susan and Mary Jane and have received no answer. I am looking for Brother John to come down to see me before I leave. It seems that he is the only one that can come very wel. I want to see some of my relations so bad before I leave the State of Ohio. I have been nearly as hoarse for some time back as I was last winter but I have recovered so I feel as wel as ever. I had some chicken for dinner to day and it was good. I have been very healthy ever since I left home. When I left Gallipollis I weighted 175 lbs. but I guess I am not so heavy now. We expect to leave here in about 8 days. Our Horses is to shoe yet then we wil have to leave and when we get to Lexington we expect to get our pay when I shal be able to send you some Money I hope and when we get there I will be with Cousin Marion Rathburn he is there.[25] I wish you would write and let me know how my Customers pays you since I left home.[26] I am afraid they wil neglect you. But I hope you wil not suffer for anything while I am gone. I have hopes that you wil be cared for while I am absent fiting for my country. I hope that ere this time my sweet Lucy wil be wel and all the rest of you And O how sincerely I hope that you wil be al right. I wish you knew the feelings of my Heart. If you did I think you would rest wel. You all my care and trouble all my hopes and fears. I care Nothing for my own hardships. Tel Johnny that Pa has got a horse like Charley that Wiseman got only he is nicer. He can run as fast as an horse in Camp I believe and jump as high. We expect to Cross the River at Maysville about 10 miles above here and then we wil have 50 miles farther to go to reach Camp.[27] We expect to get heavy Carbines when we get to Lexington. O my Dear Wife it is like parting from you every letter I close to you. O u do seem so near to me tonight and I know you are so far away that my heart feels ready to Break. I write some words of Comfort as you used to talk to me when I was sad. Nomore from your truly affectionate Husband.

    William McKnight
    to his Wife and family
    Write soon Please.

January 1, 1862[28]
Camp Ripley

Dear and Beloved Wife and family,

I seat myself to inform you that I am wel at present also the Boys are generaly well. We are still at Camp Ripley yet but one more day in Ohio is probably all that we wil be permited to remain in our beloved state as we are packed up ready to start. We are now waiting for Carbines for the Battallion. As soon as they arive we goe for Lexington which is said to be a very nice place. The 2nd Battalion is there and we expect to winter there. If we do it may be that some of us wil get to come home. If there is any chance atall you may look for me. There is not over 5 or 6 men unable to ride in our Company. There is 4 companies here at present and we bear the best name among them all. Co K is a crack Co. I tell you. We mustered for pay yesterday. I have been working on the Pay Rolls tonight. I have Copied two Hundred names on our Muster Rolls. We have 100 men all present but 2 Jo McCaskey and a man by the name Myers who are at Lexington.[29] When we al get there we expect to be Paid of. It is 65 miles to travel. The Boys are ready to go some would rather not go but they are ready to do their duty. We have the least trouble with our Boys of any Co in camp. Tel Willie that I was very glad to hear from him & tel that I wil answer it when we get through. I was awful glad to hear that our little lucy was better and the rest of you wel. I would like to be home to day we hardly know it is Newyears. There is nothing to make me think of Newyears. If I had been at home I think I would had some Rabbit for dinner but as it was we had a little extra today and went without dinner for want of water to cook it. We hav got good tents 6 for the men and 2 for the Officers.[30] The Captain says that the Orderly has to stay with him the 2 Lieutenants together so you se I wil fare with the Best of them but I do not ask it. I ask nothing better than the men. I take Notice that somehow or other my Canteen is ful of strained honey (curious). Wel Honey and good bread wil do when we are on the way but that is not all we wil have Boiled Beef and Coffee and some other nesesaries. I am in good spirits and hope you wil receive this. So do not give way to trouble atall. You must not give yourself any uneasyness about for when I cant take care of myself my friends wil take care of me. Asher has sore Eyes but they are geting Better. You may know that when I dont say any thing about our Boys that they are al wel. The Boys says that I am fat as a hog wel bout 175 lbs. I hope these few lines wil find you enjoying the best of health. We have Plenty to eat and that to that is good. It is now halfpast eleven and I must bring my letter to a close. The last for some time that I expect to write in Ohio. But write often yours is always exceptable. Good bye dear wife dear children Dear friends Dear old state. I go to defend you against al enemies. Good night.

From William to Samaria

Life as a Soldier and Divided Kentucky
(*January 8, 1863–July 8, 1863*)

After leaving Ohio, McKnight first arrived at Camp Ella Bishop near Lexington, Kentucky, in January 1863. From that point, McKnight traversed much of central and southern Kentucky and camped at several places—Danville, Harrodsburg, Monticello, Stanford, and Somerset—over the next few months. McKnight described numerous engagements throughout Kentucky against Confederate troops under Generals Roy Cluke and John Pegram. In regard to these skirmishes, McKnight rarely missed an opportunity to boast about the Seventh's accomplishments against the Rebels. On March 28, 1863, for example, McKnight writes that "our Regmt is a teror to the Rebs and pride to us they wont fight the Ohio Boys if they can help it but they dont fear the Ky troops attol."

McKnight not only discusses battles that he participated in during the time but also indirectly mentions two of the most significant events of 1863—Gettysburg and Vicksburg. In a letter dated May 24, 1863, McKnight states, "The men generaly wel and in fine spirits as we hear good news this morning from Grants Army before Vicksburg [Grant would take Vicksburg on July 4, 1863]. The news of the success of our arms is cheering to evry Union loveing heart and to none more so than the soldier who has left home and evrything thing near and dear to him and Perils his life for his Countries sake."

In addition to the accounts of military engagements, McKnight offers several descriptions of landscapes in Kentucky. McKnight on February 1, 1863, writes, "but there is a peculiar[ity] about this part of Ky that I never seen in any other place. There is great hoppers in the ground with sometimes an ackre or more that have no appearant outlet but after you pass several of these you wil sometimes come to a spring of water that would turn a mill."

In the spring of 1863, McKnight made his first trip back to Ohio. McKnight's personal diary provides many of the details regarding this trip. McKnight writes, for example, that on April 16 he "received leave of absence." Later, McKnight notes that he took the "steamer St. Patrick" from Pomeroy, Ohio, to Cincinnati on April 29–30 and arrived back in camp near Stanford, Kentucky, on May 2. Just two months after his return to Kentucky and the Seventh, Samaria delivered twin girls on July 4, 1863.

Kentucky played a pivotal role in the war and had maintained an official policy of neutrality until just months before McKnight's arrival. At the beginning of the war, Unionists in the state declared that Kentucky "ought to hold herself independent of both sides, and compel both sides to respect the innviolobility of her soil."[1] Neutrality was respected by both sides for several months in part because "each feared that an overt violation might drive Kentucky into the other camp."[2] President Lincoln clearly recognized Kentucky's importance and stated, "I think to lose Kentucky is nearly the same as to lose the whole game. Kentucky gone, we cannot hold Missouri, nor, as I think, Maryland. These all against us, and the job on our hands is too large for us. We would as well consent to separation at once, including the surrender of the capital."[3]

Kentucky's strategic location and resources—agricultural products (in particular, horses and mules)—were central to the end of neutrality. Confederate and Union generals both realized that capturing Kentucky meant controlling the Cumberland, Mississippi, and Tennessee rivers. By late summer of 1862, Confederate generals Gideon Pillow, Leonidas Polk, and Felix Zollicoffer had moved into the state, occupying several key positions. At the same time, U. S. Grant seized Paducah, and Union troops took control of other Ohio River towns.

In September 1862, the Kentucky House of Representatives and Senate voted for the Confederate troops to withdraw—a measure that Kentucky's governor, Beriah Magoffin, did not support. The motion eventually passed, and Kentucky's neutrality officially ended.

The end of Kentucky's neutrality did nothing to temper Confederate-Union divisions in the state, however, and Kentucky was sharply divided over the war.[4] Historian James Prichard states that "Kentucky was a border state in every sense of the word. Tied geographically and culturally to the South, she regarded her parent state of Virginia with much affection"; yet in the "decades prior to 1860, the increase in Ohio River traffic brought about by the rise in canal and railroad building had forged strong economic ties with the North," which created strong pro-Union sentiments.[5] Scholars Lowell Harrison and James Klotter offer some of the best examples and note that "families divided, churches split, communities differed over the issues involved. Many participants could not have explained clearly why they chose the side they did. In the Crittenden family, George became a major general in the Confederate Army; brother Thomas held the same rank in the Union army. Two of Robert J. Breckinridge's sons were in the Union army, two fought with the Confederacy. Breckinridge was a strong Unionist; his nephew John C. Breckinridge was a Confederate general and cabinet member. Editor George D. Prentice was Unionist; both of his sons were Confederates. Slaveholding Samuel McDowell Starling of Hopkinsville joined the Union Army although he was over fifty years old; he lost one son fighting for the Confederacry, another one fighting for the Union."[6]

The Confederate-Union split in Kentucky is also evident in McKnight's letters. In the chapter's first letter (January 8, 1863), McKnight writes that the "People [in Kentucky] were nearly al sesesh." McKnight frequently uses the term "Sesesh" (from "Secessionist") and notes on several occasions that he is writing from a "Sesesh farm." In a February 16, 1863, letter, McKnight identifies the Union goal for Kentucky: "Braggs Army camped handy here not long ago but there is no sesesh army in Ky now and it is thought that we wil hold the places to keep them out."

Important Civil War locations in Kentucky, Ohio, and West Virginia. *Map by Claudia K. Walters.*

January 8, 1863
Camp Ella Bishop[7]

Most Dear and beloved Wife and little ones,

Here in the center of Kentucky I hasten to break the silence of your nodout Painful suspence of waiting to hear from me. We are all here ecept one man who shot himself through the hand at Ripley all wel. We left Ripley Friday 2nd. I am in company with thre others went 4 miles Camped on Eagle Creek in the mud.[8] Halted 3 oclock this was the first night for us in tents. Plenty of Straw Slept wel. All the rest of the Boys did the same. The Cap and I ocupy one tent and the two Lieu another. The rest of the men have six tents and the Caps Waitor and 9 in al for the Co. The next morning 3d left 7½ ocl reached Aberdeen 10 a.m.[9] Raining ferried here landed in Maysville ½ past 10. 10:15 15 min of one oclock al over eccept the waggons. 2 oclock and we took on our farewel look at our Noble old state. We felt on leaving that we had changed hospitality for inhospitality and that we were in an enemies land and ready to fight.[10] We camped at a place caled Blanchards next morning 4th left at 8 o.c. past through Washington at 10 ocl.[11] The next Town we came to was Mays lick half past twelve ocl where we had quite a breese.[12] A man hurried for Davis and got himself licked.[13] I was in the mess came out all right. The People were nearly al sesesh.[14] The Agutant swore the man and let him goe with his Eyes Blacked. He said he was in fear. We told him that we took his own word for it. The morning of the 7th it rained. Though her heart would Break and there stood her little Children to by her side it told a tale of grief to me that I never wil forget as long as life lasts. You wil forgive for not writing on the way. I had no chance and now I have hardly half a chance. I would like to write more but I have to go on Dress parade and I wil to get ready soon. You can sit down and take your time to it but it is quite diferent here to sit down on a Box on the ground to write. I had a sore throat for 2 or 3 day but it is Better now. I feel very wel now. We expect to stay here a few days anyhow so direct your letters to Camp Ella Bishop Lexington Ky Care Cap Higley Co K 7th OVC. I must close. I want you to write to me as often as you can for it now ten or twelve days since I recieved a letter from you. It seems so long. I expect to get one soon. If dont I wil not know what to think. This letter I have written for you al. Tel Elliott to write to me. I am going to write him as soon as possible. Let any of your friends read this you wish to write just as you feel when you write to me but it is different with me. I do not feel like turning back yet. I want to se this great trouble settled and not left for my Babes. So good by Dear ones. May the Blessings of God rest upon you as it ever has upon us and as wel. Give my love to sisters & Brothers. Your Kisses to my Pets and retain my whole unbounded afection. Remember to that good old mother.

Wm To Samaria McKnight

In margin:
I inclose you the bean of the coffe tree allmost like Honey locust.

January 9, 1863
Camp Ella Bishop
near Lexington Ky

Dear and beloved Wife,

I hasten to answer your kind and afectionate letter. I was glad to hear from you and that you was wel as usual. For my part I never felt Better in my life. The Boys seems to enjoy themselves wel also we were inspected by an ispector General today and Co K was pronounced the Best Co in the Battallion. Ours is undoubtedly the best Co in the whole Camp of five Regiments and one Baterey of Artilery. I dont hardly know what to write for I Mailed a large letter to you this Morning. As to that likeness you ned not wory about it atal for they are going to send it to me the first chance I can take care of that myself. I do not want that to come home for if it did evry boddy would know all about it. If you thought as much of me as I do of you you would be very careful how you wound my acking heart for I have a sence of honor and a right that leads me to do wright as far as I Know how.[15] But for al I know that I am liable to err as wel as other mortals for which I am always sorry and ask forgiveness. There is always something to wory about but live in hopes I dont think I committed any great sin if it did not seem to hurt you so that is what hurts me and makes me Cry. To think that I have been the cause of one pang of sorrow to you. I hope you wil forgive me just this time and I wil do better in future if I am spared. I have recieved the most of your litters and have answered evry one and a good many more. I want you to write just as you feel dear for there is no danger but I wil get them here as easy as in Ripley and quicker to for they came by Rail. I recevied a letter from Theop today. He is five miles from Nashville and is wel and hearty. We dont expect to go far from here this Winter. The Colonel says not over twentyfive miles. We are under General Granger in the first Battalion of the Regmt.[16] I understand that our Carbines have came today. When we get them we expect to goe around and see the folks about our bed. We have a good bed and the Cap and I has seven Blankets between us that & our Overcoats makes a good Bed with straw. We Brought our cook stove with us and we have Boxes fixed up for eating and writing on. We have a cook so I have no trouble but to eat when it is ready. Our Cook sings out fal in to the Speneer when ever grub is ready. We are to get soft Bread soon and we wil get Beef again. Our stove keeps our tent warm and comfortable. I cant find Marion Rathburn at al. He is not here now. I wish you would write to Theop for me. He is in Camp Hamilton under Cap Miles.[17]

There was several soldiers buried today from old Regiment. There is no sickness in our Battalion of any consequence. The men the most of them are fat and I can hardly stoop to black my Boots without grunting. We had some pickles for supper last night. We had some grapes and fish and cheese. We had Honey and Chickens and Turkeys all the way through. Co K looks out for No 1. Part of our Regmt has been in a fight and came of first rate killed & Captured seven Hundred Rebs & over thre Hundred Horses and only lost one man.[18] Dear Wife I cant talk to you but I can write to you if I have to do so after all is asleep and I want

(upper left) Lettie McKnight. *(right)* Leila McKnight. *(lower left)* Mary Lucy McKnight. *Courtesy of Lois Mohler.*

you to write to me as often as you can. If I could come home just a few days it seems to me that it would be the greatest Pleasure in the world. I keep your likeness in my Pocket al the time and it is great comfort to look at your sweet face. Although it dont speak it seems so near & dear to me. You dont know how I prize it. It is the greatest prize I have to comfort me in my lonesome hours. Good by dear Mary good by dear Leila Thomy Lucy & Letta. God Bles you for my sake Mary my Mary my loved one.

William to Samaria

January 12, 1863
Camp Ella Bishop near Lexington

Dear Wife,

I again seat myself to communicate with you every spare hour I have. I seat myself to write to some one and it most always Comes out Dear Wife. I mis you so much that I want to hear from you every day. I have recieved 7 letters since I Came here one from you one from Theop one from Mother and one from Mary from and part from Emma Jane and from Theop that he captured from a Southern lady to her betrothed which I wil send to you. I wish you would send me some Postage stamps. I cant get any here without money. I bought one dollars worth when I went to Ripley but they are all gone used up and lent and sold. We have good beef and soft Bread and good sugar and Coffe and Beans and Pork and Crackers and Molases and we have a good Cook to Cook for us so I have nothing to do about that. But I have plenty else to tend to. I have the most of the Drilling to do. I can drill any thing in this Company. I except the Cap. He and I are like true Brothers. He sticks to me all the time. He says he Could not get along without me. I got the Praise of being the Best looking and soldier like Orderly in the whole Battalion you know that is not so. Captain is one of the Best men moraly as wel as intelectualy that ever I met with. If he was to leave the Company I would be lost for he has been a Father to me ever since I Came into the Company.[19] Our Company wears the horns for being the Best Company in the camp. We have never had one of them under guards ten minutes since we came together. There has been Considerable talk about Money. The Pay Master has gone on to pay the other Battalions at Winchester and Danvill 18 or 20 miles from here.[20] You must be of good cheer. Tell me every thing that you can think of. I do not write as I have done for I have to write in a hury and in a poor place. I have a first rate Bed and get to sleep first rate. I do not have to stand any duty atall and that is more than either of the Commishioned is exempt from. We cant get to goe into the Town atall. I have just Been down the line to Post some Guards over our forage. I find the Boys all in fine spirits some singing some laughing and others cracking jokes passing the time fine. I can lay down and sleep as sound as though I was in your arms. So sound that I dont dream of anything. . . . going to war so not like going to the Grave. Just think of our friends that have been abot so long. How wel they have fared and so far we have fared just as wel and a fair prospect. I have al confidence in God. I hope you wil pray for me as I do for you. Many a time when you was asleep have I knelt by your Bed side and prayed for you until the tears would roll down my cheeks for your welfar and to help me to love and protect you and yours so long as I live. I hope to live long to enjoy your comfort and kindness.

O my dear woman I wish I could see you and them der little ones of ours. If I could have one of them with me how pleasant it would be if I Could take care of him. Your likeness is a great Comfort to me but I do not think it is as good as it might have been for think you are sweeter looking than it is. I expect the rest of the folks are thinking that I might write to them. But when I get time write you are the all to me and the idol of my Heart and I can hardly think to write to any one else however near to me.

Dear wife I must close. You can tear of one part of this sheat if you do not want to show it to any one. I would like to know how you are tonight how you feel and how the Babies are. I have go so fat that I can hardly do any thing stooping. The Boys says that I am fatter than they ever see me. Wel I weight about (175) one hundred and seventyfive lbs. I wish I could get the childrens likenesses taken and sent to me but I supose you cant get them taken handy. Wel good you good woman you must not think of me so much. I cant come when I want to but I wil come when I can. Give my respects to father dady and Janet and all the rest. I send my Best wishes to you all my undivided love for you and the little ones. Good night god bless you and them dear little ones. You wanted to know if my washing costs me much. No it dont. I found a Motherly sort of a woman in Ripley and she only charged me five cents for shirts an socks nothing for Collars or Hankerchiefs. She gave a nice Kneedlebook thread & Buttons and everything needed.

William to Samaria

January 18, 1863
Camp Ela Bishop
Near Lexington Ky

Dearly beloved Wife,

I seat myself once more to answer yours of the 10th which Came to hand last night which was most welcome although it casts a gloom over me to think that I have left you in your hour of severe trials in which I deeply sympathise but cannot avert it is the greatest trouble I have. It is a matter of deep regret to me to reflect upon for I know that your troubles would have been lighter had it not been for me. You can cast all the Blame on me for I know that I am to blame but I hope to be forgiven.

I am very sad to hear that you have such a bad Cold. We are all wel and hearty here with few exceptions. I fare as wel and Better than I expected. We have stoves for our tents that keeps them warm although there is five or six inches of snow on the ground. The sun shone out today for the firs time for four or five days. It has been colder here than it has been known for five years but there has been no suffering in our camp. The Boys are cheerful and ful of fun. We are going erect stables here and Probably Stay all Winter. If we do we wil have easy times for the infantry stand al the grand Guards tht is al expect Camp Guards around our own camp.

I want you to have someone that owes you to cut some wood for you and have it handy and then you wil not have to expose yourself. I want you to go visiting evry chance you get never mind what People may say you can Pass of the time and forget your troubles somewhat. I thank my friends for their friendship for I know that I have many there. The hope that we may all meet again is a great support to me. I think that we wil learn each others worth by being separated so when we are permitted to enjoy each others Company there is no one that knows the worth of home untel he is deprived of it. When we get Back we wil have a great time. You need not be the least uneasy about me for I am as contented here as circumstances wil permit. We can lay down and sleep as sound as we could at home. We have first rate grub.[21] I had some soft Bread toasted today with Coffe and sugar on it. It was so good I thought how you used to fix toast for me sometimes.

I am in hopes that Captain Higley wil get to come home but for poor me there seems no chance at present.[22] I want to get out in Town some day when the snow gets of to see old Henry Clays monument and then I wil send you something to keep.[23] I will soon have to get the men out to tend Dress parade. Every Sunday after noon we have Dressparade. I must close dear Wife. It is with the depest love and affection that I close. I hope you are wel and I want you to pray for me for I know that it wil be heard. We feel perfectly safe here and you need not fear for me. So good by dear wife and little ones til I come good by.

From Wm to Samaria

January 23, 1863
Camp Ella Bishop
Near Lexington

My dear little Children,

    I thought I would sit down and write a few little lines to you to let you know that pappa is living in a white House made of white Cloth. It is about twice as big as Marvs smoke House or biger. We have a little stove in it that keeps it warm. We have a Box to sit on and one to eat of and one to write on and we have some hay down in one corner and lots of Blankets. The Captain and me have four Gray Blankets two Blue ones and two redish colored ones and two . . . Blankets and our over Coats. Alltogether we have plenty to keep us warm. Since I commenced writing we had a great Big scare. The Horses have been out in a field since yesterday morning five hundred and fifty of them and they all got scared and ran all together and it sounded like thunder. It is dark and we first thought it was the Carrs and then we thought that the mules had al ran away with the waggons. Some of the Boys got on their sabers and some their revolvers and some wanted to stay in the tents. Some thought Morgan was running on us and after they stoped for they just stoped.[24] When they got ready we had a great deal of fun about it. I got me astick and was among the first ones out there for I knew what was the matter. But it was pretty near all over but I tel you it was an awful noise. I did not think that Horses could make such a noise and it was dangerous but there was no one hurt. But I expect the Horses are hurt many of them. If my Horse is hurt I wil find it out in the morning and then I wil tel you about it some other time. If you was here you could ride him for he is so gentle. I but lashaway with my saber or shoot just as much as I please and he dont mind much and when I want him to goe al I have to do is to just close my big Brass spurs on him and he is of like a shot.

    I wish I could se you al again. You are dearer to me than my own life but I dont expect to see you for awhile. But when I come I wil Bring you all some thing nice. I want you to be good little children and do what your ma tels you and when papa comes he wil have such a good little family. I kow you are good now and papa is very sorry that he cannot be with you but we wil only have the Better times when I do come. We have a nice Cat with us that we Brought through from Ripley. She is lots of company. Ma I just recieved a letter from sister Susan. The folks are wel except Samy is lame. I have not got my money yet but I expect we wil soon from what I hear. We are all wel as usual. I feel strong as a horse and the most of the other Boys are getting fat as pigs. I feel awful Bad about you but I cant help it. I am bound to help fight it out now so that I may have a better Place for you. For if I had stayed I would not felt that I had done my duty to you or my country. Good night you dearest of al on earth to me. Kis ma for pa and ma must kiss you for me.

From your pa Wm McKnight

January 24, 1863
Comp Ella Bishop
Near Lexing K.Y.

Dear beloved Wife,

It is with feelings of deep affection and sadness that I again seat myself to adress to you a few lines to let you know that I am wel at present and I hope that my dear little family that I have left at so great a sacrafice are enjoying the same great and inestimable Blessing. I recieved your letter this evening dated Jan 18th which was received with ecstasies of joy for I had not received one before for nearly a week and I was very anxious to hear from home for I was afraid that the high water or something was the cause. But my joy was soon turned to sadness when I read your piteous Calling which I Cant hush. O if I could how quck would I take you in my armes and press you to my heart and weep tears of joy but alass this is denied us. But the happiness in store for us is some Consalation for our sever trials. You seem to think that if I was homesick I could come home but you are not awar of the difficulty of gitting out of the service. If a man Deserts and is caught he is punished even unto death for it.[25] Rather would I have my Dear little children Dear as they are to me say that Pa was killed in War rather than have it thrown up to them that yor father was a *Deserter* and had to wear the chain and ball for thre years as many are paying for the same crime here.[26] O if I could whisper in your Ear Consalation and peace so you would not take it so hard. I would be glad you know Dear I have talked and tryed to keep you from fretting about trifling things and tryed hard to make you contented but it seemed that you could not help being discontented with all I could do. I know that I was not as good to you as you deserved but I hope to live a long and happy life with you.

Yet it was not because I did not love home and family that I left. You know that there was few that stayed closer hom than I did. It was from pure motives of duty to my country that I left home and friends and evry thing Dear to me. That I did right or rong the Lord only knows but I still hope that it is for the better whether or knot dear one you wil try to be cheerful. Going to war is not so bad as you may think. Just think how many of our friends are out and have been over half their time and are safe as ever. Be cheerful as you can. The lord wil bring all things right in the end and I hope you wil not fret about me for you know that I have often told you that freting kept you poor and makes your life a burthen to you and does no good but harm. Therefore I do hope that you wil try to keep in good heart and write to me some news and consolation.

January 25, 1863

Wel dear Mary I take my pen to finish my letter I began last night. It is Sunday and the there is no mail going out today. If there had been I would have finished last night. I have just been out on inspection with the Company and have to go out again on Dress parade this after non. The weather is moderate but the mud is plenty though not so bad as it has been. We have very good times here for soldiers plenty to eat an very little to do. I took a ride yesterday to se Ben Rutherford just across the fields but he had gone to town.[27] Disappointed at not finding him. I took a ride out the Pike with Lieut Brunker and got some good fresh Butter and when we came in we had some to our steamed Crackers.[28] Wel dear I finished my dinner of good Bean soop and Coffe steamed Crackers good Butter and sugar. O it was so good yes and good beef we had day before yesterday rice soop and beef we fare very wel. I received that dreadful old Picture last night and I am going to send it to Susan so I hope you wil give yourself nomor trouble about the matter. If I had thought it was going to make so much trouble Id rather had my fingers cut of than to have it cause you so much trouble but I hope it wil all come right as far as I am concerned at least. I shal give myself as little trouble about it as possible for I dont feel as though I had committed any great crime. If I have I hope the Lord wil forgive me. It was all honest in me except I did not tel you as I should have done. It was because I knew you would be jealous of me a thing you never had any reason to be. There never was a truer Husband than I have always been to you. I would lay my life freely down for you and I do hope you wil try and rest contented. I rote to you some time ago for postage stamps and I looked for them yesterday but they have not come yet. I hope you wil send me a dollars worth or so. They are scarce here and just as good as money. I hate to send litters without them. letters come though here quicker and safer than they did to Ripley. We expect to get our money soon. You wil see. The Caunnercial says Paymaster McDowel came to Lexington to pay the 7th O.V.C. I hope it is so.[29]

O how I would like to have some of them sweet little kisses of them red cheeks but alas not for me. I am going to send you 2 sesesh Bills. Give one to Willie Saunders and one to Tomy. I gave five cts for them. Wel I wil have to go out on Dress parade. The Bugles are sounding. Wel I have got back from Dress parade and am wel satisfied. We had Dress parade and the our officers left me to take the Company to quarters. Just as I had dismounted the men the order came that the Company was to go back. I mounted the men and marched them Back and formed them in line with 8 Companies all in one line. The rest all officeered with Captains and Lietenants while there was none to represent Co K but me. Wel I did as wel as any on the Field and brought them all of rite without looseng a man but the best of it was there was a man there by the Name of Leslie Coonz who made a speech to us that cheered me very much.[30] He said that in the 1812–13 Kentucky sent five thousand five hundred Brave men from her state to defend and protect the wives and children of Ohio from the Tomhawk and scalping knife he among the rest and now says he you have come to our aid to us like gentlemen and soldiers to pay us back with interest and says he you think you have seen the Elephant.[31] Some of you have but the most of you have not. But says he I have traveled all through Ohio and been among Indians and have been in many fights among them. This I tel you says he to show that a man Can se the Elephant and not be taken up with his trunk.[32] That is a man can pass through a great deal of danger and get through safe. I have risked my life a thousand times with Horses you know dear and always got throug safe and I hope it wil always be so.

You know that I have always trusted in God and he has always protected me and you and I hope always wil. I know that all that come to him in meekness and humility he wil in nowise cast out. He has told us so. Therefore be of good cheer and al wil be right in the end.

I have never been out in town. We cant go unless we have a pass which is very dificult to get. It has been 9 days since we arived here and it seems like a month of Sundays. I have stuck to the Duties assigned me just as I always did at home.

Mary there is one thing on my mind that I Cant help but think about. That is O I cant tell shal I no wel I know you wont rest until you know now that is you did not make my home as happy as you might have done when we were together. Just because you always found something to fret about. Dont think me harsh. I trust Mary that you will take a lesson by the Past. It is with the greates kindness that I mention this. I hope you wil try and reconcile yourself and be cherful. God Bless u.

I dreamed last night that I was at home with you and the house was all upside down and ful of Boxes and straw and stuf and I thought we went up to fathers and went to the creek and there lay a great snake as big as my arm and as long as a fence rail and I thought I struck at it and missed it and it turned and Bit me on the top of the left foot for it seemed that I was barefoot and I Caught the monster by the neck and killed it and says I did it bite me. Yes and put down my hand and there shure enough right on my instep there was great teeth marks and the Blood and water runing out and I wakened up and my foot hurt and the Dream troubled so I Could hardly go to sleep. But I hope it dont mean any harm. So dearest wife I must bring my letter to a close hopeing these lines may find you all wel as it leaves us wel. I hope the day is not far distant when I wil be permitted to take you in my armes and then our trouble wil all be forgotten. God grant how soon it may come. Kiss the dear little ones for me. Recieve my love and Blessings. May the angel of peace hover around yor head forever and help you to live in happiness.

From your ever true Wm McKnight.

January 28, 1863
Camp Ella Bishop
Near Lexington Ky

Dearest Wife,

Again I take my ever faithful pen to let you know that I am wel at present and I do hope that these lines may find my Dear little family enjoying the same great Blessing. I am sory to tel you that we are under marching Orders for Danville some 30 miles from here where it is hoped that we wil have better times than here.

I have not received a letter from you for some time. I thought I would get one last night sure but I was disappointed which made me feel so bad that I had to take a good bawl to myself. I have not felt so bad since I have been here. O how I did pray for my Dear little family. O I never felt so bad in my life. I received a letter from Father and one from sister Janet tonight but none from my own Dear Dear Wife. I dont know what is the matter has she forgotten me. O no it Cant be possible. We are al ready to start in the morning. I have been takeing a ride to day I have been to the Cemetery where the Celebrated Clay was buried. O it is the most Butiful Place that I ever beheld. It is nicely laid of in paved walks. All along the side of the walks the Butiful Evergreens hangs down in Beautious grandure. The monument is a Butiful structure of gray granite some hundred and fifty ft high.[33] When I came to it I dismounted my faithful Sam and shoveled some of the granite of to send home for you to keep until I come home also some evergreen which I picked from over the graves of the Noble dead. The large leaf is Caled Oleander the other I think is Caled holly. I also send you a lithograph of our Company for you to preserve for me there places for photographs. The fellow that was seling them made me a present of it for a little trouble I was at getting signers. As soon as we get to danville we wil get our pay for four months. Our pay Rolls are being made out and the Pay master is here.

I wrote you a long letter day before yesterday and I hope you wil answer with the same. I had just sent a letter to Father before I received his. Tel him that he is too old to stand the hardships of a soldier. After I left the Cemetery I went to the Hospital to se one of our sick Boys which is the only one that we leave. I found the Nicest accomodations for them. It could scarely could be any bitter. There was about two thousand sick soldiers there the most of them getting better.[34]

I must Close. Dont wory about me dont believe half you hear and it wil all come right.

From your ever loveing and faithful husband kiss the little ones for me bless them O you dear one so Dear.

From William McKnight to his Beloved wife Samaria.

In margin:
Direct your letters the same as you did here and they wil follow me.
This is the last you wil hear from me until we get through. Dont forget the Postage stamps. It is now eleven oclock so good night Samaria. William There is one thing I want to impress on your mind and that is you must

not fret any about me for I fare first rate. We had a stuffed turkey for dinner monday and a goose tuesday. Wm

---

January 30, 1863
Camp Baird Boyle

Dearest Wife,

I again attempt to after twenty miles ride and after all details of men and attention to some 2 or thre sick Boys to write you a few lines to remove all apprehentions in respect to me from your mind. We had no trouble on our way atall but had a first rate time. I am wel and hearty. Asher is wel and Frank Sausbury and all the rest of our Boys.[35] Our Mail Came in last night or to night but no letter for poor me but I hope you have not forgotten to write. I have not time tonight Nor do I feel Competent to write on the details of our jorney. We pased through a fine County part of the way. I have often read of limestone but I never seen much before. We Passed hills of limestone one hundred and fifty ft high sollid.[36] I never seen such grand sights. To see a stream of Water thre times as large as leeding runing between two sollid Wals of limestone partly studed with Cedars and other parts shining out like a City of white houses it was the most magnifisantly grand sight that I ever was permitted to look upon.[37] But more about it hereafter. I wil write soon again. We are wel pleased with our Camp it is such a Butiful place. It has been ocupied as fair ground. We have good beds of hay and plenty of Blankets and stoves to keep us warm. You must not forget to write for when I recieve the litters to distribute I look for one evry time we get our Mails. Evry day write me al the news for it is so good and kind in friends to write to the soldiers. If theirs mothers and Wives and Brothers and sisters when they are called up by the sond of letters could se their Countenance when they are told none for you sir and knew how they felt. I think they may get more letters. Mary I believe we send 3 or four for evry one we get but I must stop. I am laying on an old trunk or leaning over one with one foot on the ground and a knee on a Box. The fire out and all my Companions in bed this long time for it is 11 oclock. So good night you dear ones. I hope you are well. God bless you all my love to al good night dear Samaria. I hop to hear from you soon.

William McKnight
to his Dear Wife Samaria

In margin:
Dont forget to kiss my Babies.
Wm. Mc

February 1, 1863
Camp Baird
Danville, Ky

Oh Samaria. Samaria. Do you hear me if you do I want you to listen to me a little while and I wil try and tel you something about our trip through here and how we got along. I wrote you a letter as soon as I arived here and gave a little outline of our trip but had not time then to write much more nor have I found time since until now. Wel we Camped as I told you or wrote you in my other letter fifteen miles from Lexington. The first night in an old log tan shop which had been Converted into a school house. We arived there just about sunset after seing to dismounting the men and feeding. I went about a mile and got a load of straw for my horse and some for myself and Cap to sleep on. There was a large stove in the house and we fired up with rails and Jack got us some super of Coffe Beef and Crackers and then we turned in we tiped the old slab Benches over and formed a Box and had a splendid bed right before the stove and O how good we slept. Our horses had al the Corn they could eat but no hay. The next day we proceeded on our journey towards this place about non we halted in Camp Dick Robison took some refreshments and fed our horses some Corn we had brought with us.[38] It is the same Camp from which I received a letter from Theop when he went through here. There is nothing remarkable about the place it is simply a nice Camp something like Higleys Sugar Camp only level almost the land is just enough rolling to lead of the matter as we would say.[39] But there is a peculiar about this part of Ky that I never seen in any other place. There is great hoppers in the ground with sometimes an ackre or more that have no appearant outlet but after you pass several of these you wil sometimes come to a spring of water that would turn a mill.[40] It showes that the water has subteraneans Passages instead of runing on top. There seems to have been formed Brooks under neath the ground through the immence Limestone Beds which exceed any thing that I ever dreampt of. After passing on some thre or four miles we Came to a Camp where old Bragg had camped.[41] He had evidently been in hury when he left.

There was any amount of Waggons and Cannon Balls on Waggons and a great many things all mashed up. We gathered up some Balls and grape shot and I am to bring or send some home when I get a chance. Do you understand eh. Wel we arived here as you know al wright and we have had a very pleasant time since. Been busy fixing up and have got things very Comfortable. Last night I recieved an order to detail 25 of our best men and horses to be ready to start this Sunday morning against seven oclock with five days rations armes and equipments one wagon and one tent. The Boys went with a will some was mad because they Could not get to go to. Tel Mrs. Entsminger that her Boy did not go in the forepart of the day.[42] I was very Busy with the Guards in the afternoon. I was ordered by the major to go with the Company to water. We had to go about 2 miles to a creek through town near where the tenth Kentucky is Camped thinking that I might not get a chance again. I sent the Co back with the first Duty seargeant and went to hunt cousin Marion Rathburn. I put spurs to my fast Horse and soon had the pleasure of finding him. He seemed very wel pleased to se me as I was him. He met me at the front of his tent and as soon as I alighted nothing would do but I must go in and sit down I had hardly got seated until he was out and gone. Presently soon he returned with thre Cans of Oysters. So we sat down together and pitched in with nothing but salt and vinegar and Crackers. We downed them raw and I tel you they were good. It was not the first dose for me. Marion is not very wel. He has a very bad cold and spits Blood sometime. His Boys like him first rate. He is comeing over to se me someday before long. I did not have much time to stay so I returned to Camp wel pleased I had found him. There is ten Companies of this Regiment here now (are you listening wel if you are I wil go on) and one Regmt of Infantry acros the road from us the 45 Ohio. The other 2 companies belonging to our Reg is one at Lexington one at Harods Burg 10 ms from here.[43] We wil stay here some time I think unless we go scouting. I recon you dont care if I should go do you. I tried to get to goe this time but the Cap was Officer of the day. Geyer was on picket and Brunker had to go so I had to stay. I have not recieved any answers from you later than the 18th of Jan I believe and I dont know what is the reason. I have written four since I got any from you. Some of the Athens men tel me they get letters in thre days. I have woried for fear the Creeks and Rivers are up so the Mail cant get through. If that aint the cause and I dont get one soon you may expect to hear from me. I have written to you for postage stamps the first about 20 days ago and have recieved no answer anything about them. What is the reason. Write and tel me if you dont want to risk them in a letters. I wil either have to quit writing or send them without being Paid. I have many things more I would like to write but I have already tried you Patience I expect. Dont forget to tel them little cherubs of ours that I am comeing home some time. Bless their little hearts. How I would like to take them all in my arms yes dear and you to but we are denied that happiness by the missfortune of our once happy but now distracted Country which I hope soon to se return to her once happy Condition. Then our Cup of happyness wil overflow. Until then good by Mary good Bles you and help you to bear up under your affliction.

So nomore sweet ones this time from your Dubly Devoted.
William Mc Knight

February 6, 1863
Camp Baird
Danville, Ky

Dearest Wife,

I again hasten to write to you to let you know that I am wel. I recieved your letters dated 26 & 28 last evening after haveing been out on one of the great scouts on the morning of the third inst 1 oclock we was Called up out of our Beds by our Major Coming to our tents. Says he . . . Cap get your men out mount them as soon as possible our help is needed. We sprang up not knowing but the Rebs was pouncing upon us. I Caled the men up out of their tents teling them to get ready as soon as possible but keep cool and they did to some of them singing as they were getting ready for drill. We were all in line in a bout twenty minits the first out always. The morning was Cold but no complaints were heard of. We went some with a cup of hot Coffe some had to leave their Coffe. 2 Battallions of our Regmt without any thing to eat but some few had Cracker. For myself I had a cracker in each sadle pocket. Pasing through Danvile we took the Crab orchard road the Cold severe and snowing. Some of the Boys got their feet frosted and got so cold that we could hardly kep from going to sleep. Against daylight we had gone 12 miles stil snowing reached Crab orchard Battle ground ten oclock and fed our horses.[44] 2 miles farther on is Crab orchard town quite a nice town.[45] A mile or so farther we left the turn pike and struck a mud Road. On we went the farther the worse until we were Compelled to dismount and lead single file over the wildest Country and roughest track ever I seen. Reached Mount Vernon County south of Rock Castle County at sundown 33 ms from Danville the most Deserted starved out looking place I ever sen. Not a straw nor any thing else to be had for our horses. Men slept in the Court house horses tied to the fences. Nothing to be obtained for the men. The People wer good Union people but the Rebs had eat them out. Some of them got something and some didnt. I got some super and slept in the Clerks Office. Next morning we had to wait for Carrs. I got some Coffe and short Cake at a tavern some might Cal it Breakfast but it was hardly worthy the name. The horses done their barn. We got under way again but in another direction. Finding no Rebs we started Back for Danvill. It being a late start we did not reach Crab Orchard until it was about midnight where we found our teams had some Provision for us but it was so late the most of the men were so tired that they turned in without super in a large Church. I hunted the Town over for some one to Boil our Coffe for us but failed. I tried to eat but I Could not. Slept in a house 2 clock when we went to bed slept wel.

Horses got no corn for super but got Breakfast. We got our Coffe Boiled but as we were ready to start I got a Cup of good warm Coffe and some Corn flitters so on we went snowing. I stoped and made a shoe for my horse and cracked it on in about fifteen minits. Over took our Company about 2 miles out. Snowed al day we reached Camp at night the Boys al in fine spirits and as glad to get back as thou it was. Some of the people cheered and welcomed us Back. O how glad I was to find your letters awaiting and good warm super Jack had prepared for us. Our company turned out 51 men there being 26 of our men out previous to the one we went on. They are out about ten miles yet we Can beat al the companies in court turning out men. The health of ours is the Best in Camp. Captain Higley is al right. Dont believe any thing unreasonable about us. There has been more lies told about us now than would sink the Nation. I have just reread your affectionaate letters and Oh Dear how I do pitty you. If it was in my power I would be with you in your afflictions but try dear and be Patient for your own sake for my sake for your Dear little childrens sake. O you dont know how it weigs me down to hear that you are unwell. I thought I had left you in comfortable circumstances. You seem to blame me for going against your wil. I would think less of you if I knew you wanted me to go and was glad I was gone but be of good cher for you wont always have to go alone. I hope you might be Proud of me to know that I had honor and spunk enough to go to defend our countryies rights.

Oh how bad it makes me fell to think of them sweet little children of mine crying for papa and especialy that dear little one puting up her little starched apron and crying for me. God bless their little hearts. It is for them that I feel the most hurt for no one but God knows who wil take Care of them if their Pa falls a victim to this rebelian but I hope for the best when this rebellion is silenced. Then O then what a happy times we wil have going to se one another. I feel so bad for you I hardly know what to do. You seem to think that it only kneeds more love on my part to bring me back but you certainly know better for you know that I have labord hard for you and always been faithful to you. If you was only wel I would not feel so bad. It is hard enough at best. I recieved with thankfulness your stamps. They came to hand just in the right time.

You want to know our Colonels name. It is Garrard pronounced Garod.[46] We are under marching orders for to morrow morning for Harrods Burg ten miles towards home from here. We expect to go into winter quarters. It is said to be a first rate place. I wil write as soon as I get there. We have been looking and hoping for our money but have not got it yet but expect it soon. There is some things conserning our scout that I thought I would not let you know but I have concluded to tel you. The morning we left Camp it was so Cold that all I could do did not prevent my feet from getting frosted as did many of the Boys. My feet is stil sore so it hurts me to walk but as good luck wil have it I have not much to do and another thing I forget yesterday when we halted the Boys had some crackers and raw pork. Harry Spires gave me some and I ate a cracker and chunk of pork about the size of a young Pup and it was the best dinner I have had. I divided my raw pork with the old Major and he said it was the first racy meat he ever ate. I tel you it was good. The next time we go scout I bet we take something to eat and to Cook in we have traveled through 7 seven or eight Counties and have not seen an armed rebel yet. Fayett at Lexington then I as amine then. Boyle the one we are in now then South through Lincoln thence through Rock Castle Co almost through the state and no Rebs yet nor are they so plenty as they have been. We would like to find some. They are not so scarce but they are not in armes. We have passed and repassed through and returned safe. It is a nice day Dear and the sun shines so nice. It seems pleasant.

When we first went to Lexington we needed washing done so we hired a yellow woman to take some to wash for us.[47] She got the fine shirt that I got from Elliott and 2 nice Collars and pair of socks and a Hankerchief and lots of things of Cap and Lieutenans and gave her monae as hunt. She did not Bring them back and I gues we did hunt for her but did not find her. She made a nice haul. Excuse my poor scribling. I must Close. Good by Deares God Bless you and yours. Respects to al from.

Wm McKnight to his loved Samaria

February 7 1863
Camp Baird

Dear Wife,

I Cant rest any longer without answering your most welcome but to me painful letter. It made such an impresion on my mind that I Cant get over it. To think that I had wrote one word that had caused you one solitary tear. O it makes me feel so bad that I Cant sleep nor rest O to think that I have caused you to shed bitter tears. O how I would like to kiss them bitter tears away. I never felt so bad about any such thing in my life. I dont know how to express myself. You say that you hope I wil enjoy myself better in my new home. I did not Come out for enjoyments nor do I enjoy myself but it is now my duty and you know that. I never flinch from that. I tryed in all my letters to Comfort you to reason with you to try to impres upon your mind that it would be better for you not to fret as you used to do about trifles. For you know dear that it used to make me feel bad to have my love fret and it was through the greatest kindness that I have written thus to you. If I have written any thing that hurts your feelings I do hop you wil forgive me for I have many times written to you. If I had not been thinking about you and loved you above all and evrything on earth I Could not have done so after haveing been on duty from before daylight until nine at night. To sit in the cold for two or thre hours to write to you to comfort you after all the rest were in Bunk it shows whether I think of you as you do of me. Many a time hav I sat and writ to you when the tears blinded me so that I could hardly write at all. You refer to the Chicken that you Cooked for me and I would not sit in the room with you. You know that I never could content myself in the House but if I was there now I gues I would not be hard to keep in the house if I was there now.

I am so glad to hear that you are al wel. I received your stamps you sent in both letters with thanks and after I got the first one I put them in the envelope and they fel on the wet ground while I was writing to you and spoiled them evry one. I had to borrow one to send the letter. I never hatted any little thing so they stuck to the envelope on each side. Mabe I can make use of some of them. I wrote that we were going to Harods burg but Cant go very wel on acount of Ice Roads being So slipery. The Roads here are as smothe as ice there being snow on the ground. We may not go now atall. I received a letter from Dady and one from Elliot last night and was glad to hear from them. I was very sorry to hear that my old customers wer so careless about Paying up. I do hope they wil pay. If they dont give the notes and acts to Alexander and tel him to push them. There is a fairer prospect for money now than there has been. I might write a great many things but evry thing is dul to me since I recieved your last letter. O if I could whisper in your ear to night it would not grieve me so much but my dear dear wife wil have to wait so long for this. O what shall I do to think that I have been the Cause of all your grief and sorrow ever since we met it nearly crushes me. O, I do hope you wont fret any more about me than you can help but then it is all my fault evry bit of it wil I Can I ever be forgiven.

February 8, 1863
Sunday morning

Dear Mary,

Dearest you say that you wil not write any of your troubles to me. What else if you do not write to me evry thing I wil feel the worse for you. I want you to write me all. Dont keep any thing back for I want to hear how you get along. Just as anxious to hear from you as you can be from me for all the comfort I have here is reading your letters. O I cant forget that letter I dont know how I got such a lars thing in my letter. For you always was good to me more than I deserved. O you blessed one you if you knew O how I feel for you. The men are al in bed and I am sitting here writing and Crying to and for you. O you dear woman you. How I do love my little family. There is few misses home more than I do.

Mary I cant se to write. I wil have to finishe in the morning. There is no mail to morrow. You wrot about my throat. It dont bother me any more lately. I have not worn my neck kerchief for thre weeks and I feel wel in boddy but O for my dear Wife what shall I do. I Cant think to write to any one else. You wil know what letters to keep to yourself dear. You talk of giving up. Never never give up the ship as long as theres life ther is hope. Good night dearest. I hope it wil not be long before I can say wel Mary you going to bed.

I set myself to finish my letters. We have just recieved orders that we wil go to Harrod Burg to day. The morning is fine and the Boys al anxious for a moove. I have morning report to make out yet and Blankets to Roll and Breakfast to eat. So I wil have to close this. This leaves us all wel with few exceptions.

I hope you wil write often and everything. Good morning dear. Give my respects to all. Love to mothers folks and except my undivided love for you and my little family.
Yours truly
William McKnight
To his Wife

February 9, 1863[48]
Herodsburg Garrard Co. Ky

Dear Wife,

We have arrived in Harrodsburg and are Camping in the grounds of the Celebrated White Sulphur springs of Ky.[49] I have been very busy al day until now or a few minits ago. I went to se the springs. It is the most butiful ground that I ever seen in the woods. It is all fixed about the springs with a circular wall of limestone. The place is all laid of in Nice Roads for Cariages al along the ways and in fact al over the whole grounds are sedars White pines and all kinds of nice trees all small and trimed up nice. O it is the nicest place for a house but it is to far from home to be attractive to me.

When I get to writing to you I hardly know where to stop nor do I know what to write to interest you most. I wrote you a letter yesterday morning and directed it to Rutland. I dont know whether you wil receive it any sooner or not. If you do let me know. The health of our Company is good. The men al cheerful and hopeful. I must write to mother soon but tel them to drop me a few lines ocationaly whether I answer evry one or no. I want Father to write me another long letter. It does me so much good to hear from him. The snow has all melted of and it looks like rain. The weather is moderate. Give my respects to Marts folks and Janetts and al the rest of my friends and relations.

Kiss them dear little ones for me and comfort them al you can and keep up your Courage and be cheerful. So no more from your ever faithful and devoted Husband. I am wel and hope you are enjoying the same great Blessing.

William McKnight
to Samaria McKnight

February 16, 1863
Camp Near Stanford, Ky[50]

Most Dear Wife,

At the Earliest opportunity I hasten to inform you that I am wel at present hopeing these few lines may find you and our dear little ones enjoying the same great Blessings. I wil proceed to inform you where we are and what we are doing. We Came here Night before last to gain our Camp and the next morning there was 40 of our men left in Connection with Cap. Higley and Lieut Brunker on a scout towards Cumberland River and I have been so busy that I have not had any possible Chance to write any sooner.[51] We lef Harrods burg on the morning of the 14th and we arrived here last night just in time to pitch out tents. We had to shovel 2 or 3 inches of snow and frozen earth of and then we cut Cedar boughs and fixed down for our beds and then covered them with straw and it was the best bed I have laid on in the state. O it was so soft and smelled so sweet. We can boast like Solomon of old of having beds of Cedar This morning we got some dors and boards out of a house and floored our chebang so with many of the rest of the tents so you se we can even find comfort in the wilderness.[52] We are about ½ mile out of town yes and we have a table fixed up to eat of. There thre cases of measels in our company none bad.[53] Al have good places to stay at and wel cared for.

It would suprise you to se what a town we can build in half an hour. Our train extends on the road about half mile. On coming through yesterday I saw the mouth of a cave that was said to extend ten miles under ground. There is many caves in the state. Mamoth Cave extends 150 miles under ground.[54] I dont know how long we wil remain here but the understanding is that we wil stay here til spring. The people here are very glad to se us. Braggs Army camped handy here not long ago but there is no sesesh army in Ky now and it is thought that we wil hold the places to keep them out. There is some hopes that when we get our pay that some of us wil get to come home.

Arrived here the same day where we found 25 of our Boys glad to se us. The Paymaster Came here and finished Paying our Company. The most of us recd Our Pay at Harrodsburg. The great trouble now is how are we going to get it home safe. It is not safe to send it in letters and we are in hopes that Cap Higley wil get to come home. If he does I wil send mine with him if not I wil express it through. I received your most welcome letter of the 10th last night. I was glad to hear that you was wel and O how I would like to se you there and help you feed them Bees. Take good Care of them but take care of yourself first and I dreamed of seeing you this morning but O how sadly mistaken. We are in the Best place we have ever been get plenty of evry thing to live on and some holsome scouting to do. I would have been out with Cap this time but the Major would not let me go. I have so much to do. 2nd Lieut had been acting Agutant of the Battalion and when he left I was appointed to fill his place much to mortification of our first Lieut. I have done 2 or 3 mens work ever since I have been here. There is an appearence of a change in the Cabinet here. If the thing works right it wil be good news for you. I would like to know what that was you would like to know that you scratched. You seem to be uneasy about my throat. I am not troubled with it as I used to be at home atall. I would be happy to have your Company but I guess you wold get tired riding stradle on a piece of dried hide. I received both your letters you spoke of the one with Collar in I received just after we got ready to start from Harrods." I had just got my shirts washed nice and Clean but had no collar and O how thoughtful in you to send it to me.

Dear wife I wil have to close as I am under orders from Major to telegraph to Danville. So I must go to town. Good by God bless you all love to you Dear good morning.

William McKnight to his wife

February 17, 1863
Camp near Stanford
Lincoln Co. Kentucky

Dear Wife,

I again hasten to pen you a few lines to let you know that I am wel as usual. Theres some of our Boys somewhat unwel in Camp. The most of the Boys are out on a scout down in Rockcastle Co. where we was some time ago. We heard from them this evening. They want 12 more men which we wil send them in the morning. The Capt rote and sent a dispatch here this evening that one of his men had been bushwhacked and wounded in the arm, his Name is Jenkins (not bad).[55] There is no great force where the Captain is only some Bushwhackers.[56] We are very anxious for his safety we Can hardly wait until morning. This is simply the facts of the feelings and apprehentions of the Company this evening. I thought there was some prospects of Cap" Comeing home and I would send my money home with him but I believe I wil risk Part of it in a letter. I dont know but it is as saf in a letter as it is here. I have more money to take Care of than I like. I dont feel any to safe laying down at Night with ten or twelve Hundred Dollars under my Head in an open tent. I sleep with 2 carbines handy and 2 Revolvers under my Head evry night. If the money reaches you you can use it to the best advantage. I shal inclose thirty Dollars if it comes through safe I wil send the rest. You had better keep silent about the import of this letters.

We are in a very pleasant place. The People used Our Boys Clever here. They say this is the place where 25 of our Boys was sometime before we came here. We have very great privileges here Can goe out in town when ever we want to. The Boys behave themselves wel not much trouble like some Companies. I think the Captain wil be sent home to hunt some Deserters. I have been rather unlucky with my watch. I loaned it and got it broke had to get it fixed and it Cost me four Dollars. The Leaver shaft was broke but it is all right now. I mailed a letter to you this morning. I have so little time to write that I have written to no one ecept you for some time. This is the best place we have ever been in get plenty to eat and plenty of forage for our Horses and good watter for our horses and selves and all the wood handy we want. I have my Horse in a stable and a man to tend him without Cost. I bought two good linnen Collars to day for twenty cts and the Lieutenant Bought some pies to night and some Cakes. I draw bread and Coffee and sugar and beef and Pork and share it with the Oficers. They share their Grub with me. I wil Close by hopeing these lines and money may find you all wel and in good spirits. Keep up good Courage. The great and good hand of Providence wil bring all things right. It is getting late so good night Dear one good night. I dream of you often. The Boys have all received their Pay except one left at Lex. That was left there reached here today. Good night good night dearest—write. I ever remain your devoted Husband.

William McKnight.

March 1, 1863
Nicholsvill, Ky[57]

Dear and beloved wife,

After ten days hard scouting I hasten to let you know that I am wel. I shal not attempt to describe the hardships we have endured at this time. I have 25 men with me. The Cap and Lieuts I do not know where they are. We seperated at Crab Orchard since which time I have not heard from them. I supose you have heard that Ky was invaded again by Rebs which is more in the imaginations of some excitable Persons than anything else.[58] We could not find any. We expect to get furloughs now sometime as I hear that Congress has repealed the act prohibiting.[59] O how I look forward with anxious hope of again takeing you in my arms again. We do not know how we wil stay here. I started thirty dollars more home by express directed to Brother John for you. He wil tend to it. This makes sixty dollars I have sent you. You can use it to the best advantage. I think you had better put in a interest in someones hands where it wil be safe. I hope that I wil get some letters from home soon. I suppose there is some somewhere her but I do not know where. I think you had better direct to Danville second Batt 7 OVC. I wil write just as soon as I get to the Company again. The Captain is out somewhere with Eight men with Colonell Runcle.[60] We are with Col Minor our own.[61] There is some of our men sick at Lexington some at Danvill ten or twelve altogether. I Cant write any at present. I fel so bad about you and the Children. I do not know what to do. I want you dear to write in answer to my letters. I must close. My tears Blinds me so I Cant write any more.

Good by. God bless you. Oh you dear ones you. I hope you wil all Pray for me. We nead the Prayers of all good. Be of good cheer. There better and happier times Comeing for us I hope. I feel as though I would as soon be dead as alive if were not for you at home. I must close. Good by again I say good by. O how my heart aches for you. It is ready to burst you know how I feel.

Yours forever
Wm McKnight

March 4, 1863
Richmond, Ky[62]

Ever Dearest and beloved Wife,

I again embrace the earliest oportunity of pening you a few lines to let you know that I am wel. We just arived here this afternoon. I have only 12 men with me the rest is I know not where. Lieut Brunker we left at Crab Orchard. Geyer went to Danville. Both sick.

We have had a long and severe march since a week ago last Saturday at that time we were situated very Comfortably at Stanford. We left there with 52 men for Crab Orchard reached there at 3 ocl snowing halted. Went into Camp not remaining long. I was detailed to go with 12 men to Mt Vernon under Command of Col Minor Com 550 men 2 canon all together.[63] Part of the 45 Ohio. This was Sunday 12 pm. We reaced there just before night laid out. Left our horses saddled al night. The Rebs had left the Place the night before. We started the next morning over the Roughest Road that I had then ever seen. We assended a mountain and traveled all day and until ten at night. This is called big hil.[64] Here we camped for the Night slept in the open air on some Boards this being the first night I slept Out of doors as tents to cold to sleep not much for breakfast. Al felt wel. Next morning pleasant. The 24th here was a battle ground where Mitkaff made a Charge and was defeated.[65] The hill that he charged up we led down and it seemed all we Could do to git down. We reached Richmond that day where we now are stayed all Night in seminary.[66] Late in the evening we were hurred of by the report that there was 900 Rebs encamped close to us. We started for Ky R.[67] After traveling on the Pike for 10 or 12 miles we struck of on a Mud Road where our mules stuck in the mud and we were compelled to remain either on our feet or in our saddles. Evry minute expecting an attack until 5½ in the morning. We got up at last after looseing some Waggons and other things we went on and ferried the Ky R and reached Nickolisvill.

This 28th stayed all all Night remained until 2nd march when we left for Lex & reached before Noon remained until morning & we left for this place which we reached after Crossing our Horses over in a little Boat Carrying thre Horses at a time feried all Night got over 150 Horses here. 3 of my men left me and went up to stanford. I forgot to mention that I left ten of my men including the ambluence Drivers at Lex.[68] When I was here before there was 8 more of our men Come to me here so I have yet with me 13 men. How long we wil remain here I do no know. I am very anxious to get to the Company and Clothes. I bought me a Pair of socks and Mittens last evening for 70 cts.

I have not received a letter from you for nearly 2 weeks. I am allmost sick to hear from home but I hope you are all wel. The Lord has been very kind to us I have not been sick a day nor have I had any serious Colds as I used to have at home. I pened you a few lines from Nickolisville teling you to direct to Danvill but I believe you had better direct to Lex to be forwarded to the Regmt. Nomore. In haste yours truly and until Death. Dearest good by love to you al.

Wm McKnight to his Wife

March 14, 1863
Sesesh farm
Ten Miles from Lexington

Dear and beloved Wife and Children,

I again hasten to pen you a few lines to let you know where I am. This day makes 21 since I left Camp have been the saddle most of the time. We have just returned from a scout 70 ms from Richmond where we had a figh and Captured about 30 Prisoners as many Horses and Revolvers saddles and Blankets and so forth.[69] I shal not attempt to give you the Particulars but the Boys recieved the Praise of old soldiers that was with us.[70] None of us recieved any injury whatever. The Enemy did not fare so well. How many we killed I do not know. 2 at least hardly knew what hurt them that I know of. I was in advance all day with 2 guides and was first in the fight. I fired my Carbine 5 times with as good aim as ever I did at a squirrel.[71] I did not see one of our Boys flince. Evry done his duty. We had to fal back on account of their artilery 2.12 lbs mountain Howitzers.[72] We returned to Richmond yesterday. I am Riding the 3rd horse since I started. The Captain and some of the rest of the Company are at Lexington. I hear we expect to get there today. I wil I hope get time to write you the Particulars and recieve some news from Home. I have not heard a word for 3 weeks. I am very anxious to recieve some letters. I wrote you a few lines from Nicholisville & sent you a Picture from Richmond and some Books for the Children and a letter. I feel a great deal Better than I did then in mind. I hope this may find you al wel.

The Boys that has been through with me are pretty near used up. I am wel except Bad cold and soreness low down in my Right side where I was hurt last spring. I hope to get to come home this summer sometime. Until then I hope you wil keep up good Courage. Tel Cous Will that I did not forget him when I sent those Presents but I could not find any thing that suited me to send but I wil ever remember him and hope we wil spend many happy days together. I hope to live a long and happy life with you Dear. I think I could content myself at home if the War was ended which I hope it wil be before long.

I must close as I do knot know how soon I may hear the Bugle. I inclose this in an envelope we go of the Sesesh prisoners. We got one Captain 2 lawyers and 1 doctor lodged them in Richmond jail.

So good by Dear ones. God Bless you from your ever loveing Husband.
    William McKnight to his Wife

March 16, 1863
Lexington, KY

Dear and beloved Wife,

I seat myself again at the erliest moment to answer your very affectionately written letter I received last night. The first I have received from one for 25 days. I left here the 3rd day of this month with 15 men for Richmond. Crossed Ky River 14 ms from Lex" succeeded in getting over in the course of the day and night all safe. The 44 drowned one man and 2 horses arrived at Richmond 26 ms from Lex before night with only 12 men bisides myself 3 have left for Camp at the Ferry 5th stayed in camp House 6th stayed in the Meeting House. The morning of the 7th we started for Harzel Green 75 or 80 miles distant 5 days rations went 20 ms Campe in an old Iron works.[73] Went 4 ms for our Breakfast fed our Horses and got plenty of sesesh Corns. Took our Breakfast in a grave yard. On we went pressed our Horse.

At noon we had assended an awful mountin expicting a fight. Loded our Carbines that night we halted a mile from town Called Campton.[74] Next morning the 9th we went towards Red River.[75] Captured Rebels al the way. I had Command of the advance gards that day and had the satisfaction of Captureing six Rebs thre myself with 3 Enfields 2 Horses and Equipments.[76] Marched them to the Head of the Column. We got a Brigade surgeon Captain 2 Gunners 2 lawyers 17 Privates besides 28 Revolvers as many Horses and Equipments when within ½ mile of Reed River we halted to take Care of some Prisoners when the first thing we knew the Rebs Came in sight. We were ordered to dismount. The Infantry was deployed to the left on foot while we the Cavalry wer to go to the Right. Haveing been ahead I knew we could not Cross a stream that lay in our way unobserved by Colonel Moore I told him of the obstruction and he ordered us to mount and we did mount for certain.[77] We were after them as fast as our Horses could Carry us. The time we had taken in mounting and dismounting had given the Rebs time to reach the ford before we could fire on them. As soon however as we came up we comenced fireing (after dismounting) on them with our Carbines and Revolvers killing 2 and wounding several.[78] They had on reaching the stream plunged their Horses in and Crossed on a foot log some swimming over on their Horses. They wer consequently in great confution they however Rallied and fired on us with Enfield and springfield Rifles & muskets.[79] They all sang very nice something like a big Musket in your ear but we did not mind them. They did not disturb me any more than the Rasping of an ol saw. Our Boys stood up to the scratch like soldiers. The first thing we knew a 12 lb shell Came hissing and screeching among us just over our Heads doing no harm however. We were ordered to mount and fall back as we could not cross the stream without swimming and that in the face of their 2:12 Howitzers. We did so in good order. Few seemed very much excited. The bugle was Sounded and all Brought their Horses to a stand for a moment when we wer ordered forward the shells stil faling thickly around us. Being in the rear I was ordered to take thre men and assend the hill that over looked the ford and enemy and await the sound of the bugle. I did so haveing hitch my Horse and fed him I proceeded cautiously to recounter. I had not been Posted very long before we were discovered consequently received their fire until they found that they could not touch us. They ordered their artilery down nearer us so as to fire mor against the Hill. The first shot went clear over the trees over our Heads. The next burst about 30 yds from one of my Boys who had a Red Cap. The sharpshoters still fireing when ever they could get a chance. I remained here an hour and a half hearing no bugle. The Boys insisted that our Collum had gone and we had not heard the signal so I fel back to the next part of the Hill so I could discover our forces part of the 45th 44th 7 Ohio and 14th Ky had gone on.[80] No one left to sound the bugle as was Promised by the Colonell. We withdrew Cautiously leaving them Blazeing away at the Hil we had just left. We overtook the Colum halted at six miles from the ford where the fight accured. We reached Richmond the 13th and Lex Saturday the 14th. The Roads very dusty and we jailed all our Prisoners but the doctor and one who made his escape. The rest of the Regmt is here now and probably ten thousand others. I received Elliots letter which informs me that you are sick which make feel so bad that I am no man atall but I hope you are Better by this time. I am just able to walk Round. I feel so bad with Cold but am better than I have been. I was out to the Clay farm yesterday and got some Murtle and English Ivy which I enclose hopeing you wil be able to make them grow. I wil answer your letters more fuly soon.

    Your truly

    Wm McKnight to his wife

In margin:

All for you dear that thirty dollars. I was glad to hear from as wel as that I sent John.

                                  March 19, 1863

                              Camp near Lexington Ky

Ever and beloved Wife,

    I again after a busy days work hasten to write you a few lines to let you know that I am Considerable recovered from my arduous scout. There is few soldiers who have seen harder times than we have or who have undergone hardships with so much cheerfulness as the men who I have the honor to be with. Through all our route they semed to enjoy themselves. For my part I had no idea what men and Horses could endure and what is more I realy liked the chase. I rode my Horse down before I had any idea of it in my eagerness to ketch and prevent any Rebs from escapeing to give the alarm but I have the satisfaction of knowing that there was not one escaped to give the alarm. We took them completly on surprise and if we had been managed right we could have captured 40 or 50 more just as wel as not. But I am runing of from the idea I started out on. I have felt so bad about you since I recieved Elliotts letter informing me that you was unwel. It makes me forget evry thing else. I would be glad to hear from you. I fear that you are stil ill. Oh how I wish to be with you. If I could settle this war with the Union restored I would give five Hundred Dollars but it wil have to be settled by the strength of Arms now I expect.[81] (God speed the day).

We have been situated here since Tuesday. We are on the Russelvill Pike about one and half ms from Lex in a very nice Place Close to the R.R.[82] It is very nice to see the Carrs go by thre or four times a day. The thought that they bear and return our letters is cheering. I recieved a letter from John in regard to some money (30) thirty dollars which I hope you have ere this recieved. The whole Regmt is all here Camped together. I was so horse that I could hardly talk but I went out on all the drills today. We are recieving new clothing and I have been very busy the most of the day and yesterday isuing clothing to the men and we have not got through by 20 men yet. We are getting nice clothing. I hope these lines may find you better. You wil have to hire some one to help you. I do not want you to work when you do not feel like it. I hope to be with you this summer sometime. I have a fine Enfield gun and several other things I would like to send home. The Capt talkes of sending for his wife. If he does and she comes I can send somethings to you. Maby you may have something that you would like to send to me. If you have all right. If you are only wel and the children I can content myself but when I hear that you are ill I do not know what to do but hope you wil be able by the help of God to be cheerful and bear up under your troubles until it Pleases him to return me to the Bosom of my Family.

I recieved a letter from Leon the other day. He is wel. This leaves me in good health except cold which is getting better. You need not give yourself any uneasyness about me. I forgot to say the Cap was out all the time I was out on another route. He to was in a fight near Mt Steriling.[83] They Captured over fifty Prisoners also without any loss of life.

So good by dear. Oh how I long to se you once more and recieve your kind Blessings. (I recieved Leilas letter also the Post stamp).

From your ever loveing
William McKnight

March 20, 1863
Camp near Lexington, Ky

Dear Samaria & Children,

It is under Painful curcumstances that I again atempt to write to you. I wrote a letter yesterday to you but since I received a letter from Elliott informing me of your ill Health which I hoped you had recovered from before this time, I had made considerable Preparation for comeing home but Pressing as is the need and trying as is the circumstances I am doomed to disappointment.

I shoed your letter to the Captain and he took it immediately to the Colonell. He seemed to simpathise deeply with me in my affliction but all to no purpose. General Gillmore is anxiously awaiting an order in conformity with the late law to Furlough Soldiers home and our Colonell says he wil at the earliest moment furlough as many as he can until then I must nesesariely wait althoug the suspence seems almost unbearable.[84] If there was any chance to get a Pass I would come but in that I failed. Some of our Boys have left for home no doubt but that is only bringing misery on themselves and Family. I would rather and I think you would have me stay and come home Honorably (when the Officers are doing all they can to get us furloughs and a fair Prospect for it) than to steal away and incur a heavy Penalty and disgrace. I hope it wil not be long before I can come. If you was wel I would not feel so bad about home for it seems to me if I am permited to come it would be very hard to part with home again.

I am allmost as wel as ever. This morning we have a very good Place to stay a first rate Bed to sleep on and plenty to eat and wear. More nice clothes than we know what to do with. I am going to send some of mine home when the weather gets warmer. We have had very nice weather for some time but last night it thundred lightning and rained hard. This morning it is cool but I think it is going to clear of. I do hope that ere this reaches you that you wil be better if you are not write and let me know for I shal expect to hear from you often by some of the folks if you cant let me know yourself. I do not know what to write or what to do. I hope you wil not be uneasy about me for there is no nead to any uneasy whatever for me. I am very glad to hear that good Mother is with you. I know that you wil be wel cared for as long as she is able. Mother I know what it is to have a good Mother and to want a good mother. If it were not for the faith I have in you I would be allmost without an anchor. Samaria you may rest assured that I wil loose no time in coming home. Oh how I wish I was there to watch over you and comfort you. I expect you feel worse on account of not hearing from me but I wrote evry chance I had and even when I had not half a chance it was impossible for me to have written oftener as we were sometimes 10 or 20 miles from Post Offices. We rode for days and nothing but woods just a Cow Path to travel on. Wel I must close. I like to write to you it is the nearest I can come to talking to you. Hopeing that all things are for the Best I close with the most sincere hope that you may spedily recover to your former health and we may permitted to live a long and happy life together when the Clash of Arms shal be hushed and Peace and happiness Reign ore the land.

Yours sincerly
Wm McKnight to his Wife

March 24, 1863
Lexington, Ky

Ever Dear and beloved Wife,

I again hasten to pen you a few lines to let you know that the spare moments are spent in writing to you. I am thankful to inform you that I am almost wel again and I hope that these few lines may find the same Blessing resting upon you and ours. We are now situated in a butiful Place near Lex. Our Boys have just returned from a thre days scout to Mt. sterling where they had a runing fight with the Rebs. They ran them about five miles took several prisoners and killed six theire Horses. Becomeing became exausted they returned to camp. More of our Boys hurt I escaped without any injury. Frank sansbury tells me that Marion Rathburn was taken prisoner with several Others of his Regmt. 2 of our Regmt received slight wounds. I dont know who they are. Our Cap is unable for Duty. Several of the men are unwell some six in the Hospital al getting Better I believe.

I am very anxious to hear from home. I have not heard from you for so long that I am fearful that you are stil Confined. O dear how I wish I Could be with you to wait on you although I never could content myself in the hose when at home but I think I could if I were there now but I hope you wil be as wel taken care of as though I was there. Dear Wife if you cant write yourself get Elliott to write for I am very much troubled about you. Poor Susan writes me that she has not been out of the house for ten weeks. The rest of the folks are well she says. I answered her letter on Sunday.

I have been thinking of sending some of my old clothes home and I thought of sending you some nice Cautan Drawers. I can draw as many as I want. When I send them I wil let you know. We expect to have stiring times we are anxious for it dont dred it the least. We feel confident of our strength. I have just received the Pay Rolls which indicates that we are to have our Pay soon. You may Probably wish to know how we fare wel we have a nice green sod for a floor and stable door and straw and plenty of Blankets for a bed a Boy to cook for us so we have things fixed up prety wel for Camp life. Can sleep first rate and dream sweet dreams about home and wake up and find it only a dream. But there is a better time comeing I hope for us.

R. T. Andrews and Wm Burns has Deserted yes and Harry spires and E. Andrews the have reached home.[85] They have disgraced themselves by their conduct. Our Regmt is a teror to the Rebs and pride to us they wont fight the Ohio Boys if they can help it but they dont fear the Ky troops attol. Asher has been very much afflicted with Boils but he is getting better haveing the report of the company to make out and the Rolls to make out too. I must close withhe mast since hopes for your spedy recovery to health.

I hasten to mail this letter direct to Lexington to be forwarded to the Regmt. I can hardly think of any thing else to ad so good by give my respect to our relations, love to you and the children and dont forget good mother I must again say close from your ever loveing and faithful Husband. Let the world say what they wil it makes no difference in my love for you and home. You are my thoughts by day and dreams but Night and I hope the giver of all and every Blessing may permit us to live together again after the Clamor of War shal have hushed and Peace reigns supreme if not in this world in the world to come where Parting is nomore and where the weary are at rest.

So nomore from your
William

In margin:
Write soon

March 29, 1863
Camp Near Ky River 11 miles from Nichalisville

most Dear Wife,

I sit down to pen you a few lines in great Haste. I am well and in fine spirits. The Cap and 17 men are with me here. The rest of the Boys are out after the Rebs.[86] Just makeing them git they took yesterday 100 Prisoners over 150 head of Beef Cattle and are Pushing them hard. They the Rebs are just stealing through here to live. They are hard put to live. Their Prisoners say that they would just as soon be taken Prisoners as not and they are accomodated very often. They think that 7 OVC must be 3 or 4,000 thousand strong for they say they cant go any place but the d—d seventh is after them.[87] I left Lex saturday morning. Before I left I sent some things with the Cap things which you wil wil be notified of by the Cap Wife. I sent some Brass Cartriges which is full of powder which you must be very careful of. I sent an Enfield Rifle which I captured on Red River for Tomy also a saber thre Blankets 2 shirts 2 pair of new drawers. A spoon that has the initials of your on that I bought from one of the Boys for 30 cts to send to you. Many cup of coffe have I suped with it. It is pure silver. I sent my cap. Tomy can wear that to I guess if he cant give it William saunders. My stable & rack you can use for gowns if you wish. That old saber you can keep for me when I come home to Practice with. I feel first rate this morning. Had a good wash and got on a clean shirt and Drawers. It is a cold morning but the sun shines. I have a great many things I would like to write but have not time now as the mail is nearly ready to start.

I hope you have become strong and wel again. Asher told me that you was lots Better which did me more good than anything I have heard for a long time. In fact it made me feel like another man. Tel mother that I received her letter. Thanks to her soul and also dear sister maries. But have not had time to answer them. I must close so dear wife be of good cheer. The Georgia Prisoners and men that have fled from the South say that the People are fast becomeing determined to stay this warr in Georgia. Pork is worth over $1.00 pr Pnd.

So good by god Bless
from William

In margin:
thirty-two more Prisoners just Passed.
Direct Lex.

April 1, 1862[88]
Camp Near Ky River
Garard Co

Stil Ever Dear Wife,

    I sit down to Pen you a few lines to let you know that I am wearying for a letter from you. I am wel at Present and in great hopes and fine spirits. Our men have taken near Crab Orchard Eighteen Hundred Prisoners and any amount of Beef Cattle.[89] This to us is cheering news. If the People at Home would do their duty it would not be long before we could return to our Dear families. This is butiful morning. The sun shines out in al his Beauty and grandure. I hope ere another Aprill sun shines upon us that we wil be Permitted to return to our fire sides.

    I went yesterday to hunt a chicken for the Captain. Found one and was just in time for Dinner. Had a kind invitation and accepted and partook of splendid Diner which you are aware is quite a treat to a soldier and have an invitation to go back to day and take the Captain which I intend to do as I have nothing to do today. Our Boys are all out eccept twenty that remained here with me. I recieved a letter from Cousin William McMaster last night.[90] He is wel and is Oposite Vicksburg.[91] I also got one from Theop. He is at Murfreesburough and is also wel.[92] I do want to hear from you so bad. Evry letter I get I hasten to se if it is your Hand write and am Disappointed very often. I am more hopeful now in regard to our National Dificulty than I have ever been since the War comenced. I hope you have recovered your health again. The Mail Boy leaves in a few minutes and I must close with the best wishes for you all. I remain your affectionate.

    Husband William McKnight

In margin:
Write as soon as you recieve this.

April 4, 1862[93]
Crab Orchard

Dear Wife,

    At the Earliest available opportunity I hasten to talk to you a little through the Mails to let you know that I am wel as ever again thanks to Providence but I have serious forebodings that you have not recovered yet as you would have written to me before this time. But I am hopeful that you may have written and it has not reached me. We left Lex 28 inst for Crab Orchard. All the able men left the tents and Regimental Property where I last wrote to you and Proceeded on towards Somerset where they Overtook the Rebs scotts and Ashbys Cavalry where they had a four hours fight with them Completely Dressing them on their own ground.[94] Our Battallion (Nortons) made the charge and our Company led the Charge right up a steep hill under a shower of Bullets and strange as it may appear not one of our Boys were wounded but alas the Butternut Devils did not share the same fortune for our Boys shot to kill and they did to for noless than 20 fell under the first charge besides heaps of Horses as soon as our men reached the summit of the hill.[95] The Enemy Broke and fled in great confusion here the sport comenced. The Rebs finding themselves whiped they was glad to beg for mercy which they recieved as soon as they threw down their arms.[96] Not being permitted to be Present I am sorry to say that I cannot give you a Detailed account of the fight but you nodout wil have seen in the Papers before this time all about it. But this much Our Boys was told by the Prisoners they never had been whiped before that the 7 O.V.C must be old soldiers. When told that we had only been out 6 months they would not believe us. The Enemies loss Could not have been less than Eight Hundred in killed wounded and Prisoners. A great many officers were among the Prisoners. The People at Home may be Proud of their soldier friends. They recieved the Cheers of the rest of the soldiers and General Gilmore said they were the Best in the field that is the best Regmt in Ky. The Cap is going to send for his wife and if you want to send me any thing you can send by her. O how I wish you could come to. Oh am I to be permitted to se you any more I think so. It buoys me up to think of the happiness of meeting you all again. O wont it be joyful to those who hold out faithful to the end.

We have been very busy makeing out new Pay Rolls. We expect to get our pay next week. The Rebs hav got such a severe Punishment this time that I think they wil not try it again very soon. If they do we wil I think serve them worse next time. I heard that they have come down to the Point and attacked our troops. I would like to know how it is. I wish they would send for the seventh or part of it at least. We feel quite safe here. No uneasyness felt here for we have plenty of soldiers here to Defend the state against any ordinary forse. The Rebs say they were compelled to Come to Ky to obtain something to live upon and their looks shows it for they are the hardest set of men that I ever seen. You have seen a sample of them Passing from Virginia to Jackson.[97] They are clothed generaly in Butternut. They have no uniform. Each one finds his own clothing. They dont look like soldiers but they know how to fight but they say the 7 is to much for them. Quite a compliment to us for they have been in the service 2 years and never was whiped before. Bully for us.

I hope that those fellows that Deserted us will recieve no countenance from the People. They told People in this state that they were going home to fight. If they do I would be glad to hear of them being taken Prisoners. But I must close. We are in fine spirits and good condition. In them things I sent home if they reach you you wil find a horse Brush which you may Present to Father. The Blankets are somewhat dirty but you wil find them quite nice if you get them washed.

Write and let me know how the Bees are doing. Let me know how you get along with evry thing. Let me know how you are and mother and Father and the children and Willie and all the Rest are. I hope these few lines may find you enjoying the Best of health. So god Bless you all. Good by from your ever loveing husband.

William McKnight
to his Wife Samaria

In margin:
Write soon.

April 10, 1863
Lexington

Dearest Samaria,

I again hasten to Pen you a few lines to let you know that I am wel and sincerely hope this may find you still mending and almost wel for I do not expect you Can be wel yet. I recieved your Penciled letter Night before last the night we arived here from Crab orchard. It was the first I had seen from your hand for more than a month. Oh you dont know how glad I was to hear from you. I wrote to you from near Camp dick Robison and then at Crab Orchard which I hope you have recieved in due time. I would have written to you yesterday but was busy. The Paymaster being here I thought I would not write until I sent my money but he did not get to our Company last night. So as soon as I got my

Breakfast I determined to wait no longer. We wil be paid as soon the Paymaster gets Back from Town. When I get it I wil send it in a letter unless I get a Private Conveyance. The Boys are in good health and fine spirits generaly. The Deserters are flocking back to the Army evry day. We are not under any orders for Marching so we may stay here some time but it is uncertain if we stay here long. We wil get letters regular. We wil get some new Horses before we leave. There is a talk that part of our Regmt wil go on to big Sandy and part to Mt sterling.[98] I supose that you wil se in the Papers that Walfords Cavalry made the Charge at somerset which is false.[99] They were not nearer than thre miles of the Place. The 7th O.V.C. made the charge and Co K took the lead and kept it. Carried it out right and just in the right time. As soon as you know several things and dont hear from the letters I write 2 or 3 times a week when ever I can get a chance. Please look over my letters when you go to write to me. I do not know what else to write at present only I am comeing home as soon as I can get a pass.

It seems to be the general impression that the war is vergeing to a close. Evry one seems cheerful in antisipation of the Prospects before us. Oh what a Millenium it wil be when friends and relations wil be permitted to embrace each other. God speed the day. I shal look for a letter from you to day. I want to hear from you so bad. Tel Mother that I am very thankful for a few lines from her. They are always acceptable. Tel Mary to write. Hers are always acceptable to. It is Butiful weather here. The Roads are very dusty here. They are far better here than they are with you. Most of the main roads are turnpike Paved with Broken limestone.[100]

You seem to dout whether I can read your very kind little letter. Read it yes I could. Guess the half of it. I am very sorry to hear of Poor Uncle Williams Misfortune. He is left again lonely and alone. He seem to have a great deal of trouble. I deeply sumpathise with him. Dear Samaria this leaves me wel. The next letter you get from me I hope wil be better than this one as I have written in a hury. Pencil me a few more lines when ever you feel like it. It cheers me to se your hand writing. Let me know whether you get my letters any sooner by Directing to Bulland or not. Let me know how you get along whether you have got your bee hives or not from stansburies.[101] Give my respects to al enquiring friends. Retain my undying love for you and the little ones at home.

From Wm to Samaria McKnight

Willie Saunders write to me Please.

In margin:
I enclose some songs sent to me from Uncle John of Cincinnati.[102]
Give one to sister Mary and one to Emma.[103]
I hope poor little Lucy wil be wel by this time.

April 12, 1863
Lexington
Sunday Morning

Dear and beloved Wife,

We are al Ready to start for Stanford. I sit down to Pencil you a few lines to let you know that I am wel and that you are ever uppermost in my mind. I went to the Colonell this morning for leave of absence but he has not the power to grant it but wil do all he can to obtain it for me. I did not sleep much last for thinking about you and the Dear ones at home. It is a butiful morning and I can hear the Church Bells tolling and I feel as if I would like to go but I have not the Privlege.

There goes some Horses and waggons Reining of there they go over Horses and evrything out in to the Road. Back they come towards camp. There they have got them stoped no harm done. Further than 2 or 3 Horses cripled. Asher just Past me as I sit flat on the ground. He says put in a few words for me. Wel Asher looks bad. He is very much afflicted with Boils but is getting Better. The Bugle sounds Boots and Saddles and I must close.[104] So good by for the Present. May Heven Protect you and comfort you and yours and restore the loved ones to each others Company again is my Prays.

May 2, 1863[105]
Stanford
Saturday morning

Ever dear and beloved Wife,

I hasten to inform you that I have arived at my Destination and find Cap Higley in Command of the Camp the most of our Boys being in camp. I find Asher almost wel and many of the rest of the Boys better and some worse. I heard that Wiseman Zachariah is dead.[106] Whether it is so or not I cant say.

I stayed with Uncle John McKay night before last in Cincinnati.[107] His Family is wel. I have not seen Cap Higley yet but understand he is better. I want to hear from you so bad I hardly know what to do with myself. It seems to me that you are a thousand times nearer and dearer to me. I can hardly keep from sheding tears before the Publick. It completely unmans me to reflect on your situation. I never shal forget our Parting. O those sweet Piteous faces rises up before me as a guardian angel to make me a wiser and I hope better man. The Boys are to get furloughs now. Five per ct of of each Co at a time. So you may look for some of Boys home soon and I hope that I may get to come & se you again this sumer. Get your father to write to me imediately direct to Stanford Lincoln Co via Lex Ky. My expences through was twelve dollars. I did not buy anything for myself but two collars and two hankerchiefs and a neck string. You must be as composed in your mind and take things as easy as possible dont take things hard. Content yourself to let things slide along as easy as posible. I do hope to hear that you are beter but if you are not let me know. I want to know just how you are.

You must send and get such things as you want. Dont put it of a day nor an hour. I must close so take good care of yourself. Let the memory of the past and the hopes of the future bear you up under your severe afflictions. Put your trust in him who is able and willing to save and who has always showered Blessings on our heads. Surely goodness and mercy has followed us al the days of our lives. So dear one I must close. Good morning. God Bless you and Protect you and comfort you in the hour of need.

From your unworthy but ever loveing Husband
William McKnight
1st Sergt Co K 7th O.V.C.

May 4, 1863
Camp Near Stanford Ky

Ever Dear Samaria,

I again sit down to pen you a few lines to let you know that I am wel and find the rest of the Boys the same. I find the Camp where I left it the Cap in comand of the whole Concern. He is Better than he has been for some time. The greater part of our Regmt has gone on to Monticello.[108] They have driven the Rebs before them without loss on our part except one man from Co L Cap Leper his name was smith Bugler of the Co.[109] There is a fair prospect of our Co staying here to do Provost guard duty in Stanford. I hope that this fine weather may improve your health so that you can walk round and once in awhile pen me a few lines. O how glad I would be to se a letter from you. Since I came back I have been weighed down with a dul melancholy feeling that it seems imposible for me to shake of. I am not worth a cent. I cant do anything. I cant write I do not know what to say. I recieved all those letters that you told me about also one from Cousin Wm and Lenox McMaster.[110] Wm says that they hav lost several men by sickness more than they had lost previous to going there. Yes and I got a letter from sister susan. She has not been wel for a long time. Her arm troubles her very much. She is under the doctors care all the time. She is ver much troubled about the Negroes.[111] Asher is in the Hospital at stanford. Franklin Sansbury is waiting on the sick boys there. We have four Boys sick there. That is thre besides Asher and he is almost as wel as ever. I was surprised to find him as wel as he is. The understanding now is that Colonel Garrard has recieved Orders to Grant Furlough and as soon as he gets back of that Reconaisance he wil give five per ct of the Companies leave at a time until al have been home. So may it be. I recieved those other letters I told you about and intend that no such thing shal ever cost me any more trouble while I live. The Cap just tels that our men have had another fight down below Sumerset and whiped the Rebles Bad and we are to move down day after tomorrow. The Quartermaster has just Come Back from the seat of war and says that the Rebs have been run clear out of State and we wil go down there for a while and the Probabililty is that we wil be in Lexington again before long. There is Eight thousand men of ours down there enough it is thought for safe operations. Our men have mustered again for Pay.

O dear wife can I ever get back to se you again. I hope so. I want you to let me know how you feel since I left whether it made you feel worse of not. O how my Heart throbs for you. All the Consolation is that God in his infinite Mercy doeth all things wel. His wil be done.

From your affectionate Husband
Wm McKnight
to his wife Samaria

May 7, 1863
Camp near Stanford
7th O.V.C.

Ever Dear Samaria and little ones,

I seat myself this Rainy morning to let you know that I am wel as usual and my great wish and Prayer is that these few lines may find you enjoying better health and the rest wel. I cannot hope that you are wel but I do hope that you may be able to go around the House and in no pain so you can enjoy yourself better than lying in bed Confined. I am very sory that I did not stay with you longer for our company being here doing nothing. I might as wel been there as here. But you know that I expected that all our company would be with the Regmt but after our company went as far as Sumerset Cap Higley was ordered back to Stanford to do Provost Duty which he has been doing ever since which dont amount to much being a very easy job. We have turned over our large tents and drawn new ones Called shilter tents each being capable of accomodating two men. The Captain being reduced to a servants tent large enough for four. The shelter tents it is intended wil be caried on horseback each man carying half of each tent. They are just about as large as two table cloths buttoned together. They dont leak. 23 of our men are in Stanford 16 have gone to Lexington to guard Prisoners through. Lieut Brunker has gone to the Regmt to obtain leave to come home. I wrote the other day to you under the impression that we were going on to Monticello beyond the cumberland River but now our forces are returning and the Prospect is that we may be in Lexing before long. I am very sorry that that I wrote it to you for we are here yet. I have not seen John Foose since I came back.[112] He met with a little Bad luck. He started with Sargeant Ross with a lot of old Horses for Lex when at dick Robinson they halted for the night.[113] In the morning they started before daylight suposeing as they had the number of Horses that they were all right but when daylight came they discovered that they had a horse along that did not belong to them. Sargeant told John that they would take him on through and bring him back but before he had gone far after daylight a Seargeant from a Battery arrested John and detained him. He is between here and Sumerset. The Cap says there is no dout but John is Clar and wil only be detained for a hearing which wil result in his release. The Cap did al he could to get them to let him go but they sid he would have to have a trial. I have written as near the facts as I can as I get them from the Captn as you wil be likely to hear al kinds of stories about him. His wife need give herself no uneasyness about him. Capt sends his money home by Lieut Geyer. It is in Pomeroy. I got that Blanket from Mrs Higley and left it at Pomeroy and told John to send it out along with the Saddle to you. Take care of that saddle. Dont lend it. Have it taken apart and put away for I expect to wride it again if I am spared. Colonel Miner says that the Probabilities are that we may be called to Western Virginia.[114] If so we wil get home again this summer. If we dont we wil be nearer home. I had rather a narrow escape when I came home. Just before I went through there was ten Rebs near Blue lick and the second night after I crossed the Bridge over Licing River they Burned the Bridge.[115] It cost forty five thousand Dollars to build. If I had been two days later starting I would have had fun getting across. As it is I feel thankful to a kind Providence for his mercies shown. He has shown his mercies to me all the days of my life and this severe affliction I hope wil work together for our good. I can say what ever may befal me his will be done. Dear Samaria I want you to put your trust in he who is able and willing to save he who has ever been mindful of us ever merciful to us. I can say shurely goodnes and mercy hath followed us all the days of our lives. So we have much reason to be thankful.

Just Picture to your imagination five Hundred Table cloths streached over a large woods Pasture in the shape of an A and you wil have a Birds Eye view of our Camp at present with here and there a few Horses and mules grazing around them. The Grass is very good pasture now and our Horses are doing wel. We have plenty of it here. The fences laid down giveing our Horses plenty of room for grazeing. The Boys have a great deal of fun about our little Dog tents. I think they wil answer a very good purpose. They wil be handy if not conveniant. I recieved a letter from Theop since I came back. He is wel says that he has learned where his father is. Some place in new mexico.[116] Charles Lewis is in camp and is wel.[117] I have not seen Asher for a few days but hear from him evry day. He is stil mending. So I must close by requesting you to direct to Stanford. From your Devoted loveing husband. Give my love to our folks. Kiss the Babes dear. May God Bless you.

Good by for the Present
William McKnight

May 9, 1863
Stanford Ky

Ever Dear Samaria,

We have just moved into or new town this morning and while here on Business I take this opportunity to let you know that I am well and Hearty and in good spirits. The Prospect seems favorable for our camp to stay here some time. We have a butiful Place to camp on and our Boys are doing Provost Duty in Town. The Boys are mostly in good health. The weather is fine and Pleasant evrything quiet.

Lieut Brunker has no doubt reached home before this time. He is Comeing to se you. I sent you my Watch by him and also a ring that I want you to wear in remembrance of me. It cost . . . dollars but I got it for two. Keep that to yourself. The watch take care of until I come home. If I never come give it to Thomas. I have not heard from you since I left home. I am very anxious to hear and to know how you are. I suppose there is letters on the Road but I expect they al goe to the Regmt. We wil get them in time.

Thomas McKnight.
Courtesy of Lois Mohler.

The Balance of our Regmt is at Somerset. Have not heard from them for some time. Asher is stil mending he wrote to day. I have nothing more to say only write as often as you can. Direct to Stanford Ky Co K care of Cap Higly. Leave the Regmt of and your letters wil not follow the Regmt. Remember to mother and all the rest. Accepe my undivided love for yourself and Pray for me for I kneed your Prayers now more than ever I did. Send me something to remember you by by Liet Brunker if you have any thing and think I deserve any thing. So nomore at Present from your ever loveing husband.

Wm McKnight

In margin:
in great hast excuse.

May 15, 1863
Camp of the 7th O.V.C.
Somerset

Dearest Samaria,

I again seat myself to let you know that I am enjoying good health and sincerely hope to hear that you are enjoying the same great & inestimable Blessings. We left Stanford day before yesterday arived here last night Distance 33 ms. We left 23 of our men at Stanford includind Asher and Frank Savage & Sansbury.[118] They are nurseing. Asher is quite wel again only and he cant ride yet. The Health of our Boys is very good. Our Horses are in fine condition but how long it wil be so I cant say as this is rather a hard Place for forage. We have to grase Our Horses and mules. We are within six miles of the River. The Enemy reported strong. Our Pickets are quite near the Reble Pickets but they are not so Friendly as they were. Five of our men are on Picket today. We may be said to be laying in front of the Enemy. We may be Called at any time to fight him. We are ready and confident. We have about as near as I can find out ten thousand men here. The sound of the Drum is as comon as the ring of the old Anvil and as little noticed but oh what an awful Contrast. The one portends Peace Pleasure Home Happiness and evrything pertaining to the comforts of this world whilst the other portends war with all its accompaing results of Carnage of Bloodshed sighs and tears widows and Orphants misery poverty and destruction and even this language to an Ohioan conveys not the least idea of the terible sufferings of the poor dependants of the Suthern Union soldier who has had to flee his country to escape imediate destruction. They are the persons whou can tel you of miseries seldom equaled in this World and there is no help for them only from the Government. God speed the day when Peace shal unfold her wings and extend them over us from maine to the Gulf of mexico.

    I have nothing of importance to write to you. I have not recieved any letters from you nor heard one word since I left Home. Oh how long is the time it seems an age. The suspence is awful. Let me hear from you. I wrote four days ago directing you to direct to Stanford. Now direct to Care Capt Higley 7th OVC Sumerset Ky and your letters wil follow me. I have not had very good opportunities for writing so you I know wil excuse me. I wil write as often as I can. Let me hear how al the folks are. Our Boys are getting furloughs at the rate of one to 20. That is four to ours at one time. It wil take a long time to get round but it wil do a great deal to prevent Desertions.[119] There is some talk of our Regmt being sent on to big Sandy but there is no certainty of anything in war but death but we have no reason to complain. Our Regmt has only lost two men in battle. They were both Buglers one from Co D first Batt and the other Co L 2nd Batt Cap Leper Gallipolis.[120] The Capn is appearantly very much Disheartened at the stories about him at home. The last one is that he was at home and was caught in Bed with another mans wife. There is just as much truth in it as there is in many of the same slanderous sort Raised him and the rest of us myself included. I feel that Such People are or should be beneath the notice of evry honest citizen as far as I am concerned if they would pul their teeth and sugar their lie Blacked gums they should not have the Privelige of kissing my United States Calvary Crowns if they wanted to but enough of this. I have enough to do without stooping into malice such infernal slanders. Let he who is fre from sin cast the first stone and I gues there would be les done. It is nothing but envy that makes the folks lie so it is some of the Caps own relations that helps to keep it up. He was once the Poorest of them all his Father dying when he was only twelve years old left the whole responcibility of the support of the Family on him. He has battled against the world all his life. He has out done them al and thats whats the matter. He cares not for their howls on his own account but for his wifes sake. I wish this world contained more men of Captain Higleys qualities. He is writing to his wife. I wish she could come and se you but thanks to a merciful God you dont suffer for friends. You are surrounded with the Best of them.

John Fosse has got back. They never brought him to a trial atal but withdrew their charges against him and sent him back to the company.

I have nothing more to ad but close by asking you to remember me to Our friends. Kiss the Babes for me and accept my best wishes and warmest love. May God bless you Comfort you and yours. Restore us to each other is the Prayer of your ever devoted but unworthy.

William

1st Sergt Comp K 7th OVC

PS We have 2 fine springs of water close at the door and about ten steps the other about 20. It is so cool and good. Wm

In margin:
Write soon.

May 20, 1863
Camp of 7th OVC
Somerset

Dear Wife and little Ones,

I again seat myself to pen you a few lines to inform you that I am wel at present and hope these lines may find you better. I cannot hope that you are well but that you are comfortable. The rest of you I hope are well. The first thing I want to know is how are you. Here I have been from home 23 days and have not heard one word from you since I parted with you. I have written thre letters to you recieved none. The Question arises is there none left at home that thinks enough of me to let me know how you are. The Cap has written and recd letters since I came back but for poor me there is not one line of consalation. But yet I hope and look forward to the next mail. I wold have written oftener but there being no books kept while I was absent it has taken my attention and a great deal of labor to set them right. Besides it took me most of two days to make out our monthly return. Also we have made out new pay rolls and expect to get our pay before long. The weather continues fine and not much to do. We are haveing a very good time for soldiers generaly. We have to take our Horses 10 miles to grase and get 4 pints of corn for each once a day which is pretty hard fare. We have a fine army here. The Egsact number it would be hard to tel but there is 15 regmts four Cavalry and more Infantry being mounted Rapidly.[121] The Enemy is laying in our front. Six miles of our pickets are posted near Enough to exchange shots occationaly. If it were not for this we would hardly know that two great Enemies stand faceing each other. The silence seems to portend something awful. It seems like a powerful Beast lying quiet to gather strength for a fearful leap when it does come sombody wil get hurt for our men are in fine condition. Our Company is in fine health and are only awaiting to be led on to victory or death. I report 64 men present none sick all able for duty their Arms and Accouterments laying in convenient places to enable them to be Ready at a moments notice. General Carter is here in imediate Comand.[122] This is the hardest part of the world to live in that I have ever seen yet for to be inhabited. It seems perfectly Destitute of evry thing pertaining to the comforts of man eccept I may say fine springs of Water which is abundnt. There stil remains at Stanford 21 of our men including Sansbury Savage and Entsminger.[123] We have just ordered more clothing. Tel Tomy that I have a nice Horse now the same one I drew at Gallipolis. He has don little since I started home and he is the Best Horse in the Company can run like a deer.

I have not written to any body at home since I left for want of time. I would be glad to recieve a few lines from any one. If I had the same opportunity of writing that my friends have I would write evry day. Dear Samaria do try and let me hear from you as often as you can since I have been overwhelmed with work. The melancholy feeling has somewhat worn of and if I could hear from you once a week I would feel very much relieved.

Give my respects Relations and friends as I stil feel that I have left some behind. If any of them wants to hear from me let them send me their name enclosed and if possible I wil try and repay them for their trouble as letters are all the source of news that is accesible to a soldier. The folks at home might do much to ad to the comforts of the soldier by dropping them their Read newspapers which would only cost one cent and the trouble of mailing.[124] Samaria do you know what I would like to se. It is a letter from your own hand write and let me know how you are all the particulars how you have been since I left you whether you are better or worse. I am very sorry that I did not stay with you but it is al right with the Col and officers and I hope to get to come again. God speed the day. May he Bless and comfort you in your hour of need. Accept my sincere love and tenderest regard. Kiss those Babies for yours.

William McKnight
1st Sergt Co K 7th OVC
Somerset Ky

May 24, 1863
Somerset Camp of 7th OVC

Dear as ever Dear Samaria,

Again on this Butiful Sabath morning I seat myself to inform you that I am enjoying good health. The men generaly wel and in fine spirits as we hear good news this morning from Grants Army before Vicksburg.[125] The news of the success of our arms is cheering to evry Union loveing heart and to none more so than the soldier who has left home and evrything thing near and dear to him and Perils his life for his Countries sake. We are haveing very easy times here. The weather continues fine. Our Horses keeps up very wel considering the keeping. There is nothing new here or exciting that I know of. Evry thing seems quiet but from appearances ther is to be something done soon. The General keeps posted in regard to the effective strength of our Regiments. There is stil a squad of our men at Stanford on Provost Duty. Asher has got quite wel again. Frank Sansbury is troubled some with Reumatisms. The great absorbing thought of my mind is how is my dear Wife and little ones at home. What can be the matter that I dont hear from them 27 days from home and not one breath nor scratch of a pen from home nor from any one near to let me know how my dear sick wife is. O how hard thus to know that the Bosom friend of my life is sick at home and cant learn how she is. O cruel fate thus to seperate us under such painful circumstances is the severest stroke that ever befel us. It is hard thus to part but I hope it wont be long. Wele kep up our Hearts as were marching along for God and our country were marching along.

I am in trouble again this morning. They started a story on the Cap in Middleport that he was caught at midnight and now they have it that it was at noon day there is as much truth in the one as there is in the other. There never was a more slanderous report on any innocent persons. It grieves me to think that such infamous lies are afloat and most all seem ready to circulate them. You know very wel that I have more respect for you than to fool away my reputation in any such away. You know to that I never did run after Bad Women but even if I did there is no reason for any such report to get afloat about me. I told you about being there. The Whole family was there. The man of the House and all Cousin James Johnson was with me when I was there.[126] He can tel whether I am guilty of any impropriety or not but I feel that there is little use in me trying to justify myself to you for you know that all such stuff is lies. If you dont I do. They are gotten up and circulated by Desineing people that have fear that our Reputation wil rise above theirs. They find that they cant rise to a level with us so they are trying to degrade and drag us down to a level with them. McRaskey told that there was a report that I was caught in Bed with Miss Huff in Middleport on Broad day light.[127] Pretty bold trick and her man and mother in the House was it not if I had ever been gulty of such a thing I would feel different but I feel bad enough about it on your account the way it is.[128] O how I wis I could se you again hopeing things are not as bad there as I hear them here. I wil close by wishing you the Best wises in the world. Accept my sincere love. Kis the Babes for your absent and almost Broken Hearted William.

In margin:
O how I long to hear from you. Give my respects to mother. Keep this to your self. You can tel them what news there is in it concerning others. If you have a few postage stamps I would be thankful for them. O how my heart aches for you Dear. You are the Dearest creature to me in this world. Bless you and the Babes for ever.
    Wm McK

May 29, 1863
Camp 7th O.V.C
Somerset Ky

My ever Dear Samaria,
    I take the Present opportunity to pen you a few lines to let you know that I am wel hopeing these few lines may find you enjoying Comfortable health. I wil proceed to finish them as soon as I can. We have been in hourly expectation of marching Orders for 36 Hours haveing been notified to hold our selves ready to move at a moments notice but we take things coole I have just completed a Bunk of forks Poles & bushes to sleep on in our Tent and it is comfortable and nice with a few Coffe sack for carpet. We feel quite at home again with thre of our little pup Tents made into one. It is large enough to accomodate 3 or 4 men.
    Lieut Brunker arived here yesterday. I was glad to hear from home. He says that you was walking around and of course you are better which gives me much relief of mind although I would have felt as though you had not forgotten me if you had sent me a few lines by him. O how I

would like to get a good letter from you once more. If you cant write get someone to write for you for I feel neglected. I recieved your nice present in an envelope. It is a very nice little Hankerchief. O how thankful for it. Wel I have just been up and got 25 more men ready to go on a scout and they are gone. Lieut Brunker has gone with them. The Capt is out on Officer of the day of the Brigade. They have great performances at Guard Mount. I had my Horse Fed to go but the Adjutant would not let me leave the Camp. There is 47 of our men out at present besides 23 at Stanford 9 on picket the rest scouting. The last that went out went with 175 others under Liut Colonel Miner.[129] Wel I have been to Head Qurters again and I expect you wil find it dificult to keep the rim of my letter. I have so much on my mind that I cant think of any thing to write to make my letter interesting but I know you wil excuse me. Cousin Will Halliday has just arived from Stanford.[130] He tels me that there was a letter there sometime ago for me but I never recieved it. John fosse is here sitting by me reading all right. I recieved a letter from Bro John by Brunker. Geyer says he is not comeing back to the Regmt until he is sent for. He wil be apt to stay some time if I am any judge. Things are stil developing themselves a little at a time. The Colonel is wel pleased with us since we came here. We have got along and evry thing goes along smothe and nice and agreable. We have the nicest place in the whole camp. The water is so handy. When we want a drink we just go out and get it fresh from the spring with a tin. We get plenty for our Horses now and ours look the best of any in the Regmt. The health of our Regmt never was better. I hear of very little sickness in the Division here. O Dear I do hope you are all well. Give my respects to all. Tel them and remember that what ever they hear about me that I am the same man that used to cary on shop at McMasters mill.[131] Accept my prayers and love sincerely. Tell the Children that I never forget them when I write. They are good I know and always expect to find them so. May the Blessing of God rest upon them from your unworthy Husband.
   Wm McKnight

June 2, 1863
Camp of the 7th O.V.C
Somerset Ky

January 8, 1863–July 8, 1863

Dearest Samaria,

    I seat myself this morning to pen you a few lines to let you know that I am enjoying good health this morning and I most sincerely hope these may find you enjoying the same great and inestimable Blessing. It is with melancholy forebodings and heavy heart that I now write to you. We recieved orders last night to dispose of all extra Clothing carpet sacks and evry thing but one suit of Clothing and a change of shirts & one Blanket. We Boxed up all our things and sent them back to Hickman Bridge on the Ky River near Nicholasville where our Hospital is.[132] I sent my jacket and sash and 2 pair of drawers 2 pair of socks neck Hankerchief 2 shirts & several other things in my Carpet sack. I kept plenty to do me. I do not expect to se them again even if I should get back.

    Wel Samaria I feel a great deal better this afternoon than I did this morning. Things have put on Quite a different face. The future seems much brighter to me than it did. I felt very bad at parting with my things but there is amelorating circumstances and brighter prospects ahead to cheer us onward. There seems to be a strong outside presure working against some of the Officers in this Regmt that they have brought upon themselves that wil make things come right after awhile. I think you can guess what the matter. We expect to make things interesting here before long. The Rebs are vry saucy. They make their appearance to our pickets and exchange shots often with us. We feel confident of success. We have a fine Army here now I think and in good condition. The health of our Company is good. We have been out on two scouts since we came here one I mentioned in my last letter that time they captured 33 Rebs and Horses without looseing a man. On Sunday our company was ordered out again. They nearly all went but me. I started but the Adjutant turned me back to do some company writing which I executed to his satisfaction. The company came in the same day. Did not encounter any Enemy. Asher Entsminger and Frank Savage are here now. Asher is on Camp Duty to day for the first time. It is easy. Samaria have you entirely forgotten me or why is it that I get no letters. Others gets letters. Asher recieved one from home only a week after date and here I am and have not recieved one line from you since I left home. Oh why did you not send me a letter by Brunker. He would have brought one through for me. Oh how I study over it think of evry thing but cant imagine why I am so neglected. I know I deserve nothing better but stil I did not expect to be entirely neglected by evry one. I have not written as often as usual but it is because my opportunities have been limited. We have been kept busy since we came here fixing up the books being knocked around so much we had got behind with our Books. Evrything has to be accounted for that has been ishued to the company as wel as all that is ishued to the men. The Colonel reported our Company in good Condition and our Horses are the best in the Regmt and I think we have the best Company also the best capt and the most men. We have to bear a hard warr but when we know that we are only stigmatised at home by unprincipaled persons knowing that we do our duty like men and soldiers we care not. We feel that if the slanderers at home would clear their own skirts they would find less time to trouble themselves about the solders. It is a bad state of things when a soldier has to defend his caracter at home and his life abroad one at a time is enough.

I cant think of much more to write at Present. You can do as you think fit about showing this letter to evry Boddy. There is several things I would like to write but I wil await a letter from you with great impatience and hope. Oh if I can only hear from you before we leave here I wil be one of the most thankfulest of men. Do write to me please do if it is only two lines just to let me know how you are and that you have not forgotten one that is ever mindful of you ever hopeful of being permitted to enjoy the company of once more. May the day soon come when the absent may be permitted to return to their Families and Friends when Peace shal be restored to our once happy but now distracted Country. God speed the day.

Isaac Meanor died last Saturday 30th of May at Stanford of Consumption.[133] He was one of the best soldiers we had. Peace to his ashes poor fellow. We lament his loss and deeply smypathise with his Bereaved Relatives. The Cap had sent a Furlough to Cincinnatti to be countersigned for Isaac but he that giveth and he that can take away gave him an everlasting one. One that we are all shure of sooner or later. If we get no Furloughs to meet here on this Earth may we so live that we may meet where parting is nomore. Remember me to Parents and Friends. Kis the little ones for me. Write to me. Pray for me. Hope for the best. Accept my sincere undiing love. I cannot forget you *never never.* I claim a place in your affections and ever shal. Can you say as much for your absent Husband until death.

William McKnight
to his wife Samaria

In margin:
I enclose my feather for Thomas my only Son. Bles him & the rest.

> June 4, 1863
> Camp of 7th O.V.C.
> Somerset

Dear Samaria,

It is with heartfelt gratitude that I seat myself this butiful Thursday morning to pen you a few lines in answer to your most affectionate and welcome letter which came to hand last night being the first I have recieved from your hand since the 24th Feb the date of which is May 17th. You have no idea with what anxiety I devoured its contents. I am sorry to hear that you have taken Cold again for expect you have been obliged to wait on yourself for want of help that has brought it on. O how I wish I could be with you. I think that I could wait on you better than I ever did. This causes me many bitter and sad reflections when I think how you need me and I Cant help you. My Heart seems as though it would burst up through my Throat any how but I hope that this state of things wont last forever. If I thought it would life would be a burthen to me as it seems as it is some times. You must take good care of yourself if possible if others are neglected. I am glad to hear that Aunt Janett has been to se you and that Dear good mother of ours. God Bless her. She never wil forsake you. I am pleased that your Ring suits you. I hope by it you wil remember the humbl giver whose heart is ever turning towards *you*. The starr of my life the being of my thoughts by day and dreams by night and if we were spared to live on Hundred years I feel as thou it would ever be the same with me.

That Old Watch you need not feel bad about atall for it is safer with you than me for I lost it out of my pocket often in the night. I have the same wish to express to be with you. There is nothing in this world would give me more pleasure than to be with you especialy in your lonely hours of need. You say you have nothing to send me to compare with the present I sent you. Your affectionate letter is a trible compensation for such a present though I shal thankfuly recieve any memento of love from you and you may rest asured that any thing you may chose to send if recieved wil be sacredly kept. Your Likeness I carry in my pocket al the time and would not be deprived of for any thing unless it was the original herself. God bless her.

I am glad you have such good Children for I know they are a comfort to you in my absence. There is some talk that we may stop in Ky this sumer. If we do it wil be better for our health. If we stay here ten or twelve days longer I wil be able to write you some thing that may cheer you and my Friends if I have any left. If I have none there I have plenty here. I do not feel at liberty to write all the good news to you but rest asured that there is a brighter prospect ahead than there has been for me. If I know any thing I feel contented that there is going to be a change here that wil give a man a better chance to come home if he wants to for good without waiting to the end of the War or if he has to stay he can suport his family better at home and himself too. So look up look on the bright side of the picture. Mind not what slanderous tatlers may say about me or you. Al we have to do is laid down before us what our Creator designed of us that we are and wil be. Let man and the Devil be against us notwithstanding. I have always felt that the Hand of the Lord has been with us and trust it all to him.

A part of our pickets have just came in. Nothing new or interesting. All seems quiet. I sent out 2 squads of pickets this morning one for thre days the other for one. One went out thre days ago. They wil be in today with Lieut Brunker. He is in charge. They are out 18 ms Patroll Guards towards Stanford. One of our Seargent and four men started away day before yesterday and the patrolls picked them up and sent them to jail. They returned yesterday looking down their noses. The Capt tels me just now that one Brigade started out this mornging. I expect they are going to cross the River as the Pontoon Bridges arived here the other day for crossing the army.[134] The 9th Army Corpse wil probably go but the 23rd to which we belong may stay at least that seems to be the talk in camp and from what I se in the papers is probable.[135] Frank Sansbury is sick at Hickman Bridge with Rheumatisms how bad I dont know. General Burnsides had his Headquarters there.[136]

You say that you would give me a kiss if I would come home and if that wasn't enough you would give me a mouth full. Wel kisses must be scarcer than they used to be with you if you cant spare more than one. I could spare a thousand for you and not mis them but I would come home all the way if it was only for one kiss from you.

I have reasons to be thankful for good health. I never felt stronger and better in my life than I have the most of the time. Since we came here the only fault is I am too much confined not exersize enough. It is nearly dinner time and I must close by wising you good health and many Blessings. Remember me to our friends. Accept my tenderest and abiding love for yourself. Remember your absent Husband is never forgetful of you. We expect to get our pay soon. Send me a few Stamps Please as this is the last I have. I sent you a letter day before yesterday with my feather in it for Tommy. So nomore at present from your affectionate and loveing Husband.

 William McKnight
 to his ever dear Samaria

In margin:
The Boys are generaly wel and in fine spirits. The weather is very fine nights cool had some rain.
I am hungry. Dinner is ready.
I have had my dinner. It was good pork crackers sugar & coffe. Be sure to get that saddl and let no one have it.

June 10, 1863
Camp of 7th O.V.C.
near Somerset Ky

Dear as ever Dear Samaria,

I take this opportunity to let you know that I am wel and I hope these few lines may find you all enjoying the same inestimable blessing. I have just returned from Cumberland where we had been on picket for 4 day. We went down there on the 6th Saturday with Capt & Brunker & 25 men besides myself. We were Posted at the mouth of Fish Creek at the junction on the Cumberland Sunday nothing happened.[137] I forgot to say in the proper place that on Saturday the 45 Boys from the next post above us went over and Captured the Reble pickets oposite to or a little below us while some of our Boys talked to them across the River. They had Captured them and were hurying to cross the ford where we were when Asher espied them from the lookout post. He pronounced them Rebles. We all flew to our Horses and expected to have some fun but when they came on to the Barr we discovered the white Flag. I saw the Butternuts mixed up with our Boys so I thought it was a trick the Rebs were trying to play on us to try to catch us so we all thought. So the Cap halted under a threat to fire on them which we were all ready for. They complied and sent out a man to make an explanation. We were soon satisfied that they were all right and they were soon among us with their

Prisoners 1 Capt 1 Liut 3 seargts and 10 men. They were North Carolina Troops. They had told our Boys that they intended takeing their 4th of July in Lexington. We had a good deal of fun with them. Told them they were starting early for the 4th. This was on Saturday. On Monday I got permision to reconaiter the other side of the River to se what had become of the Rebs. I took 11 men with me and crossed the ford and proceeded in to the Country 2 or 3 miles but did not discover an pickets but found the Enemy were camped some 4 miles farther in at a town called Stubenville and found out they had sent no pickets since Saturday. Haveing already gone farther the Capt had given me leave I returned recrossed the River to Camp without haveing encountered any oposition.[138] In the next day 4 of our men were over the River and learned that 17 Rebles followed us back to within ½ mile of the Ford the day before. Lucky for us and the Rebs too far. We had a trap laid for them. Early in the morning we heard heavy fireing in the direction of the Rebel Camp both of Artilery and small Arms indicating heavy fighting. I timed the Artilerys reports and they varied from 4 to 12 seconds apart and I think they must have fired nearly an Hundred Rounds. On the next morning that is yesterday we came into Camp and find some of Boys that we had lef in camp. Just in informed us that they had harder fight than any they had been in. We lost only 2 men from our Regmt but non from our camp. I saw several wounded men this morning. How many of our men are wounded you wil know as soon as me. Our men whiped them out and killed a great many of them and then withdrew and came back across the River last night and are most al back again in Camp.[139] But how long we are to remain in I know not nor care not. I never felt so anxious to be any place in this State as I did to be on the Battle field when I heard the Guns yesterday. We run out of provisions yesterday and I went a House along with a lot more of our Boys and got some Dinner and found some Cotton there which I enclose. Just as it is picked from the Bowls here. The people pick it and card it and manufacture their own Clothing.[140] I saw growing it resembles Buck Wheat plant it and try it. Give good old mother some of it. I saw an old woman picking just such stuff as this. The squd that was not with us recd the pay this morning. We were all ready to go across the River again today but after standing waiting for 2 or 3 hours we were ordered to unsaddle and here we are.

I am afraid to risk my money by mail. It seems so uncertain here. I expect to get a private conveyance before long as there are Furloughs waiting to be signed. I received a letter from Daddy last Night and tel him I am very thankful for it but dont know how soon I wil be able to answer it.

I got 50 cts worth of postage Stamps today. I am uneasy to know how you wil get along without Willie. Let me know what he left for and how you get along. I recieved a letter the other day from you dated the 11th May. You say that I did say any thing about how I get along. Wel you have not got one letter that I wrote for I wrote the particulars. I got a Boat that day at thre oclock and got into Cincinnati the next day at 4 oclock and stayed with Uncl McKay all night. The next day I got into Stanford all right and am not sorry now that I came back as soon as I did. O your letters are so kind. It makes me feel as thoug you thought as much of me as ever. O how my Heart ackes for you. Your kindness makes me feel better. If all the world forsakes me you wil always be my friend. O how I long to se you. When we wil be permitted stay with you. Oh if you was only wel again I would think that you could get along better without me but I put my trust in him who is able and willing to save. He is my Savior and my all. He doeth all things wel therefore be cheerful and hope for me Pray for me and God wil Bless us. Give my respects to all. Accept my unbounded love. Kis the Babes for your absent one. Oh how long will this unholy Rebellion last. May God Bless you and Protect you and comfort you all is the prayer of your Absent but ever loveing Husband.
    William McKnight
    to his own dear Samaria

In margin:
I am in such a hurry that I cant half write. You will excuse me. I send a little Ring to Liela. A Pedlar gave it to me a little while ago. Wm McKnight

---

                                             June 12, 1863
                                             Somerset Ky

Dear Samaria,

    I size this opportunity to let you know that I am wel at present hopeing these few lines may find you enjoying the same. I hasten to let you know that I have not as much money to send you as I wish I had. You know I sent my clothes back consequently I had to buy some more. I bought me a Blouse and vest the reason is we cant draw any here. I send you ten dollars and sorry that I have not more. I have just 4 dollars left.

I have got another good watch. We expect to go acros the River again. Lieut B has resigned and is comeing home soon. Keep this to yourself until you hear from me again. I recieved a letter from Brother John since the Boy was Born.

James Haley the Bearer of this is just ready to start and I wil have to close.[141] Wishing you evry thing that is good in this world. I have a cry over your letters evry day nearly. They are so kindly written. I have to go out by myself and read them and cry over them until I am nearly sick but stil I am cheerful to all appearances and I hope for the best. So good by until I se you. God bless you and help you your sorrow to bear. In hast respects and love to all.
   William McKnight
   to his wife Samaria

                                                   June 15, 1863
                                         Camp of the 7th O.V.C.
                                                       Somerset Ky

Derer than ever Dear Samaria,
   Seated in the woods adjoining the Camp I seclude myself to pen you a few thoughts of the Heart. It was with great pleasure that I perused your very kind and affectionate letter of the 7th inst which I recieved last evening. This makes the 3rd one I have recd since Ive been in this Camp from you. One from Daddy and one from Theop is all. My Head does not feel overly clear this afternoon as I was out since one in the morning with Capt visiting the pickets as Sergt of the Grand rounds but otherway I feel quite wel and have no reasons to complain but much reasons as far as my health is concerned for thanks. I have remarkable good health and feel strong as a Horse. Would to god I could say the same of my dear wife. Nothing in the world would give me more infinite pleasure than to be with you and your health as good as it was in 53 when I started for Indiana but allass the memory of those days are among the bygones and never can be recalled. But they bring up on me feelings of joy and sadness. I hope these few lines may find you enjoying good heath or at least comfortable. The little ones I am glad to hear are well. Tel Leila paa is sorry that she cut her foot for I know that mama needs her help. Your helpless condition gives me a great deal of anxiety. It seems that my little

home is almost broken up. Oh but my heart ackes for you. You say that if it was not for me that you would give up. Never give up the ship. If it does leak it wil bring us to land if not in this world. I am trying harder than ever I did to live so we may have an inheritance not mad with Hand eternal in the Heavens where sorrow never comes and parting is nomore and dear mary I hope you wil not neglect our little flock. Bring them up in they way that they should go and you never wil have cause to regret it. I regret very much that you missed to send me that Bible for I should have appreciated such a gift especially from such a source. The time does not seem I expect as long to me as to you for you are sick and that makes the great difference but I hope that I wont have to stay in war to thre years out. There is nothing new transpireing here of interest that I know of. I have my regular picket & Camp Guards evry day. Things goes on as though there was no war here. There are some companies here that have a great many sick. Ours have very few. James Denison is very sick about 8 miles this side of Stanford not expected to live.[142] Oh how I would enjoy myself to take a walk in the Garden and get some of those Straw Berries but you can eat my share. Put a little sugar on them if you can and give them to them sweet little children. You say they did not send you that Blanket. I told Brunker about it this morning. He dont know any thing about it but Ben Raster knows all about it for I left it with him and told him not to use it that I would send for it and I did not expect but they would send it with the saddle.[143] I am going to write to Brother John about it. It is there and they cant deny it and it is a good Blanket and they cant have it. I think that Raster can find it and poore me is all alone with the little ones. Oh how that rings in my Ears and Oh Billy dont forget us forget there never was there ever a man more attentive to the wants of his family or more mindful of them in my absence. I hope that I shal cease to live when I cease to love my Family. I am very anxious about your sore throut. Take good care of it. Geyer tells the truth about Brunker as wel as himself. There is not much reason for complaint between them. You think just as I told the captain when I told me he stoped and seen how you was it did not relieve me for I did not believe a word of it and now your letter confirms what I only surmised. The Deserters did not get any money this time. I among the rest they find Frenching home is rather expencive after all.[144] You wish to know where I got that Ring. I bought it at Stanford from a Watchmaker that I had some acquaintance with last winter. When I was there in camp there was some juelers came in to camp with inferior juelry Watches &c and I told them to leave or they might get into trouble an inquireing who I was and that I was acting Sergt Major of the Battalion they left in a hury this Stanford watchmaker told me he would remember me for it. So he sold me that ring for less than it cost. There is the whole history. I bought it for you with the last 2 dollars I had. You must get along the best you can. Have Hanes pay you as much as you can.[145] Tell Elliott I sympathise deeply with him in his affliction that a few lines is ever acceptable from him. He says Hanes talks of going west if he does he wil serve me a mean trick but not if I can help it. Is that all Boasted Patriotism amounts is to. To take the advantage of an absent soldier would be the highth of meanness. I am very sory willie has left but evry thing works together for our good. So do the best you can. Be watchful cheerful and hopeful. Asher went to Lexington this morning for Horses. John Foose is here wel and hearty. Cousin Halliday is well. He left for Stanford last night. Frank Sansbury I believe is Detailed as Hospital Nurce at Stanford. George Spires is comeing home on furlough.[146] If James Haley comes with the money I sent you treat him wel He is a fine man. You can trust him with any thing you want to send. I bought me a vest and Blouse coat. They cost me 20 dollars. You may think them dear but they are very nice. The vest is deep Blue the Blouse is Black Blue. You may think it extravegent but I could not help it. So good by remember to one all my kind friends. Remember this is from one to whom you are the dearest being on this green Earth.

    William McKnight
    to Samaria

> June 18, 1863
> Camp of the 7th OVC
> Somerset

Dearest Samaria,

    I seat myself once more to hastely pen you a few lines to let you know that we are all as wel here as usual. We have just returned from a two days scout over the Cumberland. We expected to have found the Enemy but did not except six four of which the Capt took prisoners. I found thre of their Guns and traps and a kit of Cannoniers Tools.[147] We asertained that the Rebs had gone beyond where we went some 20 ms and we were within 12 ms of the Tenn. line. I passed over the Battle Field of Mill Springs where Zacahriah fel.[148] The marks of canon shot are stil very visible. I also passed over the Battle Grounds of the last fight which consisted wheat field oat field and all other kind of fields and the roughest Woods where it seemed the overplus Rocks of Creation had been spilled. The stench of dead Horses and we thought probibly of men was the most sickning that I ever endured. We asertained allso that Genl Pegram said that he lost allready found 100 men killed which we had no reasons to doubt for we discovered a number of graves away of the Road.[149] We only lost 4 men an our side as far as I can learn we had our artilery playing on them while they were unable to bring theirs to bear on us at any time. We are again under marching Orders in what direction I am not able to say but the supposition is as the Rebles have gone beyond easy transportation. We are more likely to come towards Ohio a name which I honor and love where I am sorry to say we are neaded. I understand that we wil be sent to the Border by sanction of the Governor sooner or later. Tel Father that I recieved his paper today thanks to a kind parent. Tel Brother John if you se him to get that Blanket for you from Rasters.

The money I sent by Haley I expect has gave up for he had just time to have been at Maysvill when the Rebs were in there. Write and let me hear from you as often as you can. Remember me to kind Friends and relations, accept my depest sympathy and purest devotion and truest love. Kis the little ones and tel it is for your absent and anxious Husband. Yours forever. May God have mercy on you and yours is the prayer of yours in great haste as it is mail time.

William McKnight
to his kind Samaria

June 24, 1863
Camp of the 7th OVC
Somerset

Dearer than ever Dear Samaria,

I seat myself this rainy morning to let you know that I am wel and hope these few lines may find you all enjoying good health. I received yours of 15th on the evening of 19th only 4 days from home. I was very glad to hear from you but was pained to hear that you as in such a helpless condition and yours throat so sore but I hope all this reaches you may be better I do hope your Friends wil not let you suffer while I am away fighting their Battles. Early on the morning of the 20th the whole Regmt was ordered out by day light 44 of our company with the Capt. Forded crossed the Cumberland and proceeded in the direction of Monticello with the 45th 2nd Ohio 1st Ky 4 pieces of Laws Mountain Howitzer and Wilders Indiana Rifled Battery with the 103rd Infantry all mounted except the 103rd.[150] We proceeded on to Monticello 18 miles and found no enemy went 5 miles farther and went in to camp for the night. Water very scare hardly get enough for coffe. The next morning we started for Travis Mill Tenessee we proceeded onward anxiously expecting a fight but the Rebs had heard of our forces that had been sent in their rear playing the mischief with their railroads and trains and had skedadled in great haste hauling their Artilery away with them by hand.[151] We followed on crossed the Tennesee line at 2 clock 21st we found the people very glad to se us they were destitute of many nesesaries of life salt there was none one man offered ten dollars in Sesesh money for Coffee enough for suffer the early Harvest all ready being but wil relieve the poor suffering women and children. There are few men left many women and children just shouted when they found out who we were we halted 3 miles in Tenn when we were ordered to take our company and go stil farther into the State. We went across Wolf River but found no enemy.[152] They had gone thre days before we got there. We returned to camp turned in and slept until morning. It being very cold almost cold enough for frost. Nothing to feed our Horses haveing fed the last grain the previous morning we started back for camp we found ripe cheries and Berries and potatoes peas and it wont be long until the Blue Berries wil be ripe but as a general thing the country is presents a Deserted poverty stricken place. The people would only be to glad to get away if they could but it is as much as they could but it is as much as they can do to stay. As old Uncl or Louis said about holding on when the Horses was runing of it is destruction any way returning we arived in Monticello before night where got feed for our Horses being 36 hours since they had any haveing gone about 60 miles without food. The next morning we started for camp recrosed the Cumberland al safe arived in somerset fore night very much fatigued the Roads wer such as we would think impassable in Ohio we had rode to Monticello 24 ms thence to Travismill 21 ms thence to Wolf River 10 ms making 55 ms and back 110 of travel al in thre days ariving here last night haveing 13 ms into Tennessee.

I received an avangelist from you last night and was glad to se your pencil marks on it. Lieut Brunker is here yet awaiting his resignation he says if they dont accept it he wil leave any how and there is no doubt but Geyer wil have to leave either by court marshal by board of examination and that is about the way the matter stands. Geyer may come back but he is a fool if he does. I have felt very much disheartened since I received your last letter I dream about you nearly evry minite I sleep I dreamed I seen you the other night and you looked as hearty as could be I am afraid I cant come home to se you before fall & maybe for good then who can tell put your trust in him who doeth all things wel. I received your stamps I shal keep them pined on that little Piece of Paper the way you sent it. I am in hopes that God wil permit me to return to dear little family again Oh how I wil strive to make them happy and comfortable if I am spare to enjoy their company again they are so precios to me I do not think there is a man in Regmt thinks more of his family than your unworthy Billy I know that they are to good for me but stil I hope God in his mercy wil help me to be better I hope that God wil help you to bear up under your severe affliction he is my Father and my guide. I go to him with all my sorros and trials and he always bears me through. Remember me to Father & Mother Brothers and sister and friends accept my most sincere love for yourself and little ones God Bless them. Oh how my Heart swels with emotion for you I can hardly hide my weakness (get some one to cut some wood for you) I must close by requesting you to write to me often read my letters before writing to me answer parts of them so I may know what ones you get so nomore at Present but remains your most affectionate Husband.

William McKnight
1st Sergt Co K 7th OVC
to Samaria McKnight of Rutland

June 28, 1863
Camp of the 7th OVC
Somerset Ky

Dear beloved Samaria,

I hasten to answer yours of the 24th inst which just came to hand. It fills my heart with mingled emotion to peruse the very kind expressions of your Noble and love abiding Heart. It impresses on my mind that there is nothing in thought more abiding than Womans love even to an erring Husband if all the world forsake them a faithful Wife wil not. I feel that I am blessed with such but Oh the sad thought that forces itself upon me unhidden. She is alone and never kneeded me before and circumstances are such that I cannot assist her direct. But God be praised we have been Blessed with our share of this worlds comforts and pleasure. Therefore let the memory of the past and the hopes of the future cheer us in this seemingly dark hour. The sunshine wil Break through and scatter all this darkness I hope. Then will we have learned each others worth and the blessings of domestick Happyness.

I am glad to know that you are better than you have been. I hope the not far distant when you wil have gained your former strength again. I am sorry to inform you that there is no possible chance for me to come as you request but be assured you have my deepest sympathy and would only be to glad to be with you once more. But you must not give away to melancholy forebodings. I am glad to hear the little ones are wel. Sorry to hear of Brother Johns illness. I am allso glad to know that you received my letters money &c. I wil enclose you $5.00 more and wil send you some more as soon as I can get it. I sometimes get money between pay days trading round. I sent my Commission home last week. You wil preserve it if it gets home. Maybe I may have another before long.

Speaking of the Draft I do hope it wil be executed.[153] It is the only way to get out a certain class of men that are doing no good at home.[154] I can tell you what Lieut Brunkers resigned for the Colonell was going to have him sent before a boar of examiners. He was not the only one. He wouldnt stand it. He is daily expecting his papers from the General.

I am very anxious to know what you hinted at that you had heard. Your letters come in four days now. I am glad that your Sisters comes to se you. They ought to come often. I would like to hear of them being there often. It seems strange that my shop has become so disgraced. I know that it is a source of vexation to you. Never mind wait until I come & straighten things up if I live to get back. You did not say what was in the letter of the 18th. The next time you get supper you might ask me to share it with you. Maybe you would like to know what we have for dinner. Wel I went out and picked 3 pints of Dew Berries and we had some nice white sugar to eat on them with plenty of good Beans and nice Roasted fresh pork. We made a very good dinner. The most of our

Co. went out yesterday. Lucky for me they ordered me to remain to do some company Business drawing some Horses and Quarterly returns Requisitions &c. It has rained allmost 4 days yesterday and last night very hard. Our Regmt and 2nd Ohio & 1st Ky has gone to millspring 2 Reble Regmts made an attack on our troops at the springs and got completly whipped. Our Boys that was over into Tenn did a great deal of damage. They were under Saunders.[155] You wil see it in the papers.

It may not be disagreeable for you to know that I have got me a new horse a fine pacing Iron Grey (mare). It wont be so hard on me to ride now. I have always had a hard traveler. Little Charley Louis is not very wel but getting better. Asher is here. I heard from Frank Sansbury the other day. He is at Hickman Bridge Hospital Nurse. I am looking for Hally back again today, Sunday. Tel Ellliott and Jannett to drop me aline when they can. My respects to them. Tel Poor little Emma that I carry that little kneede case in my vest pocket all the time is so handy. The health of our company is good although we are in need of some clothing which we are expecting evry day. There is quite a display of galler in camp. Evry non commissioned officer has to stripe his Pants and Blouse. Many had never worn the required strypes. I have nothing more to ad of interest. I received a letter from mother and answered it last week. I sent her $2.00 dollars in it. Remember me to all our friends. Be particular and let me know how you get along. Have John B. get you wood. Tel him I said do the best you can and may the Blessings of the Ruler of all rest and abide with you and yours is the Prayer of your loveing Husband. Remember to tel the little ones how much papa thinks of them. With my tenderest wishes I remain yours until the end. Samaria be cheerful you have my love and simpathy.

William McKnight

1st Sergt. Co. K. 7th OVC

In margin:

I received that litle rose and prise it hily.

I must go and tend to my Grey and have a little ride.

July 8, 1863[156]
Danville, Ky

Dear Samaria,

We arived here last night & the rest of the camp is out with the Capt near Lebanon.[157] They have been in a fight none lost cause of Congerass

27 whiped 65 Rebs. I am in Command of the Balance of the camp there and very anxious to hear from you. There is some letters gone on to the camp. Dont be the least concerned about me. I am all right and well direct to 7th OVC via Lexington.

Write to me as soon as possible. Respects to all. Dont believe half you hear about our disasters. We come of well evry time the company of 27 whiped 65 Rebs in a fair fight.

From your most affectionate Husband
Wm McKnight
1st Sergt Co K 7th OVC

In margin:
Direct to Lexington to be forwarded to the Regmt.
In great haste.

The Fourth of July Presents and John Hunt Morgan's Raid
(July 11, 1863–August 20, 1863)

July and August 1863 are central to the McKnight story. During this brief, two-month period, McKnight learned that Samaria had given birth to twins—Martha and Myrtha—on July 4 and that Confederate general John Hunt Morgan, the "Thunderbolt of the Confederacy," had spent time at McKnight's home in Ohio during his infamous raid.

McKnight was informed by a "W. Braley" (most likely Samaria's father) that Samaria had successfully delivered twin girls. On July 11, McKnight states, "it surprises me so to hear that you have two little girls. Is it possible oh how I would like to see them.... You must let me know what you are going to call those little fourth of July Presents." Later, on July 24, McKnight closes a letter with these words: "So wishing you the greatest happiness imaginable with your little pets and the best of health hoping that I may soon se you all and that the Blessing of God may be showered uppon you is the Prayer of your ever faithful and loveing Husband."

Morgan's raid in July of 1863 was not his first or last raid—the raids were conducted to recruit troops, disrupt Union plans, and gather supplies. Starting in Knoxville in July 1862, Morgan made a pass through central Kentucky, reaching as far north as Cynthiana. In the fall of 1862, the Rebel Raider made another trek through central Kentucky behind Union lines. Historians Lowell Harrison and James Klotter contend that "despite the hard riding and the danger involved, there was an air of romance and adventure about his early forays."[1] Morgan's third raid came in the summer of 1863. Morgan, ignoring General Braxton Bragg's order not to cross the Ohio River, led his troops into southern Indiana and Ohio.

As "Morgan's Raid" advanced across southern Ohio, Morgan and his men passed through McKnight's hometown of Langsville; Morgan actually stayed for a while at William McKnight's residence. Despite the fact that other scholars have placed McKnight in pursuit of Morgan across Ohio, that was not the case. On July 24, 1863, McKnight told Samaria that he "would have given any thing ... to have been at home when Morgan was there"; a more conclusive indication that he remained in Kentucky during this period is his statement in that same letter that he "would liked to have been with the Capt.," who was in Ohio pursuing Morgan. Several days later, on August 4, 1863, McKnight expressed his frustration over his absence at that critical time: "what hurts me the worst is that for all we were goten up expresly for the Protection of our Homes we were absent and our homes disgraced and Country overund and destruction spread far and wide."

John Hunt Morgan's raid threatened Ohio's security, especially that of the border counties. As a result, "General Burnside declared martial law and the governor [Tod] called out the state militia. Approximately fifty thousand men responded."[2] Militia "poured into the countryside in hot pursuit of the Confederate raider; in all, over 50,000 Ohioans took the field against Morgan, and not half of them ever got within 60 miles of their quarry."[3] Although Morgan was able to escape capture for nearly two weeks, he eventually surrendered in northern Ohio after approximately 1,100 miles on the run. The unsuccessful raid "quelled sympathy for the Southern cause in Indiana and Ohio, encouraged Northern enlistment, and stimulated patriotism and support for the United States government."[4] Following Morgan's Raid, residents in twenty-nine Ohio counties filed 4,375 claims for damages. The state ultimately settled the claims, totaling $576,225—of this figure, $428,168 was for damages done by Morgan's men, and the remaining $148,057 stemmed from actions traced to Union troops.[5]

After escaping from prison at Camp Chase, Morgan gathered his scattered troops along with new recruits and conducted a fourth raid in June 1864. During this raid, Morgan lost command of his men, which resulted in considerable looting. This ultimately led to Morgan's being relieved of his command on August 30, 1864. The always-defiant Morgan once again disobeyed orders and took command of his troops in early September in response to reports of advancing Union soldiers. Morgan and his men were taken by surprise on September 4, 1864, near Greeneville, Tennessee—it was in this action that John Hunt Morgan lost his life.

July 11, 1863
Camp near danvill Ky

Dear Wife,

I have just received a letter from W. Braley in which I learn that you have playing hab all by your self. It surprises me so to hear that you have two little girls.[6] Is it possible oh how I would like to see them. It cant be so I cant hardly believe it. Wel I am somewhat relieved for I was ver uneasy. I was afraid your health being so poor that you could not recover. Oh how glad I am to know that the ankious time is over and that you so smart. That is a thing that I never expected to take place in our little family but if it is the will of the Ruler of Destinies all is well. I dont know what to write. There so much news afloat. I received a letter from you dated July 1st and was glad to hear that the Neigbors were so clever. I started out on the 2nd for Jim Town to try to reach the Regmt leaving the dismounted men in Camp.[7] I arrived in Jim Town on the 3rd found the Regmt but the Capt had gone out and the Colonel said it was very insafe and would not permit to go but sent me back to camp in command of 33 men. I arived on the ever memorable 4th. Since that time I we have moved the camp to this place. We have been here for 4 days. I have been scouting. There is 22 men here with me. How long we wil stay I dont know. It is a butiful Place. The men are al in good health. The Capt is with the Regmt reported to be in Indiana after Morgan.[8] The have followed him clear from Jim Town on the cumberland. The army is very active here now. I was down to Harrodsburg night before last with a part of the 7th and 2nd Ohio. We captured 20 Rebs and thirty today near Craborchard. I cant write to day. We just moved here in this place to day and I have been very busy takeing care of the camp Property and I feel very nervous. The army is in fine spirits at the news. We get papers the same day they are printed. The Rebs captured our sutler last night and a few wagons in Craborchard.[9] There was 50 of them and Boys got 30 of them today.

You must let me know what you are going to call those little fourth of July Presents. Write me of a few lines at the first opportunity. Oh how I long to see you. Just imagine you nursing 2 little Babes. Wel I must close for I cant write a sencible letter. I am writing out under an old Oak tree just back of the Town ½ mile. Oh yes I have some hopes that we may be sent to Cincinnati for Provs Guards. There is such a report. We are not Brigaded atall. Wel take good care of yourself until you get strong again. I hope it wont be long if you keep on you will have as many Babes as you can kiss. I wil have to come and help you. Sure so good by. Dont fret one bit about me. From your anxious Husband.

William McKnight to his wife

> July 15, 1863
> Camp 7th OVC
> Danville, Ky

Belove Samaria,

I take the present opportunity of once more pening you a few lines to let you know that I am wel at present and hope these few lines may find you enjoying the best of spirits as I am wel aware that it is impossible for you to enjoy the same so soon but I hope it wil not be long until you can write to me and say that we are all wel at home. Oh how I would like to be with you and to se them little 4th of July presents. I think you might let me know something about it. I expect you wil feel disappointed that they were not Boys but it is all for the better. I wil look with great anxiety for a letter from you. Oh how I do want to hear from your own hand. I expect you wil feel so set up that I could hardly touch you with a ten foot pole. Wel so be it. Inclosed you wil find a five dollar bill to buy dresses for them or to use as you se fit. I do not want you to let yourself suffer for anything for I know that there is plenty due you there to meet all your demands besides what little I can send you. I wil send you evry dollar

The twins—Martha and Myrtha. *Courtesy of Susan Hayes.*

Mattie (Martha) McKnight. *Courtesy of Susan Hayes.*

that I can spare but I have to have some money to pay for washing for if we dont change often here they soon get filthy and more. Sometimes when we are out we cant get Rations and have to buy of the Farmers and then sometimes we have no appetite for Crackers and pork. Than this is least for we generaly have good appetites when were there are 33 men here at present all in good health Leiut Brunker is here anxiously awaiting for his papers to return. One Lieutenants papers come in day before yesterday and he has gone home. He was from Clinton.[10] I have no news of any importance to write further than we are hily elated with the news and in great hopes of the war being soon.

July 24, 1863
Camp of the 7th OVC
Danville, KY

Dear & beloved Samaria,

I seat myself this butiful morning to dedicate a few thoughts and moments in words to the darling of my heart hopeing they may find you and the dear little ones enjoying health and all the Comforts of happy life. I have not heard from you since the 4th inst and I thought after answering the letters I recieved then that I would wait to hear from you before writing any more as I knew that you were likely to be in such a suspence about the Morgan thieves & that the mails would be likely to be interupted.[11] I thought that it would be little use to write. I thought you would have news to write me as soon as there was any chance to send so I have waited with all the anxiety imaginable to hear from you. I would have given any thing that I possessed to have been at home when Morgan was there for I know you would feel dreadful streaked to say nothing of the rest of the trouble you must have had. I would liked to have been with the Capt and would have been had I been permitted to do so.[12] It seems to me a very unfortunate circumstance to have been obliged to remain with the camp when there was work at home. The invader at my own door and here I must stay the pleasure of my superiors. Wel I hope its all for the better but I cant se it. It was expected that Lieut Brunker would have left before this time but I expect he wil stay until Capt comes back.

There has been a strong feeling & hope that we would all be sent where we belong we have not a Horse but what has been condemned as unfit for service but if we were to get marching orders for Ohio we would all walk cheerfully. There has been orders for us to go or come back but were not considered reliable by the Major but evry thing seems to indicate a movement that way. God grant that we may for I never would have left my little Family unless compelled to. If I had thought or known that we could be denied the privelige of comeing home once in a while to attend to our families but such is warr.

I sent you five dollars from Somerset & five from here but have not heard from either. There is a prospect for pay again soon as we are working on our pay Rolls. We have been very busy inspecting Arms and Saddles Carbines and pistols has been going for thre days and we have turned over all unserviceable property and wil get rid of it to day I suppose. Oh how anxiously I wil wait for a few lines from you as soon as you can write and tell me all the news and what about the Shop and what has been done. Consult your Father about any change likely to take place take his advice I wil abide his decisions. We get the Papers here every day the same date of ishue. We are glad to hear that Morgan has done so little injury and has been Cut to pieces so I expect the Capt (God Bles him) wil get to se his family and if he does he wil certainly come to se you I am anxious to hear from him.[13] If you se him tel him that I want him be sure and write to me for I dont expect to se him for thirty days. The news from the Army is truly cheering and gratifying to evry lover of the Union.

Wel Dear you must not forget to tell me all about them little 4th of July Celebrities of yours. I think you rather slited me that you did not even say you was going to have a fourth of July there. Well well all right. Ile remember you for that. I wil forgive you this time but if you have any more such Cut ups without letting me know about it you may expect to hear from me.

Well I hardly know what else to write unless I may say that we never enjoyed better health since we came out than we have for some time Charley Lewis has been sick but he is Better and was on duty yesterday. We have very easy times for being so near played for Horses. We only have 2 men on Picket Duty per day. I have enough Company work to keep me out of mischief so we are not bad of atall. Oh if I knew that you were suffering for nothing how much Better I would feel. Wel I guess I must close as I have a Shirt and pr Drawers need washing. I must get at it before it gets to hot. So wishing you the greatest happiness imaginable with your little pets and the best of health hoping that I may soon se you all and that the Blessing of God may be showered uppon you is the Prayer of your ever faithful and loveing Husband.

William McKnight

1st Sergt Co K 7th OVC

In margin:
Remember me to all enquiring friends and the Dear little ones Bless them. Elowese Nettie Jeny Annie Maria Martha & Maggie are Pretty names.

Undated Letter[14]

Dear Mary,

I hope these few lines may find you all wel. We are well here. Better health health I never have seen in Camp. You wil readily percieve that I made a mistanke in turning my Paper . . . but you can Paste a sheat on the Back of the song if you want to let any one se the song and not the reading. About ten days ago I sent this song to Plants but fearing he would not Print it I thought I would send it to you it is very much admired here among the soldiers.

You did not write whether you Recevd five Dollars at two different times. When the Rebles were in here ten days ago they took the Clothing and burned the Tents of the Boys that were at Stanford and came very near getting their old Capt Simpson biger than old Nate. Had to mount without my saddle he just came into . . . flieing white Pants on low quartered shoes white socks they did not reach his Pants by 2 feet. All together something like Old Bullen and Sut Livengoods Lizard.[15] So good by may the Blessings of Providence rest and be with you and yours (Bless you).

Wm. to Smaria

In margin:
excuse me.
No. 2

This leaves me alone with the men 40 in Camp and 14 in Town half mile from here. But I hope it wont be long the Captain wil be here today or tomorrow with the balance of the Ohio Raiders which I expect you know more about than you wish to again under the same circumstances. But I hope this wil be a warning to our men at home & not to Preach

Reble Sympathy nor remain idle and marganized.[16] We expect to be all mounted and armed anew. Our Saddles are here and other Horse Equipments. I forgot to tell you in my other letter that I got my old Carpet and Clothes from Hickman when I was there. It is a great deal better to have something to put your clothes in. I rote you about sending me a pair of Boots but I expect you wil not get a chance so you need not Bother your already overtaxed mind about it. I do not keed them yet any how. The Pay master is here.

Dont forget to let me know how you get along about money. Wel here I am writing again. I have to get up so often than it is impossible to write an inteligible letter even since I sat down to write these last two lines there have been two aflications for Passes and one wants an Order to get a little whiskey feels very . . . had fase all rinkled looks awful.[17] Well I am going to send you a piece of poetry. You must do the best you can. My heart aches for you my love to you all from your loveing Husband.

William McKnight to his wife

August 4, 1863
Camp 7th OVC
Danville KY

Ever Dear and beloved Samaria,

Haveing just Recieved and read your most welcome letter of 24th July I hasten to answer it. Oh I am so glad to hear from you. I had not heard from you for so long I did not know but the Reebs had got you. But I am glad you are wel and you did the best thing you could have done to stay at home. But one thing sertain if I had thought you were going to accomodate Rebs in my House I would have been there to accomodate him to a dose of lead the infamous thieving hounds of h—l. It makes my Blood boil to think that they were mean enough to impose their dirty Pictures on a poor defenceless helpless Family and what hurts me the worst is that for all we were goten up expresty for the Protection of our Homes we were absent and our homes disgraced and Country overund and destruction spread far and wide. Well its all come right I hope yet I should have been there had I been permitted to come but its al for the better I hope. I have been very busy here haveing all the writing to tend as wel as other duties. We have turned over to the Quartermaster nearly all our Company property which has taken a great deal Care and writing. I have been working five days on the Camp Pay Rolls. Just finished last night and sent them to Cincinnati this morning. I wrote at a House close to camp and they gave me dinner evry day and would not charge one cent and the very best of dinners too good ham milk Potatoes & Corn Bread & Butter. We have no accomodations for writing in camp. You have to pick up a Piece of a Cracker Box or something of the kind. I received a letter from the Capt the other day. He said he was comeing to se you in a few days and I know what he says he means. I wish I was there to welcome him and this Cruel Warr over. There has been stranger things than that happened and I expect to se that very thing take place. Thats the way I feel and always have and the day is not very far distant. I feel very sory for the sufferers of our neighborhood but there are men no doubt that invited and welcomed them. Thats what I have feared and have written about to you long ago but I hope the loyal Citizens wil take care that their Rights and safty are not endangered that they wil take care of the Sympathisers.[18] I hear that they are tending to them that they have taken old Rickely and are going to hang him.[19] Wel good he ought to swung long ago. We have been to Hickman Bridge since we came here thought the Rebs were comeing in and we were unarmed so they run us Back for to be safe Hickman or camp Nelson is 18 miles from here towards Lexington.[20] It is very stronly fortified artificialy as well as puturially. There has been little else talked of or Dreamed of here but Ohio. We were in great hopes of comeing back but now our hopes sinks within us and we have given it up for the Present but we think that we ought to be sent back at least and there is yet a bare possibility that we may come yet. There has been some Rebles in here but have been whiped out about thre Hundred Captured. The rest are fleeing for Dear life and our men after them just fighting them all the time with a fair prospect of Captureing the whole forse this side of the Cumberland.[21] They come in to help Morgan out not knowing he was played out and gave up. Wel I have just had my dinner and I feel better. Maby you would like to know what we had. Wel we had Honey good Buiscuts Coffe Crackers Beef Pork & Sugar. Not so bad is it. You are right the Boys dont suffer for anything. We are in a Butiful Place Blue Grass knee deep all around.[22] We have three shady Elms along our line of Tents which is very enviting in the heat of the day. The weather is fine and much like our own climate except the nights is cooler. We can sleep with one and sometimes two Blankets over us. The fruit is beginning to Ripen and Rosting Ears and Potatoes and we get our share we are Bound to have if we have to protect we wil partake. I would like to know whether you have money enough and how you get along. Whether the Bridge was burned or not I have not heard any particulars from there and very anxious to hear from there all about it

I deeply sympathise with you in your severe trials and long Confinement and illness but I hope you wil soon be as healthy as ever. Oh how I would like to be with you for I know you must have your hands ful but God bless their hearts. They are the best little things in this world Poor little Lettie Susan I never shal forget her the most Pityful Face that ever I beheld in all my life was hers the morning I left home last if I should forget the Countenances of all the rest I never can erase from my memory that look. Oh dear my Heart almost hurts when I allow myself to give way to my feelings. I cant think of any pretty names for your little Pets. You can find some that wil suit. Dont be to nice about it I sent some in my last letter. Thomas and Leila & Lettie I know wil be good to Ma for Pa's sake. Tell them I know that they dont kneed any telling to be good for I know they wil do al they can for you. Be kind to Lettie (*I cant forget* hers)
Between lines:

Write soon and let me know whether Hanes got my letter or not and what he intends to do and how he gets along and whether he pays you any money or not.[23] How much he has paid you how brother James is and how Fathers Folks gets along how your Father is and the folks generally. I do not expect you to write evry thing but stil I would like to hear from them all. Lieut Brunker is still here but how long he wil stay I do not know. He telegraphed to Burnsides today to know what had become of his papers. He wil not stay an hour if he gets them. Let me know if Geyer has been heard from latly. Tel me what you did with the traps I left at home when the Rebs came in. Now I dont expect you to answer all these questions at once but any of them you think of importance. Wel I know your patience wil be pretty wel tried if you have followed my Zig Zag letter this far. So kiss the Babies for me.

I hope the friends wil be kind enough to assist you when your are knedy but you must depend on your Neighbors to much. I must close. The mail is most ready to go out so good by until I write again. Be as cheerful as you can. Dont be afraid to stay at home if the Rebs come again but I think they are played out comeing to Ohio. Remember me to Mother and Father and Brother & sister Uncle and all enquireing Friends.

So good by. May the Blessings of God rest and abide with you and yours is the Prayer of your Faithful Husband.

William Mc Knight to his beloved Samaria

In margin:
I enclose you a piece of our company flag or Guidon the wind has torn of.[24] Id like to have a good pair of double Calfskin Boots No 8s if you could get them and send them with the Captain. If you cant get them handy never mind now. We expect to be paid soon and then I wil send you all the money I can. I was afraid the Rebs would find my over coat or something and Destroy evrything they could get their hands on but it is a good thing they did not.

August 17, 1863
Camp of the 7th OVC
Stanford Ky

Dear and beloved Wife,

It is with feelings of deep emotion that I seat myself this morning to pen you a few lines to let you know that I am wel this morning. It is not daylight yet and we move at 7 oclock to Crab Orchard where it is expected we wil get a lot of new clothing and Horses and get ready for active work. We wil be there in a better place for water. Here the it is very scarce. We drew new Carbines yesterday of the Burnsides pattern also were paid of and I am going to send you ten dollars this time.[25] I think it a risk to send and therefore I wil send only a little at a time and hope you wil get it. Lieut Geyer is here but has resigned and is going home whether he gets his papers now or not. You invite me over and seem to think I would come any se you if I could. God bless you dear. You dont know the pleasure it would be for me to do so. There is no place on this green Earth that my Heart ackes for as it does for my little Cottage Home and dear Ones there. I am sorry to know that your hip hurts you. I hope it is Better by this time and that your health fully recovered and the rest of the Family wel and that we wil be permitted to meet once more and spend a happe lif together. This is the great wish of your loveing and Husband until death. God bless you all. Good by until I se you again. Your Beloved Companion forever.

William McKnight
1st Sergt Co K OVC
PS I received the letter you sent by the Capt.

August 20, 1863
Camp Near Mt Vernon

Dear Samaria,

I seat myself to pen you a few lines to let you know that I am wel at present and hope these few lines may find you and the Dear little ones enjoying the same. I am weariing for a letter. Have not heard from you for so long. I begin to feel as though I was forgotten but stil I know that you cannot write when you want to. We are all mounted and armed now and Brigaded and the general talk now is that we are on our way to Knoxville.[26] How it wil be I dont know But I think that it is altogether likely. I know that it wil be a hard lick and Heartsickning letter to you to think of going farther away is a sad thought but there are men here with us that are going right home that have away from their Families for two years who Have been left to the mercy of the Sesesh and are in a suffering condition. Therefore when I think that we are going to relieve a down trodden people it does not seem so hard to think of. The men seem anxious to go as a general thing. We are just waiting for the Horse shoeing to be done and are expecting to be ordered out evry minute or have been. We came in last evening from the Orchard. I supose you have heard that Lieut Geyers has resigned and gone home and the Colonel has Ordered me to take his place so I wil be relieved of the Onerous Duties of an Orderly and get the pay that I have been earning. I have been doing the work and the Lieutenants getting the pay. Geyer drew 4 four Hundred and sixty dollars and had been absent al the time and I drew thirty eight that is the difference.[27]

I sent ten dollars in a letter some 4 days ago and I payed a debt for Brunker of nine dollars which he pay you. I have just ten dollars left and if we go into Tennesse I wil keed it and more but I want to send you and wil send you evry cent I can. A soldier would suffer if he had not money through this inhospitable country. I feel bad to think of leaving a place that I can hear from you in a few days but is all for the Better. I put my trust in the giver of evry good and gracious Gift and submit evry thing to his wil knowing that he doeth al things wel and hope you wil do the same. Tel them little dears that Pappa is comeing home some day if he lives to se them and stay with them. Remember me to all and remember that your loveing Husband never forgets you in his prayers. So hopeing that we wil soon meet each other and this cruel war is over and peace once more spreads her mantle ore this distructed country. Then wil there be rejoiceing. God speed the day so be of good cheer keep up the Heart hope and pray and dont forget your Constant Husband.

  William McKnight
  1st Sergt Co K OVC
  direct to Mt Vernon

Going for Dixie
(*August 25, 1863–March 28, 1864*)

𝒰p until this point, McKnight and the Seventh Ohio Volunteer Cavalry were organizing and preparing for battle, seeing only limited action in Kentucky. During the fall of 1863 and the following winter, however, McKnight's unit would be "going for Dixie." Although McKnight refers to this region as Dixie in his letters, many in eastern Tennessee remained loyal to the Union cause. Prior to the war, eastern Tennessee had voted against secession—out of 48,000 votes cast, 33,000 were opposed to separation.[1] During the war, many Confederate leaders questioned the allegiance of eastern Tennessee. In a note to President Jefferson Davis, General A. G. Graham stated, "Civil war has broken out at the length of East Tennessee....They look confidently for the re-establishment of the Federal authority in the South with as much confidence as the Jews look for the coming of the Messiah."[2] Colonel W. B. Wood also summarized the situation in eastern Tennessee in a letter to Judah Philip Benjamin, Confederate secretary of war, "I have been here at this station for three months, half the time in command of the post, and I have had a good opportunity of learning the feeling pervading this country. It is hostile to the Confederate Government."[3] In early 1862, Confederate general Edmund Kirby Smith of the Army of East Tennessee declared, "East Tennessee is an enemy's country."

McKnight's letters written during the winter months of 1863–64 provide detailed and vivid accounts of several battles and skirmishes. Throughout this time, the Seventh engaged the Confederates in eastern and southern Tennessee at Beans Station, Creeks Cross Road, Dandridge, Knoxville, and Mossy Creek. McKnight's letter dated September 14, 1863, also describes the operations and events that led to the capture of the Cumberland Gap—the strategic thoroughfare referred to as the "gateway to East Tennessee." Collectively, these actions were part of the larger effort to remove the Confederates from eastern Tennessee.

One of the most compelling descriptions McKnight pens is that of the losses of his "beloved" Captain Joel P. Higley and good friend Levi Little in the battle of Blue Springs (October 1863). A month later, the Union forces at Rogersville (November 1863) were routed by the Confederate forces under General James Longstreet. During the demoralizing defeat, more than five hundred Union soldiers were captured, including many from McKnight's unit. Some of these men were eventually sent to the infamous Andersonville prison in Georgia. Israel Garrard, commander of the Seventh, briefly described the affair in a brief note to General Burnside: "I was attacked this a.m. and totally defeated. I lost my guns and two-thirds of my command; rebel force not known, as they were continually sending troops forward. I think the whole of the Second Tenneessee is lost. About one-half of the Seventh [Ohio] Cavalry is lost."[4] Daniel Carpenter of the Second East Tennessee Mounted Infantry had a different opinion of the fighting at Rogersville; he claimed that the Seventh Ohio troops acted shamefully and were in full retreat, with some of the men throwing down their weapons in great confusion.[5] In the same report, Carpenter requested an inquiry into Colonel Garrard's actions, suggesting that Garrard left the battlefield, leaving Carpenter's men to either flee, die, or be taken prisoner.[6]

In his letters, McKnight also shares several accounts of the destruction and poverty that the Seventh encountered in Tennessee. McKnight previously (June 24, 1863) had confessed that the citizens in eastern Tennessee were "destitute of many

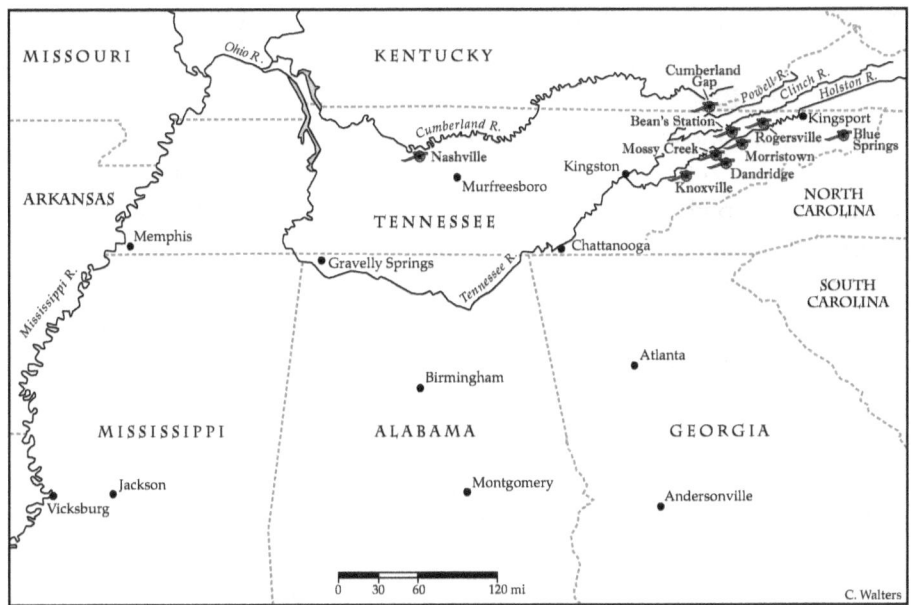

Important Civil War locations in Alabama, Georgia, Mississippi, and Tennessee. Map by Claudia K. Walters.

nesesaries of life salt there was none one man offered ten dollars in Sesesh money for Coffee enough for suffer the early Harvest all ready being but wil relieve the poor suffering women and children. There are few men left many women and children just shouted when they found out who we were.... As a general thing the country is presents a Deserted poverty stricken place." McKnight's last letter in this chapter was sent from Knoxville; it begins with "I seat myself to pen to you the last letter that I ever expect to from this the most Loyal and the most Desolated part of Tenn."[7]

August 25, 1863
Williamsburgh Cumberland River[8]

Dearest Wife,

I once more seat myself to let you know that I am wel and all the rest 60 in number and in fine spirets going for Dixie.[9] I have not time to write much. We are to start in half an Hour and Oh how I wish for a letter from you. If I only new how you were I would feel more resigned to my fate.

The letters came in to day but none for poor me evry body else nearly. Some from our post office. Stil I hope for the Best. I hope you are all enjoying the Best of health.

I was out forageing today and had to take Oats from a poor Widow Woman. Oh Gods I never wis to be placed in such a position again but it Cant be helped. You must do the best you can and forget that. Let the World say what they will I am the same as ever to you and hope ever shal recieve the same Respect from you as ever and I hope we may be permitted to meet you in a world thats fre from sin. So good by God Bless you and Protect you and yours is the Prayer of your Husband.

William McKnight
1st Sergt Co K 7th OVC

In margin:
Kiss the Babes for your absent William.
In the greatest Haste.

September 14, 1863[10]
Camp 7th OVC Knoxville Tenn

Ever Dear & beloved wife,

It is with feelings of deep emotion towards you and yours and gratitude to god that I sit down this morning to embrace the present opportunity of transmiting to you a few lines to let you know that I am wel and hope these few lines may find you in good health.[11] It is the first opportunity of writing we had since you heard from me before from Williamsburg Aug 25th Capt in command of the 2nd Battallion & we started that day to assend mountains and hills on our way to this place I in comand of the company. It is useles for me to attempt to give you the Particulars of our march further than the most important. We camped that night within ½ mile of the Angelico Mountains water good 68 men of our Co along all well.[12] Here old Burnside passed our column he said that ours was the best Regmnt in the State. The next day we started at 10 ock to assend the Mt 16 mi of the line with much dificulty. We arived at the summit made 10 miles that day and camped. The mt is 7 mi long Both sides over it camped and mustered for pay in camp for 2 nights and 1 day Left this camp 28th 1 ock camped at one at night. Next morning went 4 miles for breakfast and feed this being 29th traveled 6 miles Crosed New River 6 miles further we took supper at the foot of the

Brimstone Mt.¹³ Just at dark we comenced climbing and at midnight we were on the summit of a Mt that it was al we could do to lead our Horses up. 6 horses gave out on the mt.¹⁴ Our teams haveing gone another Road before reaching the mt. We were 5 hours crossing went into camp & I went on Picket as Lieut of the Guards 20 men. Rebels reported at a Town 3 miles ahead at Mt Gomery. Next morning we got Breakfast and foraged for our Horses and proceeded to Town but fund neither Town or Rebs the town being like Yanke doodles you couldent se it & the Rebs had taken french leave.

I may here remark that the Towns and Houses are mostly Deserted along the Roads. We here remained until 2 ock Sunday (nex morning.) We started out went 1 mile took a hasty Breakfast and traveled 15 miles went into camp 2 ock pm got some dinner and remained all night. 20,000 Rebels reported 4 miles ahead at a Town Called Kingston.¹⁵ Our strength estimated at 50,000 180 pieces of Artilery enough to sweep Eastern Tenesse. Sep 1st in camp on Emery Creek until eleven ock started out Crossed Poplar Creek traveled 10 miles went into camp 1 mile from Clinch River.¹⁶ Rebels stil reported ahead of us sighn where they had been all along the Road. Clinch River is about 3 times as large as Leding Creek and is a butiful stream. Several days previous to this we had to use water that our Horses would hardly drink the nastiest you ever se taken from old swails where nothing but lizards Snakes & frogs would stay but here and ever since we Crossed the Clinch we have had good water E Tenn is wel watered by springs. The 2nd we started out at 5 in the morning Crosed the River & proceeded to Lenoir Station on the R.R.¹⁷ Here we found the Rebs had left and gone to London Brige 6 ms below on the R.R.¹⁸ This Bridge was of great importance to us as wel as the Rebs. We got some dinner here captured Sugar Bacon Barley & Salt to a smal amt. We had hardly had time to eat our dinner until we heard cannon in the direction of the Bridge to Horse was sounded and off we went double quick for the scene in high Spirits hopeing the Enemy had been bayed and brought into a fight. We all felt sure we were going to have a fight. Wel on we went the day was hot the dust in Road about 6 inshes deep and such another time as you never seen. The dust flew so thick you could not se a man and Horse ten feet ahead. When we arrived within 1½ miles of the Bridge we discovered a large smoke which told the story. The Rebs had retreated across the Holston River and fired the Bridge.¹⁹ We sheled them a while and drove them Back killing 8 or 10 of them. This was a magnificent structure Cost 2 millions of dollars. We were disapointed and had to turn around and go back as the River is almost as large as the Ohio. This Bridge was just above the junction of Clinch & Holston Rivers forming the Tennessee.[20] The next morning the 3rd we took up our march for Knoxville where we arrived before night being 20 miles. The next morning we drew 5 days Rations and at 5 ock we started for the Cumberland gap.[21] Our course this far had been nearly south now we took nearly a north course a little East of north marched 16 miles Camped for the night. The next morning we started without Breakfast marched 20 miles recrossed the Clinch River. Coffee Roasting Ears and Beef for supper & Breakfast. Started out this morning the 6th went 2 miles halted & took Breakfast and fed 12 miles from the Gap at a Town called Taswell which had been burned by the Rebs.[22] Proceeded on toward the gap skirmished all the way to the Gap Camped on the Howell River 5 ms from the Gap.[23] Started out next morning. shelled the Rebs back. Corn and Coffee for Breakfast we arrived in the sight of the Rebel Works on either side of the Gap on the mountains some 1200 feet high we went into camp under the Rebel Guns as cool as though they were the best friends instead of enemies. We comenced bombarding them but recieved no response. Sent in a flag of truce for an unconditional surender but recieved no satisfaction. On the next day we bombarded the enemy again and burned their mill. The Rebels fired on me as I was going to water with the company but their shels fel short & did no harm. In the evening I & Capt went on a Reconaisance under the Reb works with the Colonell and the rest of the officers of the 7th. We had a fine view of the gap and all of their forts and entrenchments. When I returned it was dark and the company had gone on Picket & I was to take charge of them. I took supper & proceeded to the Picket Post. Posted my guards and walked & rode about all night not being allowed to sleep. The next morning I took half of an old Reb canteen and a Horse shoe nail an hammer an made a graiter and we had great times making mush I tell you. Reinforcements came in all day. Another flag sent in & the Rebs surendered without fireing a gun (exception the little fight they had the might we burnt the mill they killed 1 man belonging to Tennessee). With 2025 Prisoners all their smal arms 10 pieces of artilery mules Waggons Horses camp and Garrison Equipage.[24] Flour was the most in way of provisions. The 7th OVC had the Honor of being the first Regmt from the South side of the mt to enter the Gap. Thursday Sep 10th might have seen me at 8½ ock at the very top of the C"mt viewing the Giberalter of the Rebels. Here one can look into Tennessee to the south Virginia to the North East & Ky to the North West with seven ranges of mountains in sight. It is one of the strongest fortifications naturealy that one can concieve of. It is no use for me to attempt a discription. It cant be described nor imagined it is the Grandest sight that I ever expect to witness.[25]

With 10,000 troops wel provisioned we might defy the whole Sothern Confederacy. The Prisoners were generaly lusty looking and hearty and glad to fall into our hand and are takeing the Oath.[26] Those that are known to be loyal and are enlisting into the Tenessee Regmts.[27] Burnsides brought Guns along on purpose. The Rebs had no Coffee not sugar and all the Rice they had was to make coffe of their Pork. Gracious what pork it looked like it had been butchard by starvation and killn dried. Coffee $5.00 per lb Corn $1.00 per 10 ears Cigars 50 cts a piece salt 40 cts per lb womens shoes 20 to 22 dollars per pair Boots 50 to 75 dollars per pair & evry thing in proportion. Paid by our Boys 2.00 dollars for Bakeing 12 flat cakes that a dog could hardly bite or cat scratch and so on and articles were very dear til we opened up the Direct Rout to stanford and Ky. The Gap is 55 miles from here and 75 from Stanford by way of Richmond Ky. Burnsides has established his head Quarters here and we are in no great danger I dont think. While I write the sond of our Locomotives shows that trade & business is reviving. The people are flocking to us from their hiding places & joining us in Arms by Hundreds. Those that were able brought evry thing that you could wish to Eat here and gave it freely and our Boys bring in bush whackers and our armies are sweeping before them here like a whirl wind evry thing before them. We are welcomed here by the mothers with tears in her eyes and I think they feel very much like our folks did at the sight of the Noble Sons of the States not long since.[28]

I cant give you all the particulars this time but I hope it wil not be long until I can. I think the time very very long to hear from you. You wil write as often as you can. Keep in good heart and dont forget that you are the Idol of my Heart and the object of my life and ambition and I hope this wil find you all well. Remember me to sister Janett and mother and all the rest and remember you have one who wil never forget that I hav a dear little family at home. Oh how I would like to se you all. I hope the time wont be long until I can se you and that God wil Bless and Protect us to meet again is the prayers of your William.

In margin:
Direct to Knoxville Tennessee via Lexington.
I received a letter from you this evening. We left Williamburg.
I am riding my old saddle again.
I want you to write me a good long letter as soon as you get this and tell me all the news how you get along for money and how the rest of the folks get along. Though I feel they dont care much for me maybe I am mistaken.
When we were at the Gap I got a pair of Boots for $8.00 I have plenty of clothes to do as long as they last. I want to come home this fall if I can Get leave.
Since I have been relieved of an Orderlies Duties I have more time to myself although we have been in the Saddle for nearly a month I have been wel and we have not suffered for any thing necessary.

October 1, 1863[29]
Head Quarters 7th OVC
9 Miles E of Morrstown[30]

My ever D Samaria,

I seat myself once to pen you a few lines to let you know that I am wel and hearty and hope these lines may find you enjoying the same Blessing. I have neither Paper nor any conveniences for writing but Capt Warren of Athens is going to start for home this morning.[31] I wish you to send my Over Coat to Athens by the Hack just as soon as you get this directed to him to bring to me as I kneed it as the nights is very cool and frosty. The men are very Healthy generaly. We have had a very active time here. If you have any thing to send put it in the pockets. I recieved a letter from you dear thre days ago but as there was no date to it I cant tel how old it was. One from little Emma and one from Lieut McMaster. Was very glad to hear from you all. My heart Ackes for you. I never felt so bad about you in my life. There is no chance for to help you as I am out of money. I have the best Horse in the Regmt that I would send home but I cant share him now but hope to put him into market soon and then I wil be able to help you a little. You must do the best you can. I hope to be with you again. It is the one great and uppermost thought of my Heart. If the lord only spares me to spend the balance of balance of the days he has allotted to me with you when this Cruel war is over.

I care not what the Hardships may be it is all I ask and pray for is to be restored to my dear dear little family with health to support them and bring them up in the way they should go. Tel Emma I will answer her kind letter as soon as possible. Give my respects to sisters and Brothers Mother & Father and friends. Tel them to write for I have no chance.

Dear Samaria,

You wil excuse me for the paper I use. It the best I have and remember your absent husband is ever mindful of you and oh ho I would like to se you all. You seem to talk encouraging about the close of the war. I hope your anticipations may be realised and that it may not be long until we may be permitted to return to the ones we love. Until the good by God bless you and comfort you. Let the memory of the past and hopes of the future sustain you. I hope you wil not suffer you nor the little ones allthou it seems that our neighbors are apt to turn a cold shoulder to those to whom charity due. Brunker owes me $9.00 nine dollars. He was to pay you. Tel him I recieved his letter & I want him to pay you the nine dollars as Hoyt (Sergeant in our Co) wrote to his Father to pay him Brunker the 4 dollars that he owed him that he wil have to look to Old Hoyt for Sergt Hoyts debt.[32] So good by. God bles you all and help us to live that we may be permitted to meet in another if not in this world.
From your very affectionate Husband
   Wm McKnight
   Lieut Co K 7th OVC

                            September 23, 1863
                            Hd Qs 4 Cav Div

Lieut McKnight,

You will take charge of team of twenty (20) wagons and proceed to Henderson Station and load them for Rations. If there is nothing but Hard Bread & Bacon load them up if Coffee & Sugar bring half of Each kind. You will take with you a guard of 20 men. Be as precaitous as possible.
   Respectly
   Jo. P. Santmyer[33]
   1st Lieut 4 Cav Div

PS I want the Head of Cattle driven up to within a mile of my head quarters and let the sergt in charge report to me as soon as he gets up. Leave the balance of your men (5) with the sergt. Report to me with the Rations on your return.

October 9, 1863
Camp 7th OVC on the E T & Va R R[34]
12 miles from Greenville[35]

Ever Dear Samaria,

    I seat myself once more on Mother Earth to let you know that I have not forgotten you. I am wel at present and hope this may find you & the dear little ones al well. We are & have been laying here in front of the Enemy for 7 days skirmishing almost evry day. Last Monday we had a heavy skirmish with him & lost 8 men in killed & wounded.[36] The Enemies lost must have been greater although not known as they carried theirs of the field. Our company was in suport of the Battery & was not imediately in the fight if but in plain sight the 103rd Ohio Infantry was in the skirmish. Came in quietly. They lost thre men our Regmt none eccept one by accident in the first Battallion. We have been on picket and sent skirmishing evry day for a week. We are awaiting Reinforcements which are being forward rappidly. The Rebs are about ten thousand strong in front of us in sight of us evry day and saucy creeping up in our pickets & fireing on them and recieving fire in turn. We captured 20 waggons and Horses & drivers yesterday on a Road south of one camp a little. I Scouted the same road for 7 miles thre days ago but found no Enemy. But they are on the alert in front of us. They wil have to skadadle when our Reinforcements gets up with us. It is reported that Genl Wilcocks is Getting around them above and on the left or north of us but whether or not we wil give them Hail Columbia in a few days.[37] I must close. I have to go on picket with the Company one mile from here so I must close Comending evry thing to the care of our heavenly Father hopeing & trusting that he may return me to you once more is the Prayer of my heart. I dreamed a sweet dream about you. I thought I was seated on our bended knees with my dear little Family around me. Oh what a sweet dream but alas it is al mans Delusion but I hope the time wil come when we knel together. Until then I Comend you to to his care. Remember to all. Kis the little ones & tell them that I love them & pray for them. Oh if you had seen me crying over your old likeness & heard me pray for you you would know how love you. I must close. I much more to write but have no time at present. Write to me as often as you can and tel the rest to write to me for I cant get any thing to write. So good by. God Bless you & yours.

From your loveing Husband
William McKnight
Lieut Co K 7th OVC

October 21, 1863[38]
Rogersville Tenessee[39]

My Dear and ever beloved Wife,

I hasten to let you know that I am enjoying the best of health at present & have been ever since I came into the State. The men that are with me are very healthy only two being left sick at Knoxville. Warren Coulter & Peter Bechtel how they are I do knot know but they are not deserters.[40] I think I have not had an opportunity since the 3rd of this

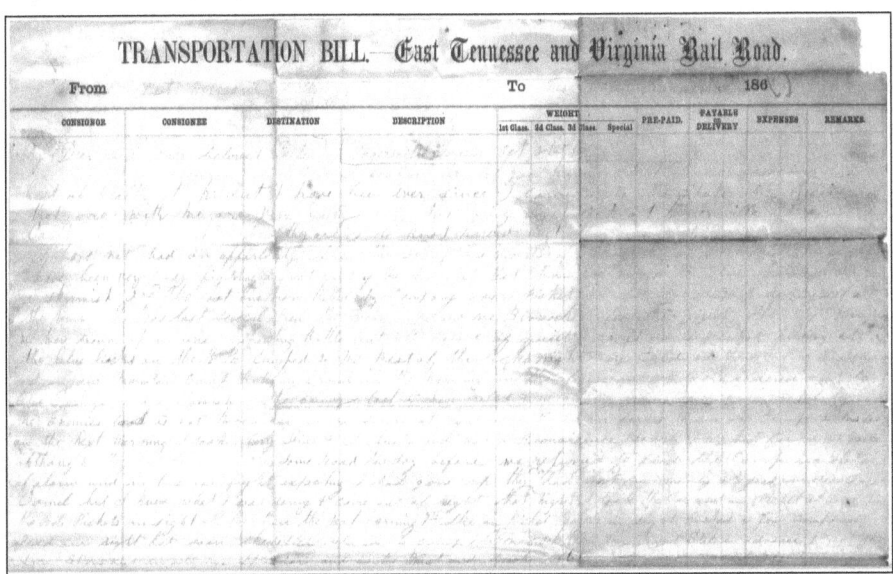

Letter from William to Samaria written on paper from the East Tennessee and Virginia Railroad ledger book. *Courtesy of Terry Hauger.*

month of writing to you since that we all have been very busy fighting a great part of the time. At that time we moved to blue licks.[41] Had a skirmish 2nd Ohio lost one man killed. My company was on picket near but none present but myself at the time. The Rebs lost several men. The rebs withdrew. We Bivwacked for the night.[42] The next morning we were drawn up in line expecting Battle but all passed of quietly except some picket firing at the blue licks on the RR. Camped 2 ms west of the licks. Night very cold on the 5th. The sun shone out on our mountain Camp Butifully Grand in the morning. In the afternoon we were ordered out to Blue Springs had a skirmish withhe Enemy.[43] Lost 5 men Killed and 13 missing from the 10th Ohio Infantry.[44] The Enemies loss is not known but it was severe. At night we withdrew our forces to our old camp 2 ms bak. On the next morning I took Harry Spires & A Austin and mad a Reconaisance South 7 ms but found no Enemy although they had been on the same Road the day before.[45] We returned to find the Camp in a state of alarm and in line for fight. Expecting I had gone up they Capt Higley had sent for me by a squad under Capt Comel but I knew what I was doing & came out al right.[46]

That night I took the Co went out on picket at Blue Springs. The Reb Pickets in sight all the time. The next morning 7th stil on picket. Rebels in sight Pushed a few companies pased our right but soon skadadled. Returned to camp 7 PM. 8ock PM our Regmt Stil in advance.

9th Oct the sun Shone out in all her splendor and as the mist and smoke lifted itself from the Mt tops the sight was magnificently Grand. I was again ordered out with the comp" on picket remained all night. Early on the morning of the 10th we moved forward with the Brigade was ordered out on the left as skirmishers Dismounted my men & double quced them one mile me being on picket & haveing my men to relieve after the Brigd came up we were behind. With great difficulty we got up with the Battalion just as we met the Enemy in force. My Company being on the left of Batt" we were decieved when the Enemy advanced on us they sung out not to fire on our own men thinking that it was the left of our Batt swinging round. I ordered the men not to fire thus the Enemy were able to advance within 40 yds of us before we discovered the mistake. Capt Higley discovered it at the same time I did ordered the men to fire & fall back. The Enemy fired first from our front & right thus subjecting us to a rakeing fire. The lead just showered around us. I was thre Rods in advance of the Company & within 30 yds of the

Rebs. Seeing that the whole Batt had falen back I ordered my men to fall back also.[47] This they had already done eccept one Corp by my side. On turning to assend the Ravine I discover to my Horror our Brave & Noble Capt laying upon his Face upon the Ground. Hastening to him & speaking kindly to him Receiving no answer I seen he was mortaly wounded. He never spoke. The feeling that came over me at that moment I never can Describe. I raised him gently in my arms walking bacwards I draged him 3 Rods up the hill laid him behind a log unable to move him further. I sat or partly fel by his side Determined to die withe him.[48] But seeing he was dead I knew that I could do him no good so I with drew a little the Enemy stil Pouring their fire into us or me as there was not a man to be seen eccept Levi Little & Martin Rupe.[49] Rupe being only stuned but

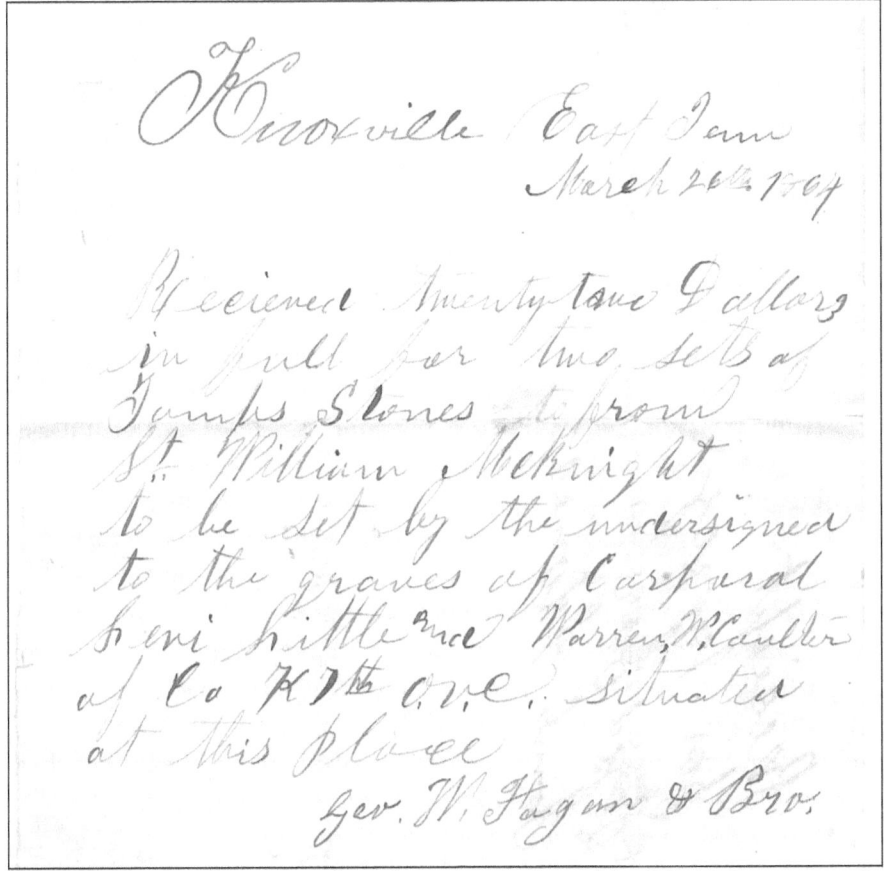

Tombstone receipt for Levi Little and Warren Coulter of the 7th OVC. *Courtesy of Terry Hauger.*

not so fortunate with our Noble Corporal who had Recieved a mortal wound and was lying groaning some 25 yards to the left & front out of my Reach.

With my Heart sinking within me I withdrew a little farther up the side of the Ravine. Here on a Ridge at the head of the Ravine I found the Bat halted. I called on the men to come with me & rescue our men. They done so & we got the captains Boddy. The rebs had not found atall but Levi they Robed of evry thing eccept clothing. Rupe haveing got out himself the Capt had just turned on his Horse (the Rest were dismounted) when a minnie Ball took affect under his right Shoulder Passing throug his Body & lodgeing one inch from his left Nipple Breast killing him instantly. He was at the head of his comand the 2nd Battallion.

Levis wounds were through his left shoulder joint & another Ball entered his leg below the Knee & lodged near the knee joint. He suffered dreadfuly for a while but died like he was going to sleep at 10 PM. 9½ Hours after the Battle I carried them both of the field and got them well taken care of.[50]

The night was spent in taken care of them and the next morning with great difficulty I suceded in obtaining transportation for them Both to Knoxville.[51] Procureing the best coffins possible I sent them on the carrs in charge of Sergt Carr & Wm McBurns with instructions to inter them there & mark their resting place.[52] Peace to their ashes. Better men never lived. We feel their loss & Deeply sympathise with the bereaved families of our Noble men. Two better men & Soldiers never was sacrificed in this cruel Rebellion. The Whole Regmt mourns their loss but hope to live to avenge their loss.

My company was the first that was fired on this being 11 am. The Battle continued to Rage until night fireing sounded like a thousand wood chopers only as much louder as the imagination can concieve. In the afternoon the 9th army core came up on the right & charged them at the same time. We opened on them with Canon from two Batteries. Our Boys went for them with a yel on the Right. We maintained the left while the Batteries opened on them from the rear & center carried evry thing before them. The crash of arms the Boom of canon & Bursting of shels was terrifically Grand.[53] The darkness closed the awful scene. The next morning we drove the Enemy 25 miles captureing Horses, Waggons, Provisions & Prisoners and killing many of the Rebs. Went into camp 10 miles from Jonesburough.[54] Entered Jonesburough next morning 13th.

Moved towards Blountsville went into camp 4 ms from Town.[55] Lost one man from 1st Batt.

The next morning we moved out met the enemy 6½ AM Dismounted & went out on the right. The Enemy shelled us. Canon opened on the Enemy from 3 Batteries. We drove them in the fore noon. In the afternoon we went forward dismounted and skirmished 2 ms on the left. Took Blountsville on the morning of 15 our Regmt went to Zolicoffr took the place captured Comisary Stores & Arms Burned 2 Forts 2 Block Houses & one RR Bridge across Holstein River.[56] Destroyed a great many arms that night. We started for Bristol 11 ms distant arrived near and went into camp 1 ock in the night.[57] Next morning we went into Town captured 25 RR Carrs any amt of salt, sugar, Rice, Tobacco, Dried Fruit & many other Comisary Stores. We Burned the carrs, 2 Locomotives, tore up the track & played smash genaraly.[58]

Thence we moved to Kingsport on the 18th.[59] We passed throug Blountsville captured about 100 Horses. On the 19th 8 AM we started marched 10 miles camped at Rogersville where we are. The carrs come in here evry day. We expect to get clothing here before we march any more. Yesterday I was out in command of the 2nd Battallion. There is scarcely any thing but Rebs here.

I have not heard from you since sometime in august. There was a mail come through for the Regmt. All the Boys got letters but me. I dont see why that I am slited. I write evry chance I get. There is some talk that our Regmt may go back to Ky. I hope it may so we can hear from home. The men are very healthy & have been ever since we came into State. I wil have to close for the present. Hopeing that this wil find you all enjoying the best of Health & spirits and that we may be permitted to meet again soon. I remain your Ever Devoted Husband until this life shal end in blissful eternity. God bless you all. Respects to Friends & love to you all. Good by Dear Samaria.

   From William McKnight
   Lt Comanding Co K OVC
   3rd Brig 4th Div 23

In margin:
Excuse my paper & scribling. Oh how I long to meet you again in fond embrace. Wm.

McKnight wrote in a diary almost daily throughout the war. Most of the entries were brief; however, on November 6, 1863, McKnight penned his longest entry. The following is a verbatim transcription of that entry:

November 6, 1863
Rogersville fight the 7th O.V.C. and 2nd E. Tennessee were surprised.[60]
4 miles from this Place on what is called Big Creek.[61] *Early in the morning the enemy fireing on our pickets first. E" of where we were and then on our advance Guards. W" on the Town Road we here turned our Train around and went back under first of Enemy across the Creek. Planting a Section of our Battery and opened on the advancing collums of the enemy but before the Cavalry could get up to their support the Rebs charged and captured it not however without the loss of many of their men after which we fell back across the Creek again and Planted the 2 remaining Guns on a small Hill and opened but on the Enemy again across the Creek with Canon and Musketry but the Rebs Come on in solid column the Cannoniers Double shooting their guns and fireing right into their ranks but on they came. They knew that they had a force all around us and see that we were confused and that encouraged them. They captured our last Gun and were closeing in on us from every direction we retreated across a field to the left towards the Holstein River between a ford and a Ferry and succeeded in Getting over the most of the 7th the 2nd takeing to the Mountains before were al over Rebs fired on us and took some Prisoners. We Proceed to Buls Gap then to Morris Town a Distance of 30 Ms the Men without Breakfast or Diner Horses unfed.*[62] *3 P.M. upon Colecting the men together I ascertained that I lost 12 men, but on the next day 7ths thre came in. Stil Missing Duston Harper.*[63] *Killed Henry Shiner John Foose Orellana Williams Royal Hoyt . . . William F. Walker William Johnson, Issac Nelson missing.*[64] *We lost all our Train Baggage Co." Books Papers Pay Rolls and evry thing in the Train accep a few Mules. Co" Property all Tents 5 Burnside Rifles besides what the 9 Prisoners lost they lost all 9 Carbines 9 Revolvers 9 Cartrige Bts. 9 Carbine Slings 9 Pistol Belts 9 Pistol Holsters 0 Cap Pouches 9 Swivels 9 Horses 9 Saddles 9 Bridles 9 Halters 9 Blankets Horse 9 Brushes 9 Curry Combs . . . 9 Sleeping*

Blankets I lost my Saber in the Train. Fountain lost evrything eccept Revolver. I lost Revolver 2 Valises 5 Shirts 4 Pr. Drawers 4 pr Socks 1 prs Trousers 1 Hankerchief 1 Talma 1 Horse 1 Horse Brush 1 Comb 2 Blankets. R.D. Andrews lost his Horse and Equipment also his Arms. A.D. Davis lost his Arms in the River 1 Saddle 1 Bridle 1 Brush and Comb 1 Great Coat 1 Cartrige Bt and Sling 1 Blanket. R.D. Andrews also lost 3 Blankets 1 Talma 1 Pr Boots 1 pr Drawers 1 Shirt. James Smith Horse Sadle 1 Blanket 1 Talma 1 Saber 1 Shirt 1 pr Drawers . . . Robinson 2 Shirts 1 Pr Pants 1 Horse Wm M. Burns 1 Carbine 2 Blankets 2 Shirts Horse and Equipment 1 Talma and Drawers M. Nelson 1 Suit Clothese 3 Blankets 1 Horse.

November 10, 1863
Camp in the woods near Russelville[65]

Deara Samaria,

I once more seat myself on Mother Earth to let you know that I am stil in the land of the liveing in good health and thankful for it. I have long anxiously awaited a letter from you but in vain I have not heard from you since Oct 2nd. Oh what anxiety. But I expect you think that I dont write often. It is even so I have not had the Chance but you may write once a week surely. I wil get them sometime letters come through often now. We met with a severe Disaster on the 6th inst at Russelville the 7th OVC & 2nd E. Tennessee were in advance & on the morning of the 6th we were completely Surounded by an overwhelming forse before daylight.[66] They drove in our pickets on the front first then we moved our Train towards Rogersville. When all was silent an unsuspecting they opened such a volly upon us that completely surprised us here comenced a scene of horror & confusion. After the first fire they Charged on the Train & Captured a part of it. Some of the Teamsters cut a mule or Horse out and fel in with the mounted men. We then fel back about ¼ of a mile planted our Batteries & fought them until overpowered. Our Battery 4 Guns Captured many of the men Being shot down or Captured at the Guns. The Cavalry never got up to suport the them until too late. Here things looked sqully & very little Chance of esscape but fortunately we found a hole out and succeeded in fording the River that lay to the right through a heavy fire from the Enemy with the loss of our Train about 100 prisoners 4 pieces of Artillery five Officers all our Books and Company property Clothing and many Horses.[67] One of my men was shot & thought to be killed. His name is Duston Harper. Prisoners Wm L. Johnson Orrellama Williams Isaac Nelson Royal Hoyt John Foose Robert T Chapder & Henry Shiner.[68] I am in hopes that they may yet get in as many have succeded in makeing their escape. The Agut & St. Car got away from them. The Rebs were much disappointed when they saw thier game had gone. All they got Cost them very dear for they were just mowed down as they advanced in the Artillery with Double Shots of Canister and grape from our Guns. I understand they Boast very little of their atchievements although they had seven or eight thousand men. We had plenty of force but it was some distance of was ready to march to our assistance but was witheld by Genrl Wilcox the 2nd of E Tennessee I think were heavier lossers than ours. We have drawn some new Clothing & I made a Requisition this morning for enough to supply the deficiency eccept Blankets Tents & Cooking Utencils which cannot be obtained at present. We are very much in kned of Blankets as the weather is quite cool and Frosty but one great blessing were all in good health and anxious to try them again if they give us a fair chance. We have been in nearly all the fights that has taken place in the State since we came in to it. We have been somewhat misfortunate but I feel thankful that it is no worse. We lost the best captain in the Regmt & two good men & soldiers. We mourn their loss. Hope they are better of than we are and their Families wil not be permitted to suffer.

 I have 51 men with me all good and true on the 3rd inst I was appointed captain of the company by Brgdier General Garrard our former Collonell.[69] It is a Great responcibility but by the Help of God & strict attention to my duties I hope to get along but Oh how wil my little family get along without me. God have mercy on them. I wil come to you as soon as I can if the Lord wils it. You wil have to do the best you can. I sent by Amos Dyke what I hope may help you until I can.[70] I had my Pay Rolls all ready mad out for four months pay but lost them. All my Clothes valise & evry thing only what I had on & a good Horse. So I must close for the Present. Give my respects to all enquiring Friends. Accept my most sincere affection sympathy & love. Kiss the little ones for your absent Husband until Death.

 William McKnight
 Capt Co K 7th OVC to Samaria[71]

In margin:
I write laying on my Saddle Blanket on my belly a large Testament with my Feet to the fire. Some stamps please. This is the last sheet I have & none to be had.
　Wm

In his letter of November 10, 1863, McKnight accurately describes the events at Rogersville and mentions William Lemon Johnson as one of the prisoners. William Lemon Johnson was born on November 4, 1840, and died on February 28, 1933, in Pomeroy, Ohio.[72] Donald Johnson, who is William Lemon Johnson's great-grandson, still lives on the family farm near Buffington Island in Meigs County. Mr. Johnson provided a copy of his great-grandfather's story of imprisonment at Andersonville, Georgia, as recorded by Howard Blaine circa 1900.

"The morning of November 5, 1863 finds the 7th OVC encamped at a little town called Rodgersville in east Tennessee. I, as [a] member of Company K, being on detached service as one of the Brigade Cattle Guard, just after daylight an oderly brought an order to get ready to march as the Jonnies were coming and we were going to retreat. I said to the other boys of the Guard, Jonnies or no Johnnies I am going to have my breakfast. Little thinking that would be the last for 48 hours. Just as I was finished breakfast—bang, bang went several shots up in town; I jumped up and ran out of the house. As I came out of the house I could see about fifty Rebel Cavalry on a side street. My horse was in a stable so I had to run toward the Rebs to get to him. When nearing the stable I discovered the other boys getting their horses had left the stable door open. My horse was standing with his head out of the door; seeing my coming running and hearing the firing, so excited him that he ran out of the stable over towards the Jonnies. That horse had played me a trick and I was in a bad shape. I ran toward the house where some of the boys still remained and just as I got back to the house one of the Jonnies fired at us, the ball striking the cistern curb just as I passed it, making a hole in it, that I could have stuck my fist through but I did not stop to try it for I had other business to attend to and was anxious to get it done. That business was to get to the mountain, which as about a quarter mile away and if ever a boy made good time I did. I never looked back till I got to the woods at the foot of the mountain period. I stopped and looked over to the house I had left. I beheld what looked from where I was as the cattle guard still there. I could see that they had on blue clothes. I stood there and looked for some time, finally came to the conclusion that as the regiment was escaped out on the road from which the Rebs had come. About three miles from town that in falling back, the Rebs had retreated on a side road that headed in another direction. I started back to join my boys, as I supposed the ground over which I had to travel was very irregular, just as I got on top of one of the little ridges, low and behold, about twenty-five yards from me was Jonnie Rebel coming toward me, his short Enfielding across the saddle in front of him, when I saw him I stopped, so did Jonnie, he motioned me to come on down to him, as there was nothing else I could do I at once obeyed. When I came up to him he said, "Are there any more of the boys out there?" I assured him there was not. He says come on and we started back toward town. Pretty soon he spied my spur on my heal; he says you had better give me that spur as you will not need it. I removed the spur and gave it to him; he seemed quite pleased to get it. He marched me in to town where I found all the Provose Guard, which they had captured, and in a short time they brought all of the 7th Tennessee Regiment and two Illinois Battery boys, which they had captured out at camp. The 7th OVC swimming the Tennessee River and making their escape.

"I will digress a little at this time to relate the only funny thing that I recollect on this occasion, just as I came down to the road from the house, at which we were in camp, one of the boys passed me on his horse on the lope (not quite a gallop), I think it was Mart Rasp, his sheet iron frying pan, quart cup and coffee pot playing the long road; it was enough to make a hare laugh.

"After the Jonnies [got] us all together, one of officers came around and informed us, if any of the prisoners were sick, so they were unable to march they would furnish them horses to ride. That settled it for me, I was sick, so I got a horse. We marched all that day and night; about two o'clock, that night we made a short halt from some cause, all at once two shots rang out. I made inquiry what was the matter. I soon learned that Adjutant Allen and Lunt Johnson of the 7th OVC had escaped and this caused the shooting.

"The next morning just at day we came to Clinch River. I wandered what would be done as it was quite a stream running full of ice. It was soon solved by the order, jump in Prisoners, as the boys hesitated, the officer in command, drew his saber an prodded some of the boys and in the went, the water being up to their arms, after which they marched all day in their wet clothes, their feet becoming very sore. That night about ten o'clock went into camp in the timber, some distance from the road, getting our first Rebel jonnie cake. About ten o'clock the next day, we came to the main rebel army, commanded by General Longstreet. The first thing we struck was their artillery, sixty pieces; it looked like a ten-acre field full. The boys ran up against the same guns a couple of weeks later at Blans Cross Roads and Knoxville. At the latter place, General Longstreet got more than he bargained for.

"When we got to Headquarters of Longstreet, we were ordered to get into line and search began for our money. They taking name and amount and promising to pay it over at Richmond; false promise, as no one ever saw a cent again of the amount they contributed. They got $700.00 from one of the two Tennessee Regiments. One thing more before we leave Longstreet, before we were allowed to break the men came along and picked out three men, one captain and to privates; these were deserters who had joined the 2nd Tennessee Regiment. I learned later they were shot as deserters. After leaving Longstreet Camp, we went to Bristol and took cattle cars for Richmond. The first stop was Lynchburg, where we got some hardtack (real hard dry bread); after which we proceeded to Richmond land on Belle Isle."

He [William Johnson] was next sent to Lawrence, then to Libby where he spent one night and then to Andersonville where he spent about thirteen months of unbelievable conditions of hunger and taunting thirst. He was told of a natural spring running through

Private William Lemon Johnson, member of the 7th OVC captured at Rogersville, Tennessee, and later imprisoned at Andersonville, Georgia. *Courtesy of Donald and Brian Johnson.*

the prison but the guards would answer their pleas for drinking water by themselves drinking deep and long and throwing water wastefully about while making the prisoners go days on end without a drink—a cruel and needless practice. Food was practically nonexistent, it being a lucky day when one was able to catch a rat, sucking off and drinking the warm blood and eating the warm raw meat. Prisoners passed their time delousing each other. When his exchange came, he weighed only 86 pounds and was suffering from scurvy, which caused his eyes to water almost continuously, a condition which bothered him the remainder of his life. In fact, the operation for the condition of his eyes at the age of 93 caused his death. At that age he was active, hearty and strong, physically and mentally as alert as most men of 60.

November 13, 1863
Camp of 7th Ohio Vol Cavalry
near Russelville Tenn

I certify on honor that on the 6th day of Nov" 1863 near Rogersville Tenn the Regiment and Command of which my Company formed a part were attacked and overwhelmed by the Enemy loseing by Capture all the Trains in which were the Books and records of my Company and Command without which it is impossible for me to make my returns.[73]

William McKnight
Capt "Cavarly" Co. K 7th OVC

I Certify that the above is a true statement.
James McIntire Maj[74]
Comd Regiment

I certify that the above is a true Statement.
Israel Garrard
Col. Company Brigade

December 11, 1863
Camp 7th OVC
Beans Station Tenn[75]

Dear and beloved Samaria,

I hasten to Pencil you a few lines to inform you that I am enjoying the best of health and I hope that this may find you the Same. Dear we have just returned from another Battle field in which we were gloriously Victorious. The Battle was opened late yesterday afternoon near Morristown by our Brigade the Enemy haveing posted himself on the right of the Road with mounted in the woods Infantry on the left Artillery in an open field when they came up the 9th Mich was deploying Skirmishers to the right.[76] We came up Dismounted & Deployed on the left went forward in line paralel with the Road the Enemy on the same Paralel here. The Battle comenced 4 oclock pm & was hotly Contested until the shades of night closed the conflict. The Enemy skadadled from the field in great confusion leaving about 100 Killed & wounded of their number for us to care for. We did not find all killed nor wounded until this morning. My company went into them with a wil that makes me proud of them. They fired near a 1000 Rounds came out without a hair of their Heads being harmed. The Enemy played on us with 2 Pieces of Artillery the Shells Bursting over & around us harmlessly. Our Artillery at the same time Played upon them but les fortunate for them one shot killing 9 men. The rest of the Artillery fireing being less effective but such Rifle fireing for the number of men on our side I think scarcely ever was excelled. Our Burney Rifles being susceptible of being fired 8 times per minit and handled better they could not be.[77] We had the advantage of woods. The Enemy lay along a fence just across a corn field.

Saturday morning Dec 12th. Daylight I resume my writing this morning while the Boys gets Breakfast. Harry does the most of it good cook. Orderly cook was wounded severely 4 others of our Regmt slightly. The 9th Mich suffered less. It was the same men we fought at Rogersville. My camp are in fine health & spirits & wil fight. We expect to Recieve pay in a few days and as soon as this Valley is cleaned out of Rebs who are now Running for life we expect to come back to Ky. The Rebs have been putting forth evry effort to make a saf retreat out of Tenn ever since they were so badly cut up at Knoxville. The citizens say that they are the worst frightened set men they ever seen. The Prisoners we took (some 20) say that their cause is hopeless.

Charley Lewis is wel and I told him to write John Foose is a prisoner I se the paper has it J Tease.[78] William T. Walker whom I thought a prisoner is at Knoxville. Hiram Carr was left Knoxville sick when we were there & started not long ago to come to the camp not long ago & was taken prisoner so Harry was told when he was there the other Day.

Dear Molly I received your very kind & affectionate letter of 26–7 October & was very glad to hear from you. I also recd one from Sister

Mary & one from my ever kind Mother. It is impossible for me to answer them al as I would like to do but you must Remember me kindly to them all. I do not know what to advise you to do. I wil trust that your own judgement may lead you to do the best that can be done for your own comfort. I hope & pray that you may not suffer for the comforts of life. I had an invitation last night from Our Old Colonl to attend a meeting to pass Resolutions in respect to the Retirement of Maj General Burnsides from the Command of the Army of Ohio but I did not attend.[79] I expect it was a grand affair as the officers of the Whole Division were requested to attend. Old Burny as the Boys call him leaves us with Great Honors as he held Knoxville against thre times his number when he was completely surounded for 16 days.[80] We regret his loss.

I think the names of your pets very pretty suit me first rate. I would like to se them and all the rest & hope I may soon. I got me a new Hat & Boots yes & new Horse. One of my Horse is very lame worth $75.00 and I am afraid I wil have to leave him. Wel I have to close for the present as there is to be Brigade Inspection at 11 AM. Remember me kindly to al. Kiss the little ones for me & accept my sincere love and affecion.
From your affectionate Husband
   William McKnight
   Capt" Co "K" 7th, OVC
   To Samaria

December 26, 1863[81]
New Market[82]
25 miles East from Knoxville
On the E Tenn & Va RR

Ever beloved Wife,

I again take my pen to inform you that I am (by the blessings of a merciful *God*) stil permitted to live and move although I am not able to be with my Company. I hope I wil be in a day or two. I am stopping at a very Clever Farmers in a small vilage. I came here yesterday morning. I am run down with Diarhea which has been working on me for ten days or 2 weeks.[83] Wel I have just had a bite of Dinner & feel better some light Bread & Potatoe soop a quite a treat for a Soldier. We moved up here on the 23rd went into camp for the night. The next morning at 2

A.M. without Breakfast we started out marched until 10 A.M. East on RR when we halted. The Generals Aid told us that we were going on in a few minutes 1½ miles to feed but the first thing we knew our scouts came dashing in with the Rebs charging after them. On they came Bang whiz went the Balls right over our Heads. Our Boys Cool & steady ready for them as soon as they made their appearance. We Charged them with a tremendous volley & terriffic yells right down off the Ridge we were posted on which was more than they bargained for and it would done a citizen good to have seen them tack about and break like Quarter Horses fairly running out of their shoes throwing away their Muskets. Our Boys picked them up fired them at them then slam them against trees in a rather unmilitary stile rendering them useless. We followed them killing a number (besides prisoners) until we ran on to their main force throwing them into complete confusion. At this moment if we had Charged them mounted the Victory would have been complete but before we could make a Charge they rallied & haveing their Artillery planted they opened up from 2 pieces which compeled us to seek the cover of the woods but before we could get out they got range of us killing one man & one Horse within ten ft of where I was in Ranks.[84] His name was Vires from Co F of Gallipolis.[85] At this time Col Camerons Brigade on our Right advanced on them while Col Garrards Brigade attemted to make a flank movement to the left.[86] When we received a Dispatch that the Enemy had made a flank movement on our right endangering the command we therefore fell back to the Battle Ground. Here we could se that the Brigade on our right were haveing a warm time. The Rebs Charged our Battery captureing it but before they new it the 2nd Mich Charged and retook it & brought it safly off the Field.[87] The los on our side was very light that of the Enemy must have been heavy. We took 50 prisoners a number being officers. We came out in the rear. I was placed on videt on the Dandrige Road on the right of outer Road with Co I to prevent a flank movement on our way out with the 7OVC to suport me just about Dust the Rebs have in sight, in good shooting distance.[88] I had my men formed across the Road woods on either side. We did not halt the scamps but fired into them such a volley that sent them howling back some of them never to return. They made their appearance again meting the sam reception. After holding them as long as I wanted to the Regmt being ready I fel back slowly drawing them after me until I was in line with the 7th. When they recd the fire of the whole Regmt which put a quietus on them for the night & we fel back without further molestation riding 10 or 12 miles back to this place without food without Horse feed sick & exausted Bunked down without supper sick all night & Came over here yesterday.[89] The Regmt remained in camp went out to day commanding in but no news late in the Evening. Feel a great better but wil not go to the Regmt until I am well. Yours most affectionaly.

Between lines:
Dec 30 Since arriveing in camp I ascertain that our men had a hard fight here yesterday 29th. The Rebs herd that we had sent a part of our force to the right so they thought they would have an easy prey. The pitched in and gave us a pretty hard fight for a while but they got back faster than the came. They lost a great many killed & wounded. We have driven them back about six miles. We captured one of Longstreets couriers with a Dispatch to Brag saying that he was surrounded and nearly out of Ammunition and had mad three desperate efforts to get out but had failed & I did not know what in the H—l to do.[90]

I guess you never wil want me to write an other letter like this. I dont believe you ever wil be able to read it but I know you wil excuse me under the circumstances.

In margin:
Direct to 7th OVC 1st Brigade 2nd Division Cavalry Care

December 27, 1863
New Market E Ten

Ever beloved Wife,

I am happy to enjoy the pleasure of writing a few lines to you this Sabath morning. I feel a little better this morning. The Diarhea has stoped on me & I hope wil soon be able to join the Regmt which is two miles above here. The Enemy confronting them. We are wel fortified & have been trying to draw them in but they are wild & wont coax nor toll. All is quiet in front today. The weather is calm & serene being somewhat cloudy. I recd a letter from Sister Jannett & was glad to hear from her also one from Bro John and Elliott announcing the safe arrival of Sister Susan but in poor health. I sincerely hope it may improve.

I would like very much to answer all the kind letters I received but it is impossible. Nevertheless their letters are none the less acceptable. Tel them I wil answer as soon as I can. I have just heard that the Rebs have all left haveing done so in the night our forces all on the forward move in close pursuit. Good luck to them. I wil be with them ere long. It is the first time I have been absent from the Regmt since we entered E Tenn. We left a number of sick at Blanes Roads when we moved up here & a number dismounted have not heard form them since we left. Our trains were ordered to Cumberland Gap & the Colonel says that as soon as this raid is over we will go to Ky. If the Regmt dont come the men wil anyhow. There are some being furloughed 3 or 4 from our co probably.

Jannett informs me that Amos Dyke has got home but you have not seen him. This I do not understand for I sent a horse by him which he was to sell and hand you the proceeds. I also sent a blanket to you. I hope he wil do so for I did not draw any money last pay day from the fact that I never have yet been mustered by Lt" & it wil probably be some time before I can be but when I get my papers my pay wil amount to something if I am so fortunate (6 months pay being due me). This has caused me a great deal of trouble on your act." For I fear that my dear little family which are all the world to me may suffer but I pray *God* may bless & comfort them.

December 28, 1863

After passing a very restless night I again resume my pen. I am able to walk around but not able to go to the Regmt yet. I was made a present of a nice little horse about a month ago & traded him for a fine mare which is the admiration of evry one who sees her. She only cost me the boat money which was $5.00. She is very much like Leutzes more nice as a peach. I lef my old horse in camp stil lame but getting better. Mrs Higley wrote to me about sending the Captains remains home which is impossible at the present time but the R.R. wil soon be in opperation through & I wil do all in my power to have him sent home at the earliest oportunity. Tell her she wil have to employ an Attorney to obtain the balance of pay Due him. R Downing tends to such business.[91] Levi Littles widow had better employ him to settle her claims also. The Capt Recomended him to Zack Wisemans Widow & he collected hers for her. I tried but could do nothing.

Dear Molly if you are in need of means sell or trade that watch for a cow or any thing you wish. Let me know how you are getting along.

Comment a little more on my letter so that I may know what letters you Receive. Tel Sister Susana to write to me and as many more as can. I cannnot expect my friends to write much without answers but if they knew our circumstances I think they would write anyhow & sincerely hope they wil. Remember me kindly to mother & Father Sisters & Brothers Cous Will & Elliott Emma & Sally & dont forget my Dear uncle & family at the mill. Tel Tom to write to me & let me know where Cousin Lenox is. Hopeing to hear from your & wishing you all a happy New Year. I wil draw my scribling to a close hopeing this may find you all enjoying the best of health & the comforts of life. I wil bid you kind adieu for the present. Kiss the little ones in remembrance of your absent & affectionate husband.

William McKnight 2nd Lt Co K 7th OVC
to Samaria McKnight of Rutland Meigs Co Ohio

December 28, 1863

The weather is quite pleasant today. Rained considerable last night have not herd from the front today but our men drove the Enemy yesterday and have been recieving Reinforsements continually Infantry Cavalry & heavy Artillery & the general impression is that the Rebs cant very well get out and are bound to get whiped. If they loose E Tenn they acknowledge they are gone up. The Western Va Troops have the Va Passes secured & we have them cut of from Bragg & for my part I think they are bound to be killed or captured unless they scatter and take to the mountains.[92] We have had no snow here yet nor have we had any great amt of rain. Our men are all wel provided with Clothing & Blankets & soon we will have plenty of Gov Rations again as there are three Trains of cars Running Daily within 8 miles of this place with Rations & the Bridge at that junction is to be done this week.

General Foster came up last night to the front & I think he wil clean out the Rebs.[93] The Steam Boats now run from Paduka up the Tennessee River almost to Knoxville where there is a R.R. connection & it wont be long until we can come home by the Rail & Steam.[94] The importance of holding E Ten is plain to evryone who wil take the trouble to examine the map.[95] It is key to the Southern Confederacy.[96] But I am tireing your patience but I know you wil excuse me. It is so seldom that I have the

Colonel Santmyer's orders used by McKnight for a letter to Samaria. *Courtesy of Terry Hauger.*

opportunity to write & if I were to offer one dollar a sheat for paper I couldnt get it here. It is like the Southern Confederacy it is played out. Tel Dyke if you se him to write to me as soon as he can & let me know what he did & how he got along with the Capt. Things I sent the Capt more with him besides some of his Blankets & other Property & I am very anxious to hear from him.

Wm McKnight

---

late in the Evening December 28, 1863

. . . I wrote some time ago that I had been appointed Capt of the Company but the Collonel informed me that Gov Tod would not commision any more officers until our Regmt was recruited this puts a damper on me.[97] If he had not promised I would not have expected anything of the kind. Hows it wil be I do not know. Consequently I am in a great deal of trouble about it. This I communicate to you as my Bosom Companion so you may know just how I have been used for all my hardships. May just Dues from the Government set to the present amounts to over $600.00 dollars & I need it & cant get a cent.

December 30, 1863

I left my boarding this morning & arrived safe in the Regmt feel quite wel. I am writing with $5.00 Gold pen presented to me just now by one of the Boys. My Boarding cost me six Dollars 5 days myself and Horse.

January 9, 1864
New Market

Ever beloved Wife,

I seat myself once more to pen you a few lines to inform you that I am well or nearly so & I hope this may find you enjoying the best of health & the comforts of life. I have not herd from you for a long time & am very anxious to know how you are prospering. The weather here is quite cold with snow on the Ground. I have not been to the Regmt for Eight days on account of illness but I am better & think I wil go today or tomorrow. I went to the Regmt once & had to come back. Now I think I wil be able To do my duty again. The Boys are in fine spirits. Some of them have renlisted in the Gun Boat service.[98] Patrick McCan is sick but the men generaly are in good health.

I have not much of importance to write. The Enemy are stil in front but are trying to get out & have not made any demonstrations for some time. Neither do I think they wil as the Prisoners report them nearly out of amunition & a great many barefoot among them. Our forces are concentating at evry point of outlet so it is hoped they wil be compelled to surrender sooner or later. God speed the day for it certainly would be a blessing to them. I herd that Longstreet had sent in a flag of truce with terms similar to thos acceed to at Vicksburg.

It is reported that they are actualy guilty of digging up the buried & stripping them of their Clothing. The Carrs wil be up here tomorrow from the plains & when communication is opened we wil then be supplied with more Rations. We have not had full Rations of Coffe & Sugar but have not suffered. We have had Beef, Pork & Flour plenty. It is still said that we wil come to Kentucky. Some of the Regmts have already gone. A great many of the Old Regmts are renlisting. Those that have one year or less to serve ours cannot renlist only in the Boat service. There wil probably be 4 to 6 from Co K enlist three haveing already done so. There is one that wont that I know of.

My old favorite Horse has got wel again. I sold one the other day for $115.00 & wil send you some money the first chance. I have some little debts to settle but I hope to send you enough to help you until I can do better. If Dyke done any good atal he ought to have payed you enough to help you through the Winter. I am last to know why I have not heard from him. Tel him to write if he has not started back. If he has write & give me al the news. Let me know how you are provided for this winter. Nomore at present but hope that the Blessing of God may rest with my ever dear family. Remember me kindly to all. Accept my sincere love. Tommy Leila Letta Lucy & the pets from your absent but loveing.
Wm to Samaria McKnight

Feb 6 1864
Maryville Blount Co E. Ten[99]

Ever beloved Wife,

I again take my pen to inform you that I am wel & have been ever since I left Newmarket at which place I last wrote. The health of the men is good with few exceptions. John Wiseman is at Knoxville not very wel.[100] Warren Coulter Died there on the 12th of January of consumption.[101] I believe he had been sick ever since we first came to Knoxville. Sargt Carr is stil there. Sam foose is a prisoner as is also Orrellama Williams at Richmond Va.[102] Have not herd from them only by way of our Doctor who was also prisoner & has returned.

After I left Newmarket we were in a heavy Engagement at Dandrige which had just comenced as I got to the Regmt.[103] We fought until 10 PM comencing about 3 PM. We maintained our ground giveing the Enemy severe punishment. Our los was very light considering the heavy fighting being the heaviest of small Arms I have ever witnessed. We then withdrew to Strawbery Plains thence to Knoxville thence to Severville some 50 miles thence to the Smoky Mts south of Knoxville 20 ms where we are now stationed.[104] I have been on Picket duty in com of 2 Cos for 7 Days. We have plenty to eat & fare better than though we were with the Regmt. The Rebs are within 7 miles of us. The Regmt is about the same Distance. We are situated on a butiful Stream Called Little River.[105] The weather has been very Propitious a part of the time. The Shade was actualy sought for as in Sumer. A part of our forces have been over into

North Carolina & I just got back. Asher was over & just got in this morning. They Captured 52 prisoners 20 of them being Indians killed 23 in a fight.[106] It is said that our Div is comeing to Ky soon. The Div in cannection is gone started Day before yesterday. I herd that Longstreet recieved a severe Dressing yesterday. I recieved a letter from Father yesterday Dated Jan 2nd & was glad to hear from him as I have not Recieved news from home for a month by letter. I see Doctor Train & had a long talk with him.[107] He almost makes me homesick. You wanted to know whether I was comeing home or not. I think I wil not try to come from here as it would cost about $50 & a great risk besides but I think that it wil al come out right yet. I sent $50 home by way of Cincinnati by our sutler I have paid about all my Debts & have about $30 left.[108] I am very anxious that you send your Photograph as I lost your likeness January 22nd. My belt crouded it throug my vest pocket. I was very sorry to loose it. Cant hardly keep House without it. Give my love to all my Sisters Brothers & accept my most sincere affection & love for my little Family. Write soon & tel the rest to Do the same. Excuse me in great haste more anon.

Wm McKnight
2nd Lt Co K 7th OVC
1st Brigade 2nd Div C.C.

In margin:
Just as I was finishing my letter yesterday evening our pickets were fired on and we were ordered to move which we did last night 4 miles towards Knoxville. On our way Capt Lepers Horse fel with & broke his leg bad. He is from Gallipolis of Company L.
Direct of Knoxville E Tennessee

February 12, 1864
Maryville, E. Ten

Ever beloved wife,

I once more enjoy the pleasure of answering a very kind & affectionate Letter from you of Jan 30th I recd last night. It gave me great pleasure to hear from you once more as it has been some time since I herd from you direct. I have just been out withe the Regmt for Forage. I only had to go 5 miles the Lt. that was out yesterday went about 15 miles, and hasten to answer some of your enquiries in regard to my affairs. All I think it nesesary to say is that you need give yourself no uneasyness about me.

There is not a shadow of foundation for the stuff that A" has been reporting. Molly I have got plenty of money to do me til I can get more.

About punishing me at least if there are no one here knows any thing about it. The only reason for not Recieving pay is because I never have been mustered in nor is it possible for any one to muster himself into the service any more than it is to muster himself out. You spoke about sending me some stamps & paper. I have never Recieved any from you of late. We have gone into winter Quarters here been here four Days. There are three Div of Infantry here in sight and as many of Cavalry scattered about in the vicinity. We are putting up log Huts & covering them with our Tents makeing them quite comfortable. The weather has been very favorable the most of the time pleasant. The men are all in fine health that are with me. 36 in all 17 at Stanford 8 at Richmond 8 at Knoxville 2 at Camp Nelson Ky 5 Deserted including McKaskey 4 at Home sick 1 at Covington, Ky & 6 others on different Details.[109] Makeing 87 in all. This does not include Desertions previous to comeing into Ten. Say to the Relations of the members of this company that they are as good as the best & they may wel feel proud of them. You said you Recd $50 mailed at Cincinnati. If you look at the penciled Backing you wil know who sent it. You sid you got that from Brunker. You did not say what. Please let me know the next time you write.

I do not want you to stint yourself but suply yourself with the Comforts of life as wel as you can & hope it wont be long until I send you more money. Dont forget to tel me how the little ones are doing in school. You never told me how you liked your coverlid I sent to Mrs. Higley's. You would laugh to se my little House just large enough for a bed for me & the Orderly & Board to write on. We do our cooking out of doors. I have a boy to take care of my Horses so we get along first rate. Capt. Campbell has Resigned & is comeing home in a few Days & I think I wil send a letter or two with him.[110] I want you to send me your mineature by some one if you can as I want to se how you look when you are in good health & dont forget to pen me a few lines evry week. It is a great comfort to know that you are wel & I am glad that you are getting along so well.

The Col has sent to Gov. Tod for my papers as 2nd Lt & sais that he wil have them dated back to the date of Brunkers Resignation 25th June & says that I am the Ranking Officer of the Company & things are in a more satisfactory condition than they were & I am sorry that I gave you any trouble about me.[111] All the reason I did so was to explain the reason

I had changed my signature. One word about coming to Ky the Prospect at present is not as good as it was & I dont know but it is for the best as there is nothing to eat on the mts for man or Beast & Doctor Train says the Roads are almost impassable. So you wil have to suffer the great disapointment of our prolonged stay but I say Gods wil be done so be of great cheer. It is getting dark & I must close. So good night my loved ones from your affectional.

   William McKnight
   To Samaria

In margin:
I have been trading Horses & Watches & evrything & dont calculate to suffer if Uncle Sam dont pay me.

February 18, 1864
Knoxville E" Tenn

Ever beloved Wife,

   I once more embrace the oportunity of pening you a few lines to inform you that I have not forgotten you & the home I love. I recd yours with the paper & Envelopes today. Thanks to you dear.

   Our Regmt is laying within a mile of this Citty. We came in here last night from Marysville & this morning we went out on the Severeville Road five miles ran into the Rebels & drove them like Chaff before the wind. We would have given them a complete dressing but they didnt Stay to see it done. We returned to camp considerably exhilerated with our very cold ride.

   We are camped in sight of the powerful Fort Sanders & Higley and many others with all the extensive Earth works completely surrounding the Citty considered impregnable.[112] If they were so at the time of the Siege it is doubly so now. It is thought that it is intended by the Enemy to make an attack upon this place soon & everything is being done to strengthened the works that can be done to give them a warm reception. For my part I think they wil not be so fool hardy as to throw themselves upon our forts as they did before as they lost two Brigades the flower of the Southern Army at one charge. But evry one says let them come we have the Re" Re" now below & Steamboats run this far giveing us plenty of means of supply.

   There are a great many sick in the Hospitals here but not so many as there were some time ago & they are wel cared for. The Sanitary

Commission is furnishing them with all kinds of Vegatables Canned Fruits & all other kinds pickles & all kinds of Bed clothing, Pillows &c.[113] The Deaths average about five per week or one from each Hospital per week.[114] I came over here this afternoon to make out Discriptive Rolls for some of my men who are here in the convalescent camp not very sick all able to visit the camp. I am staying with Sergt Carr. He has a room & has a good situation. He attends to the effects of Deceased soldiers takes an act of evry thing so the Relatives can get them. Evry thing is done in order. If they are never called for they are turned over to the Goverment & then the Heirs Receive pay.

You said in your letter that Tommy had had one of them chokeing spells. This gives me uneasiness but I hope he wil not be troubled much more. Tell him paa sais he wants him to be a good boy & mind his mother & stay away from the creek when she tells him to. Take good care of the little dears. I hope to see them all. I can picture to my minds Eye how you look with two little ones on your lap at once. O how I long to see them. I pray for a safe return to you & have faith in God that he wil hear & answer my prairs. I feel that he has been merciful towards us goodness and mercy hath followed us al the days of our lives. O what a consolation. May he Bless & comfort you & restore us to the loved ones at home. So good night loved ones.

Wm to Samary

Good night how I long to hold you in my Arms.

In margin:

We are al as wel as usual.

I bought 36 cts worth of stamps and one Dollars worth of paper but could get no envelopes.

I bought a shirt today paid five Dollars.

Give the little Pieces to the children dont think that I forget the two least.

We have plenty to eat but little for our Horses.

I know now what you got from Brunker.

February 19, 1864
Knoxville E Ten

Dear Molly,

I have just sold one of my Horses for fifty Dollars for which I paid Thirtyfive Dollars. Enclosed you wil find Twenty Dollars for spending money. I have to keep some to speculate on and Defray my expences. I got a picture taken this morning & mailed it to Sister Susan. When I get a ful rig I intend to send you one. I expect you will hardly Recognise me as I have let my Beard grow so rough but it is a pretty fair likeness. The morning is butiful. We expect to move today. I mailed you a letter this morning written last night. I have sent acros the River for my other Horse or one of them. I am in fine spirits this morning. Evrything is hustle & Business here & I am in a great Hury so you must excus me for the present. Good by. God bless you all.

From Wm. McKnight
His wif Samaria

March 5, 1864
Head Quarters 7th OVC
E Tenn On Clinch River Knoxville[115]

My Ever beloved Samaria,

At the earliest opportunity I take my pen in Hand to inform you that I am enjoying good health & hope this may find you all in the enjoyment of the same great & inestimable Blessing. I received a letter from you of the 12 ult & was very glad to hear from you.

We moved up the country from Knox" some 30 miles & then moved back again to the same laid there over 2 nights & then we move N.W. towards the mouth of the Clinch & Holstein Rivers but the Rivers being so swolen from recent Rains we have been compelled to lay over now three Days & wil probably have to lay over as much longer before we can ford. Our Horses have become unserviceable from over hard scouting & small feeds & many have Died. I have lost within the past two weeks over half belonging to the Company consequently many of our men are walking. We have for the first time for a long time turned our faces towards Ky but whether we wil reach there or not remains somewhat doubtful but one thing certain we are nolonger fit for Duty nor wil be until we are remounted & reorganized.[116] The men are all in very good health at present & I have so much to attend to that I can hardly find time to write to any one but I hope when we get across the River that we wil settle down for a time. I have written this morning to Capt Simpson at Stanford to have the rest of the Camp Detailed but whether he can have it done or not I dont know but hope he can.[117] But keep this within your

Bosom until you hear from me concerning it. I have just recd orders to have the comp" ready for inspection. So I have to close hopeing to hear from you soon. I remain your ever affectionate Husband until Death.

Wm McKnight
2nd Lt Comd Co K OVC
Direct to Knoxville Care of Lt Col Miner 7 OVC

            March 9, 1864[118]
            Head Quarters of OVC
            Near Clinton E. Tenn[119]
           On South of Clinch River

My own Dear Wife,

 I am once more permitted the opportunity of addresing to you a few lines to inform you that we are enjoying good health at present & sincerely hope that these few lines may find you all in the enjoyment of the same. The prospect before me in some respects seem some what brighter than when I wrote you before. It seems quite probble from present indications that we may be in Ky before long. At least to me the prospect never appeared more promiseing.

 We are in the same place from which I last wrote. It is a pleasant camp. The weather is much like spring. Farmers are plowing for corn what there is left. The most of the farming being done by women and Children. I have been working on the pay Rolls for two Days past & have not finished but will get through today.

 I have not herd from you for a month or more & then only by Bro Johns letter. I have not time to write much today. Capt Green is going to Knox" & I want to send by him.[120] I am very anxious to Recieve a letter from her I love & to know how the dear little ones are. O how I long to se you all once more. Please write to me at least once a week & I wil write as often as I can if it is evry other day.

 We have lost over half of our Horses since I wrote to you from Knox" & what we have left is not serviceable. I have my old Grey yet he looks tolerable wel & if I get to come home I intend to bring him with me if he lives. He is an old war Horse been in the service ever since we left Riply.

 When you write inform me whether you Recd $20. or not I sent you from Knox" or not. Give my letters a short perusal before writing so I may know what ones you Recd.

I have not Recd my papers yet but expect them by the paymaster. The men are very anxious to come to Ky. We have been on Duty all the time ever since we entered the State & the time has come I think that wil relieve us for a time.

So dear one be of good cheer. All things worketh together for our good though the future looketh Dark & impenetrable. You are ever remembered in my prayers my thoughts by Day & Dreams by night that the Savior may guide & protect you comfort you & restore me to the loved ones at home for their sake. When peace spread her majestic wings ore this crushed & heart bleeding Country & the Clash of arms shal be herd nomore. O what a happy Day it wil be when the worn war soldier returns to the bosom of his Companions. So let the pleasures of the past & the hopes of future bear us through all troubles. From your most affectionate Husband until Death. Love to the little ones.

Wm McKinght

Lt Co K 7OVC

to his loveing Samaria

In margin:
In Haste time short.

March 15, 1864
Office Christian Commission[121]
Knoxville, Tenn

Dear Samaria,

I again snach an opportunity to let you Know that I have not forgotten you. I am enjoying good health at present & the Co is enjoying the same. We arived here last night from Clinch. We are all Dismounted & encamped 1½ miles from Town. I came in this morning to see some of the men that have been here in Hospital for a long time all strangers to our neighborhood & while I am getting my Boots fixed I thought I would spend the moment in pening you the random thoughts of my Brain. I recd a letter from sister Mary last night. She informs me that you have recd 6 letters from me lately which I am glad to hear & anxiously look for a letter from you. Then I may have something to found a letter uppon. The talk now is that we wil be sent to Ky.

I have turned over all the Saddles & Ordnance Stores belonging to the Camp. Horses and all the Genrls has moved all the available force to the front resting at Mossy Creek some 30 miles above here.[122]

O Mary I cant write I have so much embarrassing at present. I cant write sincible but I hope this may find you enjoying the best of health. When I return to camp I take with me Religious Books Papers &c for the camp. They are furnished here grattis. This is the second time I have got Books for them. Evry mess of six have a Testament in my company. They are at all times anxious to obtain reading matter & the friends at home would confer a great favor if they would just remail their old Papers to their friend here in the Army.

I am very anxious to know how you get along this Dreadful Cold winter. I hear of many freezing to Death there & other Places. If we stay here I wil write soon hopeing to hear from you soon. I close hopeing and praying that I may soon meet you all once more. My love to you all. Kiss the little ones for your absent Wm. So good by for the present Dearest.

Wm Mc
To his very Dear Samaria
Direct to Knoxville East Tenn
Care of Lt. Col. G. G. Miner 7th OVC

March 18, 1864
Head Qrtrs 7th O.V.C.
Knoxville East Tenn

My ever beloved Wife,

I again embrace (what is always a pleasure to me), the opportunity of comuneing with one who is indelibly imprinted upon my most inmost soul. My thoughts by Day & Dreams by night. O how anxiously do I look forward to the time when I may be permitted to return to the loved ones at Home the thought of which is a pleasure to your absent Husband. How fervently do I pray for my dear little family & for my restoration to them not for my sake but that I may through the Divine Mercies of a blessed Redeemer bring them up in the nurture & admonition of the Lord. I hope *Dear* one that you wil be very attentive to the instruction of your little ones. Teach them to love the *Savior* for he says in the *Holy Book* to Suffer little *Children* to *come* unto *me* & forbid *them* not for of *such* is the *Kingdom* of *heaven*, therefore the whole Duty Devolves upon you to instruct them in the right path. O that the Lord may give you grace to suport you in the hour of trouble & crown your efforts with many blessings.

I have not recieved any news letters from you for a long time ecept by Sister Marys letter of March 5. She informs me that you recieved some half Doz from me. I am glad to hear that you get a stray one once in a while for I can appreciate the value of a letter. I expected to have been on my way to Ky before this time but alas my hopes are scattered to the four winds of *heaven* & we are stil kept in the field although we are in no condition to do active service. We may build fortifications or Do Provost Duty in Town or something of the kind but we are all Dismounted eccept some 6 or 7 in Company K. I have with me here 44 men & not a Horse in the company eccept 2 of my own 1 to pack & 1 to ride.[123] I have just heard from the front all the available force is 27 miles above here & have done but very little fighting since we left. They are wel supplied with Rations. The weather here for some days past has been very much like March although it is quite Dry & not very cold. We were prety hard up for Rations a few Days but have plenty now.

 I have been over to the Grave yard this afternoon with a few of my men putting up a Tomb stone to Capt Higleys Grave.[124] We carried them on our shoulders about a mile & set them up & all returned to camp with the assurance that we had but simply done our Duty toward him & intend if we are paid of here to place to the memory of Levi Little & Warren W. Coulter the same. We did not go to the expence we would have done if we did not think that his folks wil send a Burial Case & then we wil send him home. The stone we got Cost us 12 Dollars & is of very nice marble.[125] I have made papers out prepareitory to Discharging John Wiseman & I think he wil be home if nothing happens in 30 days & now while my Comrads sleep I am humped over a Cracker Box like a Hound over a mush pot out in the night open Air by candle light how often transfering to paper the stray thoughts. Would any friends write to us under such circumstances of my Brain. Sweet dreams to you Dear one To night. I must close until morning.

March 19, 1864

 I seat myself this fine morning to finish my letter the firs thing that attracts my attention this morning is the 8 Army Corpse marching towards Town. They are from the front & indicates that we have plenty of forces in front & to spare. The 9th Corpse is turning in towards Camp & probably going into Camp near us.

 There was an opportunity given the Company to express their choice of Officers for the Company. I am happy to say that I recieved the unanimous vote of the Company not one Dissenting voice in the whole company to the first in Comand.[126] They also chose their men for Lieutenanats but I do not know whether the appointments wil be confirmed or not but one thing I am proud of after being tried for the post 18 months the men knowing me wel & when such an opportunity is given them to have their vote and respects manifested in the way it was is very gratifieing to me & worth more than the favor of Colonels or others in power who confer an gets what is Due to the men who Do the work but let this go as it wil. I have an abiding faith in an all wise providence. If we get not justice here on Earth we wil get our reward in heaven if we are faithful & upright & just.

The papers to enable me to Draw pay has never come throug yet but I stil live in hopes. You know how easy I can take trouble & seeming injustice but the great concern is for my little family so long as they do not suffer & there is a prospect for the better I wil not Dispair.

Sometime ago I sent you $20.00 in a letter. Let me know whether you recieved it or not. I shal look for a regular shower of letters soon. They wil come to Knoxville in five Days sometimes & you had better Direct all your letters to this place so long as we are in this Department.

Tel sister Mary that I wil answer her letter soon if possible. I recd a letter from Ema some time ago. I have not answered yet but wil. I wil send some papers to the Children soon. Mary I have $4.00 left yet. I have had to buy 2 shirts cost $8.00 & it costs me from one to thre Dollars a week for something to eat. I have loaned some of my money to the Boys who have become Destitute. I have got our Rolls made out for four months Pay and expect pay before long. Wel I have written most of particulars & many that are not. So I must Draw my scribling to a close. Wishing you the greatest comfort & happines & hopeing to see you all once more. I subscribe myself your most affectionate Husband. Love to all.

William McKnight
To Samaria McKnight

In margin:
Molly I wish you to understand that this is strictly confidential & dont care to have evry body see this letter for I have given ful vent to my feelings. This leaves us all well & in fine spirits. Good by God bless you all. W OVC

March 20, 1864
Head Quarters 7th O.V.C.
Knoxville East Tenn

Beloved Companion,

I once more embrace the opportunity of pening you a few lines to inform you that I am enjoying the best of health and hope this may find you all in the enjoyment of the same. Haveing just completed Furlows for Sergt Wiseman & James Elshire of my company & as they intend starting for Ohio in the morning I thought I would pen you a few lines in addition to what I wrote last night & send by Wiseman to you knowing that you would be disappointed if I did not send you something.[127] It is all I have to send you at present. I was going to send the children some papers but they cannot carry them very wel & I have no way to mail them properly.

I would be very glad if you could send by him (Wiseman) if he comes back a pair of the best Socks you can get as such things are very scarce here. If you cant get them handy never mind. I want you to se him & have a chat with him. He can give you al the particulars. I dont know that I have any thing more to write at present but wish you to do the best you can. Never Despair be patient & persevering trust in the Lord follow his precepts. Pray for me that I may soon return to the bosom of my little family to go out nomore when the thundres of warr shal be hushed & peace spred her mantle over a powerful & happy people. Good night I must close. The wind blows my candle so I cant se to write any more. My love to you all. Good night Dear ones may God bless you & comfort you is my prayer.

William McKnight
Lt Comdg Co K 7th O.V.C.
1st Brigd 2nd Div C.C.

P.S. Scend me you Mineature and let me know whether you ever Recd Col Garrards that I sent you or not.

Lt. McKnight 7 OVC

March 21, 1864
Seminary Hospital Ward 6[128]
Covington, Ky.

Dear Captain,

I embrace this oppertunity to address a few lines to inform you of my whereabouts. You will see by the above that I am at Covington Ky instead of Camp Dennison as you might suppose that I was there instead of where I am. I received a note from you dated Feb 23rd requesting me to give you my address and that you would send me my description roll. I would be very happy to have you do so in order that I may get my pay when they are paid off here again. I persume that I regret not being able to be with you as bad as you do but so it is I can not use my hand at all even to eat with.

I understand that my roll has been sent for by the authorieties but dont think that it has got here yet. I was pleased to learn that you and the rest of the company were well and hope that you may all continue to enjoy the same. Write to me occasionally. Give my respects to all and oblig yours &c.

James A. Haley

March 24, 1864
Head Qurts Co K 7th OVC
Knoxville East Tenn

Beloved Samaria,

Feeling somewhat lonesome and not very much on hand to do I thought I could best pass of the time in silent communication with one who is ever uppermost in my mind.

Dear one your memory warms my heart and monopolises my whole feelings this evening. O how I long to se you. I feel this afternoon as though my friends at home had forgotten to write for I have not Recd any letters from you for it seems to me an age. So long ago I have forgotten when it was. I have all kinds of conjectures about the reasons. Sometimes I think you have written and the mails causes the delay but then Asher and many others Recieve Letters and I think you have heard something from us that Deters you from writing. But what ever the reasons may be I wil write to you when ever I can and I sometimes think of sending some of my friends a sheet of paper and Envelope already Directed so they wil be sure to start it in the right direction.

But enough I know I am becomeing wearisum and wil change the subject. The men Recd pay last evening but I did not get a red. The reason is because I have not Recd propper papers yet but I am stil in hopes that all wil yet be made right. I am not the only one in the Regmt in some fix and as misery Loves company it is some consolation. I made reciepts and sent home through the State Agency fifteen Hundred and Eightyfive Dollars for the men and it grieves me to think that my little family may be kneeding some help pecuniarly and I am held here unable to render it to them. But it is a consolation to know that the gracious God who hears even the Ravens when they cry wil not turn a deaf Ear to your little ones when they are in kneed.

Dear one please write to me as often as you can and let me know all about how you get along and what means you have to go on if you are in kneed of money let me know. I hope against another pay Day I wil be able to Draw my pay. If justice is done I know I wil be able to help you and then I want to come home if they pay me. Since I was appointed as Comdr of Company I would recieve Eight or ten Hundred Dollars.

While I resume my writing the men from the front come poureing in. They all belong to our Brigd. They came down on the Train runing within an Hundred yds" of my Quarters. I understand that our comand has turned over their Horses Arms and Equipments and are comeing down here. What the intention is there is no telling but the Surmises are that there is realy more prospect of us comeing to Ky at present than there has been for some time. But I have written so many time about comeing to Ky that I expect you are tired of hearing anything about it. We are all as anxious to come that the least gleam of hope raises our hopes anew and we cant help talking and writing about it. Whether we come or not it matters not if God is on our side and I feel that he has shielded us and preserved our lives through all the dangers of the past.

Dear one I hope that you wil put your trust in the Lord who has always been merciful to us. I feel that he has answered our prayers and have an abiding faith in his protecting care. O how I hope to see you and the dear ones again and then I can tel you what cannot be expressed with the pen. Until then be of good cheer. Remember me in your prayers. Accept my sincere love and affection for you all and may God bless you all is my prayer.
From your affectionate
William McKnight
To his loveing Samaria

In margin:
Tell me all about the little ones.
We have had five inches of snow this week but one days sun Dispelled it. The Boys had great time killing Rabets. WMc

August 25, 1863–March 28, 1864

March 28, 1864
Head Quarters 7th OVC
Knoxville E Tenn

Beloved Wife,

I seat myself to pen to you the last letter that I ever expect to from this the most Loyal and the most Desolated part of Tenn. Upon leaveing I feel no regrets although leaveing many warm Friends but what is the friendship so Hospitably shown compared with the love friendship and Hospitality of a beloved Home with all that is near and Dear in this World anxiously awaiting us. Northward we leave tomorrow morning at 7:20 A.M. The time seems long and the greatest anxiety is felt throughout the command. As I have said there is no regret felt at leaving but we cannot forget that all who came do not return. With Due Reverence Do we realise that we leave behind the remains of thre of our beloved companions who entered this doomed State as buoyant and with as bright prospects as those that are spared as the liveing monuments of Gods mercy

In regard to Capt Joel P. Higley I feel myself incompetent to do justice. Beloved by all who knew him warm Hearted generous and faithful as a frined ture and patriotic bold and dareing but not without caution and forethought as an officer. He was to me the best and truest friend that I had this side of the great watter which I hope once more to Cross. Not only did he manifest his friendship to me but acknowledged to Com Officers of this Regmt that actualy loved me whether I was worthy or not I do not pretend to say but it is comfort to have the respect of such as he. But alas he is laid in the Cold Cold ground on the silent Breeses of the suny South lighs a requium over his unwept and untimely Grave. I have visited his grave thre times since we came here. The last time placed with my own hands a Decent tomb Stone to mark the resting place of him we all loved.

I have also with the donations of the company procured Stones for the other two which is almost ready and wil be set by the stone cutter.[129] They are all buried in the same place ½ mil North of Knoxville in a butiful place where lies over seven hundred or our fellow Countrymen who have fallen in defence their Country. They are arranged in circles now numbering five with the feet toward the Center. The men are containing 48 graves in which is the Captains there being left between the circles some five or six yds. Evry grave being marked name Regmt Co and State so when friends wish to find them there will be no dificulty in finding them.[130]

Dear one when you write Direct to Lexington Kentucky as we expect to be there in five or six days. I have not Recd any letters from you for a long time and I hope you wont send any more here. But I shal look for a shower when we get through. There is a move on foot to send us home a short time when we get through and there is . . . that it wil succed. I wil have to close as I have to be ready to start Early. I am going to send 1 Horse through by land. So be of good cheer. I am comeing towards home if I dont get through good by. May God bless you all, more again excuse in great Haste.

Yours truly

Wm To Samaria

P.S. We are Ordered to Mt Sterling Ky some 30 miles East of Lexington to recruit and refit but Direct to Lexington care of Lt Collonel Miner. Lt Col" 7th OVC

P.S. Tel Harrys folks where to direct also al the rest he wishes you to let his Wife know that he is well.

The Final Months
(April 1, 1864–June 21, 1864)

$\mathcal{U}$nlike the previous chapters, this chapter includes an array of letters from William's family. McKnight may have been killed in action before the letters reached him, or he may not have had time to destroy the correspondence before his death. In the only known existing letter from William's father, Thomas McKnight writes, "My Dear boy I cannot write my tears blind me to think of the sufering of our Dear soldiers and the desalation and suffring this cursed rebelion has caused since it comenced. God only knoes when the end will be. Oh my Dear boy all I can do for you is to put up my feble prayers to the throne of god for your safty and for the safty of our beloved land which is now steped in blood." Thomas goes on to close with these words: "I must close. I want to send this with other in the morning. So good by Dear son. May god watch over you is the prayer of your Mother. Good by Dear boy but not for ever. I hope to see you again."

McKnight's letters detail Company K's return to central Kentucky from eastern Tennessee. The railroads transported both men and equipment back to Kentucky, and McKnight was pleased to write that the Seventh was "nearer the home we love so wel."

McKnight also made a brief visit home from April 25 to May 6, 1864. This was the first and only time McKnight would see his twin daughters before his death just a few weeks later. Ironically,

McKnight was killed in action at Cynthiana, Kentucky, facing the troops of Confederate general John Hunt Morgan—the same General Morgan who had stopped at McKnight's home in Ohio nearly a year earlier during his failed raid across southern Indiana and Ohio.

Three of the final four letters in the collection inform Samaria of William's death. William Hartley, a member of Company K, writing from Maysville, Kentucky, on June 14, 1864, was the first to notify Samaria of William's fatal wounds: "your Husband is Mortly Wounded." Less than a week after Hartley's correspondence, John McKnight sent Samaria two additional letters. The first states that William's body had been sent home and that John intended to inquire about "Williams effects" at Nicholasville—the location of William McKnight's last known letter to Samaria, which indicates where the Seventh had been camped before the battle at Cynthiana. John McKnight's last letter reveals that William had initially survived his wounds at Cynthiana and that John had "paid the lady that took care of him fifteen Dollars." Samaria McKnight received these letters only shortly after receiving William's penultimate letter, in which he signed off "Yours truly until Death."

April 1st 1864
Salem[1]

Dearest Brother,

I embrace the preasant opportunity to addreys you a few lines in answer to yours of the 20th which I received last evening. We were very hapy to hear from you. We also heard from you by John Wiseman who got home on the 26th. Father went up and seen him the next day.

Sister Susan has improved some in health cince I last wrote to you and is in hopes that Brown can help if not cure her. Elliott has been very sick with his fitts for a few days. I heard from him about an hour ago and he was no better. If it was not that he has had just sutch spells before we would not have mutch hopes of his recovery. James Sandsburry has been very sick for about three weeks but is a little better today.[2] Samaria and the children are well also all the rest of our friends and relations as far as I know at presant. John has up and payed us a vissit last sabath. He says

Hannah Jane has poor health this winter and he thinks he will have to move her to the country for air as she is consumptive but I do not know whether he will or not.³ Jimmy is working down at Pomeroy now at the coal works. He intends going to Indiana with Susan when she goes as she cannot go alone. They think of starting in about three weeks if she still improves as she has been doing. Sam Brown & Aunt Jannett Sanders were up to see us last week. They and families are well. Aunt Mary was some better than when I wrote to you last.

The 4th VVI is at home now. Cousin Will is coming out in a day or so to see us. Lewis Love has not reinlisted.⁴ I suppose he cannot think to leave Enritta for three years more. Alesander Patterson & John & Washington Halliday and quite a number from the 36th of our acquaintence have reinlisted and are at home.⁵ The small Fose is very bad in . . . & Middleport we have a couple of pair of socks to send to you by Mr. Wiseman if he should live to see you, as you spoke of being in nead of some, well I believe I have writen all I can think of at presant.⁶ Father Mother and all the rest join with me in sending our best love and well wishes to you. Please write as often as you can for Mother is always uneasy to hear from you. I will bid you good night for the Preasant from your loving Sister.

Mary to William McKnight

April 5, 1864⁷
Paris In Camp Ky⁸

Ever Beloved Companion,

I hasten to inform you that we have arived safely in Ky once more & feel that we are almost in reach of home. We started from Knoxville just one week ago today. Arived at London 30 miles 11am went across the River to camp 4 PM Maj General Wm T. Sherman arived by Special Train from Chatanooga.⁹ Was saluted by 1st Ill Battery 13 guns.¹⁰ Our Regmt Drew up in line along the R.R. Cheered the Genl loudly. He stood with head uncovered on the platform of cars Saluting us in return.

Wednesday 30th left London 10 AM for Chatanooga took Dinner at Athens Alla 12 pm. 55 miles from Knox" arrived Chatanooga sundown passed through under Mission Ridge where our forces had such a heavy Battle some time ago.¹¹ The Ridge lays some 2 miles East of Town forming a kind of a Cemicircle completely lined with Earth works formerly ocupied by the Enemy mounting 60 pieces of Artillery. Our men had to charge across an open plain from Town to gain the hights of the Ridge which they did successfuly. As you wel know from accts in papers just west of Town 5 miles stands out in bold Relief Look out Mt where the Rebs had their Sige Guns.[12] Here we met T. J. Wilson & many others we knew.[13] Slept in Cars al night started out at midnight. Grant captured there 150 pieces of Artillery from Bragg altogether.[14] There Look out Mt runs in a north & south Direction terminating abruptly nearest Town where Bragg had full Comd of the Town that is the range of his Guns Comd the Town which by the has nothing preposessing about it being more of a military post than any thing else.[15] Thursday 31st we started out on the Train for Leine Ville at midnight.[16] Crossed the Tenn River at Bridge Port at Daylight.[17] Run through Cumberland Tunnel 9 AM 2288 feet through.[18] Run through a town Called Stevenson.[19] At Day light run through Tulahoma Murfreesburough Chickamunga Nashville Louville Frankfort Lex" Paris landed.[20]

This leter I comenced yesterday and looking over it I did not intend to send it atal but you can look over it and gain a few items. I did not get to finish it as we started out to this a new Camp. It seems to me I cant write a sencible letter any more. I have the blues the wost kind. You need not let any body se this miserable scrible.

Yours truly
Wm to his love

April 6, 1864
Camp 7th O.V.C Buckner Farm
Near Paris Ky

Ever Beloved Samaria,

Through the blessings of Divine Mercy I am once more permitted the pleasure of adressing to you a few lines from a point a little nearer the Home we love so wel & I am happy to inform you that we are all in the enjoyment of good health & sincerely hope this may find you all enjoying the same.

On the morning of the 29th March we shiped on board the carrs at Knox" for this place. We arived here via London Chatanooga Athens Chicamauga Look out Mt Mission Mt Ridge Murfeesburough Stone River Bride Port Tullahoma Cumberland Tunnell Stevenson Nashville Louisville Frankfort & Lexington ariveing at Paris on the 7th Day of our journey

haveing accomplished the whole journey without accident to the comand and I would be glad to give you ful particulars but I have not time at present but I want to hear from home so bad that I am almost sick. I have not Recd" any letter from you for nearly two months & I dont know what to think but I hope to hear from you soon and I want you to be sure to tel Bro John that I want him to come to Paris to se me. He can come out here in a couple of Days & I would be glad to have you come too if you can leave the little ones. O I do want to see you so bad I dont know what to Do. If you cant come tel him to come sure and any of the rest of the friends who wish to come tel them they can come out here from Cincinnatti in two or thre Hours by Rail. I have so much to Do you wil please excuse me for the present. I wil try and do better next time. Give my respects to all enquireing friends accept my sincere affection and sympathetic Love. May God Bless you & comfort you is my prayer.
From your affectionate Husband
  Wm. McKnight
  Lt Co K 7th O.V.C.
  To Samaria McKnight
PS. I seen T. J. Willson at Chatanooga. He is wel looks the same as ever.
PS. Direct to Paris Ky.
Melancholy me Molly dear O dear one.

April 8, 1864
Camp 7th O.V.C.
Near Paris Ky

Beloved Wife,

Your favor of 1st inst just came to hand and I am happy to inform you that it did not find me where it was directed as you no doubt are aware of before this time as I wrote a few days ago. You can imagine how I felt when I discovered you hand write once more if you appreciate my letters as I do yours when you have not Recd one for a couple of months. But I hope to hear from you nearly evry day now as letters come through in 48 hours.

I am sorry to hear that your health is so poor but I hope to see you soon but how soon I cant tell. The Col is doing all he can to let the Regmt come home and we are in great hopes he wil succeed and when you think that I do not care any thing about you and I could come if

I would you do me gross injustice. It almost breaks my heart to have you write thus but if you think so you have a perfect right to do so and tell me of it and I wil bear it without a murmer. I had begin to think you had not written to me thinking that we were comeing to Ky and that would have been perfectly right but it seems you have written and been returned. It is a gratification to me to know that you have written anyhow.

My mind is so engrossed with the contents of your letter that I cant think of much else at present. O how I would like to see you and the dear little ones and help them eat parched corn. I have lived on it many a day and glad to get it but thank God we have plenty now. I have no complaints to make. I have bourn it with my companions here and would not have you know at the time what hardships we endured. It is for the sake of our loved homes and families for if this government is broken down all we have that is near and dear to us is at the mercy of the outlaw the brigand and murderer but thank God the Government can with his blessing maintain itself against those whose whole purpose is to rule or ruin. I know Dear that you must have a hard time and it grieves and weigs me down because I cant help you any more than I do but you know dear that I cant help it. Would to God I could if you had seen what I have in East Tenn the suffering and devastation and starvation you certainly would feel thankful that you were in a land of peace and plenty.

I have seen whole families of women and children who had been striped of the last pound of meat and Ear of corn which they had collected & raised themselves. Yes and not a Dollar in the ward to buy and nothing to buy if they had. The principal part of what was raised in Tenn was raised by women & children the last year & they are left to starve and leave their homes without the means to do so. Just imagine for instance a poor woman perhaps barefoot with half dozen little Barefoot & nearly naked children makeing their way across a mountanous country of som hundreds of miles alone. This is no ideal picture but reality.[21] Wel dear one I must close hopeing and praying the day is not far distant when we wil be permitted to return to our peaceful firesides to enjoy the company of the loves ones forever.

From your loveing and affectionate Husband.
William To Samaria
God bless you Dear ones.

In margin:
Be sure and answer imediately. I have heard that poor Elliott was dead.[22] Poor fellow. I pitty Sister Jannett. She is nearly as bad or worse of as you. She has no man but you have a kind a one.

April 14, 1864
Paris, Ky

Dearest on Earth,

I take the present opportunity to address to you a few lines to inform you that I am enjoying good health at present and hope this may find you and the Dear little ones in the same State of health. We are once more on the move our Destination Nickolasville 12 miles from Lex.

I came to Town last evening and the Regmt comes this morning. The old Stanford Detail is here on Provo again and I have been trying to get the whole Co Detailed. I got a picture taken yesterday & wil mail it with this letter. I do not know whether it is a good picture or not but it is a fair likeness. I have written for your likeness but it seems you have never noticed it in my letters. I am very anxious to know how you get along what money you kneed and what you have to depend on. If you kneed let me know. I wil try and send you some. I sincerly hope this may find you all well & doing well.

The future brightens be cheerful and patient and above all be prayerful especialy for me. In great haste I have not had breakfast yet so you wil please excuse your loveing Husband. My love to you all. O my dear wife.
William McKnight
Lt. Co K 7th O.V.C
Direct to 7th OVC Lexington, Ky

May 4, 1864
½ past 6 PM
Cincinnati Ohio[23]

Ever beloved Wife,

I take the present opportunity to pen you a few lines to let you know where I am and how I got along. We arived here all right today. Sister Susan was very ill all night but feels better since we left the Boat. We wil stop all night at the Madison House and get the Carrs at 6 ock in the morning.

I have ascertained that I can get mustered here thereby enableing me to draw my pay. If I succeed it wil be extremely fortunately for me. I am going to give it a trial in the morning if I am spared.

I bought me a Blouse & Straps today at $15.25. My fare cost me $6.00 and I think I wil have enough to take me to the Regmt and I hope that I wil Recieve my pay so that I can send you some more money.

I sent you a pair of Shoes not such ones as I would liked to have sent but they were the best I could get of the proper size. I hope it wil not be long until I wil se you again to enjoy the pleasure of your dear company. May God bless & Comfort you in my regreted absence.

I have very little time to write at present but wil write as soon as I get to camp if I am spared. So good night Dear and bless thoss Dear little ones & wife I so much love.

From your ever loveing & faithful
Wm to Samaria

Undated Letter[24]
Meigs County, Ohio

Dear and ever beloved son,

I sit down this quite sabath morning to try to pen you a few lines to let you know that we are enjoying tolerable health at present thanks to the giver of every blessing. My Dear boy I cannot write my tears blind me to think of the sufering of our Dear soldiers and the desalation and suffring this cursed rebelion has caused since it comenced. God only knoes when the end will be. Oh my Dear boy all I can do for you is to put up my feble prayers to the throne of god for your safty and for the safty of our beloved land which is now steped in blood. Oh that God in his mercy again would smile upon our suffring children. We had a letter from Susan mail before last. She said she had been very seack on the boat she would never get along if it had not been for you. They did not reach home till friday. James was prity well pleased with the country. I wish he wase home again but I will trust in god for his safty. Tomy and lealy was up to day and brought your potograph. Oh how Dear it looks to me. Oh that god may procte that Dear form in the hour of danger and may his gairdan angle watch over you in the hour of neade. Your family is well. John has been very lame cince he came back. Joe came home sick. Frank is home sick. He is going back this weak.

I must close. I want to send this with other in the morning. So good by Dear son. May god watch over you is the prayer of your Mother. Good by Dear boy but not for ever. I hope to see you again.

Thomas McKnight

May 10, 1864
Had Quarters Co K 7th O.V.C
Nicholasville Ky

Ever beloved Wife,

I once more take my silent pen in hand to inform you that I am wel and sincerely hope this may find you all enjoying the same great and inestimeable blessing. I can hardly realise that I have paid my dear little family a visit atall. The acheing void in my heart for their absence from my sight is heavy. It is only the hope of seeing them soon again that buoyes me up through the presure of discoureaing difficulties. Things begin to look more prosperous to me but at the same time there are many who would become disconsulate even under the prospects but I have a hope that all wil yet be wright.

Wel Dear I may be writing that which does not interest you. Wel we have all been Paid of today. Yes all but poor me. I cant get pay until I get mustered. I am in hopes we wil stay here for some time to come. If we do we wil get an opportunity to get mustered. But if we do not it wil grieve me for I want to send you plenty of money to live on so if you are deprived of my Company you wil not suffer bodily nor those dear little ones come to want as I hope they never may.

I wrote to you first then to Sister Susan then mother. I hardly remember what I wrote and I am not writing very much since now but you wil excuse me I know for I have been so mixed up with evry thing today I cant half write.

But I sold old Bob for $65.00 and that wil help me to pay my debts and Dyke gave me a little more that he owed me so I wil get along very wel. My greatest concern is for my little family. God speed the Day that we soon may meet to part nomore forever.

Wel dear I am going to send my over coat home and some money enough to by the little ones and yourself some summer ware. I felt as though I had not done enough for my family but I have been in such circumstances that I could not help it. For my part I can get along some way but oh my dear little ones. May the Savior bless and protect and comfort you all. I am just as firm in the faith that I wil be spared to come home as ever throug the divine mercies of a gracious God. I hope to be with you soon. The Boys are almost ready to start for Town and I must close.

From your affectionate Husband.
Wm McKnight
2nd Lt Comdg" Co K 7th OVC

In margin:
I am stil command of company.
My heart warms when I think of the little trade you remember we talked of just before parting.
We are likely to lay here some time and I want you dear to write often.

May 13, 1864
Langsville[25]

Dearest Husband,

I hasten to answer your welcom letter of 10th that I Rec by the way of Mr Babel.[26] He stopt here this forenoon. He is quite poreley and said he did not expect that he would get home untill Tomorow. Your letter did not find us all well as you wished it. Martha is better to day than she has been since you left home. Her ear beald or broke & Lucy has a sore Throat & Ear ache. The rest of the Family is well and I hop a trust that this may find you in the best of health. I know your visit at home was but a short one but oh I am so glad you had the Privilege of coming. It leaves a new Impeion on my mind that will long be remembered. O what a nice visit it was. I think of it often. It seems to me that I could not live under such Trobel if it was not for you & hope of seeing a time when we may be permited to live a long and happy life together.

Daddy came down after you you went away. He said he would like very well to have see you again before you went away. You had not ben gon but a few minets he was here when it hailed. Samy was down day before yesterday. He said Mary is better, Martha wigels so that I cant write. Sally has left and gon for good. I have a sore finger and am going to loose a nail and it bothers me like fury. But you will excuse me will you not dear. We have some Garden made and got thoes Potatoes planted a week ago. Little Ellen Savage was buried to day she was not sick long, was around part of the day before she died I no not what aild her.[27]

We have some nabors if we cal them so down in that house that Paneth lived in. The Womans is a half sister to Dan Logan.[28] The mans name is Hougland some say they are not man & Wife but I dont know. The children was well pleased with them pretty Books. Lucys shoes is to large for her but Lettie can ware them and mine will do fine and I am very mutch obliged to you for your kindness. I Received a letter from you dated 7th and also the one you sent from Cinci and was very sorry to hear that you felt bad but hope you feel better by this time if not let me know. I have but one falt to find with your letters love and that is they ant long enough or you dont write half as mutch as I like to hear. Dont be afraid of writing things that you think would not be interesting to me for I am very anxious to know all about it. Well I guess I mite as well quit for you will see by some of my writing that I am botherd to death. You musent think hard becase I have put of writing becase I cant help it. Mary thinks if she dont write very often but when the children gets well you may expect to hear from home often. I wish you good Nights sleep and seek plesants dream. Good Night.
In margin:
That last vissit at home was the best one you ever made and dont forget our trade.

May 14th

Well dear this so bad that I dont know hardly wheather to send it or not but I cant better it now. The little ones is about the same & are so cross that I cant think of any thing. But Mary will write you a good letter before long so no more at present.

From you true Wife to Lt William McKnight Co K 7th ovc.

May 16, 1864
Head Quarters Co K 7th O.V.C.
Nicholosville Ky

Beloved and affectionate wife,

I seat myself once more to pen you a few lines to let you know that I have not forgotten you. I am and have been very anxious to hear from you and cant imagine why you have neglected writing to one that values your letters above all others. I thought I would not write any more until I heard from you but I cant wait any longer. It seems like an age since I left home and all so dear and I want to se you worse than ever. Although we are haveing very easy times here my heart is constantly turning homeward. The prospects of getting away from here are no better than they were when I started for home and hope they wil continue. Do write soon and let me know the Babes are O sweet Babes O sweet family why are we thus seperated but I hope it wil not be long before I may be permitted to enjoy your sweet Company so dear to me. Although I dared not give full sway to my feelings there is a latent feeling within my breast that I did not give ful ven to because I knew it would only tend to make our parting more severe. O the happy moments I spent with my little family are still imprinted upon my heart and ever wil be while life remains. And may heavens best blessing rest upon you.

I have drawn 32 Horses 30 Sabers and 30 Saber Belts since I returned. Paid $35.00 thirtyfive Dollars of my old debts sent you twenty Dollars and have ten left besides I have bought me a pair of Boots $7.50 seven fifty. I have plenty of clothes. I traded Coats with Jimy his being very heavy. It wil answer in place of an Over Coat. You can take the cape of that old one and make Tomy a cloak for winter and use the rest any way you chose as I can draw another when kneeded if I live. We are all getting along first rate. My morning report only shows on sick present. I have been rather unwel since I returned but I feel first rate and have for three or four days Past. It has been raining very hard today but we are tolerable comfortable.

I have a fine large wall Tent and no one to ocupy it but myself. Haveing slept alone evry night since I returned I have my bed fixed up off the Ground made of Barrel Stoves. It is very comfortable. Many of the Boys are getting Furlougs home and the Col said today he thinks they wil all get home before we leave 12 being absent now at home from Co K. Wel I believe I have written most all the interesting matter I have. I hope this may find you and the dear little ones in good health and that I may soon be permitted to return to your embrace to enjoy your company forever. Wel I have just been out to Roll Call and it is almost bed time and I wil have to turn into my Cot alone. So good night Dear one. My love to you all, and respects to the balance.

From your affectionate.
Wm McKnight
To Samaria McK

In margin:
I forgot to plague you about your letter before I went. You wrote that you hoped you would wake up and find me in your Bed some morning. Was your hopes realized, eh. Tel me. Tel Tomy that I have two of the finest Horses in camp one Black the other Bay. I accompanied the officers on a three mile ride yesterday. Had a fine ride on new horse. Had all the apples we could eat.

May 19, 1864
Head Quarters Co K 7th OVC
Nicholasville, Ky

Mary my own love,

Feeling very lonely this P.M. my mind turning homeward. I thought I could not employ my time in any beter way that to devote it you and pen to you a few stray thoughts of my mind. I am very homesick and fear it wil get me down if I dont get some proper remedy soon. The only thing that I can think of that will do any good is to come home the first opportunity that presents its self which I am fuly determined on. I have been misused and misled long enough and there seems to be no stopping place. I am stil left wholy in command with nearly all the work to do off the old company. I am very much attached to it but a great deal more attached to you and the little ones. I care not for what I have gone through it was cheerfuly done under the most arduous trials of the War. I feel proud of the attachment of the Company to me and that I have assisted so far as I was able to protect our firesides against our common enemies and am proud of my position as a Soldier and hope you feel as I do in that respect. You may feel proud that you are a Soldiers wife although your own domestic troubles may dround all such thoughts. I pitty you dear. I dont hear from you much oftener here than when in Tenn. I read one letter yesterday that was an answer to one written at Marysville with some Stamps in it. They were just to my hand. O it was such a good letter, date Feb. 26th. It had been clear to Knoxville. I am in hopes there is some more on the way. I know that you have a poor chance to write on account of so much to do but write as often as you can and if I dont get as many as I think I ought to I wil know the reason is because you have not time.

I hope the Babes are wel by this time so you wil have more leasure. I wrote to you the other day that I had paid some $35.00 of my debts.

I had paid fifty insted I have only Recd" one letter from you since I left home eccept the old one spoken of. I recd one from Cousin Will McMaster. He was wel & at Clarksburgh, Va.[29] He informed me that Bro John had been discharged (good).[30] He could not stand marching. The Boys are haveing a great time firing Sky Rockets tonight. They remind me very much of a Battle we have drawn almost Horses enough to mount the Regmt but not Saddles. I have only drawn ten & 30 sabers & Belts no other Arms.

We have been in fine spirits. The news from Grant has been so cheering for some time past.[31] The health of the Regmt never was better. I have improved considerable since returned. My pants & shirts all seem to being growing less or I am growing bigger. I hardly know which. I am expecting my muster out papers evry day. If they come soon I intend comeing to the Citty to be mustered & paid of and get some photographs taken to send home. Wel I must close as it is getting late. Being the sole ocupant of a large Tent I feel quite lonely. The Orderly is gone & all the rest belonging to the mess. Harry & Shinner left today.[32] They said they wer going to Town but I rather suspect they have gone home again. Hopeing this may find you and the Blessed little ones wel I wil bid you good night. May sweet dreams comfort you and the angels protect & comfort you is my prayer.

From your affectionate and loveing Husband
Wm McKnight
To Mary

In margin:
Give my respects to Uncle Wm and the rest of the folks generaly. N.B. says nothing about me comeing home and don't build yourself up too much about it.
Wm.

I am allowed 2 Horses by gov." I believe I told you about my 2 fine Horses 1 black 1 bay both fine. Write soon love. I have hired another Boy. I would like to be with you to night love. Do you remember what I said to you before I left. Tel me about you feel since I left. Tel dady I am sorry I did not get to talk with him more. Wel Molly it is almost ten oclock by my old turnip it is great company for me it reminds me of you evry time I take it out.

May 28th 1864
Head Quarters Co K 7th O.V.C.
Nicholasville Ky

Ever Dear and affectionate Wife,

  I seat myself at this late hour to pen you a few lines to inform you that I am in good health and hope this may find you and the dear little ones in the enjoyment of the same great and inestimeable blessing. I have been so busy for a few days that I have not had time to write to you atall being on Detail on a Court Martial in Town. I Recd a letter from you dated 20 and 21st and was very glad to hear that you was all right and think I understand but want you to write plainer next time. Dont be fearful but write just what you think and feel. You cant imagin how much good it did me to hear from you but the best of all was that little sentence (I am all right). You spoke about Babel but you did not say any thing about my Over Coat from which I infer that he had not sent it down or left it with you yet. Several of our Boys returned today. They inform me that S. S. Hanes was drafted and I want to know if he has taken the advantage of it and not settled according to last agreement if so dont forget to inform me.[33]

  I have nothing particular to write and as I expect this wil be old before it reaches you and it is getting late. I wil bring my letter to a close hopeing to hear from you imediately if not sooner as the Boys say. I wil bid you good night hopeing that the Lord may Bless and comfort you in my absence and that he may restore me to you soon is my daily prayer. O what happy moments we spent together. Can it be possible that they are the last. I hope not. Therefore pray for me be cheerful be patient be hopeful and then I know you wil consequently brave all trouble and be an armful. God Bless you love. Good night (o my own love).

  From your affectionate and Loveing Husband (kiss the Babes).
  Wm McKnight
  2nd Lt Comdg Co K 7th O.V.C.

In margin:
N.B. I was happy to hear that the Babes were better. Write soon please Doooo.
N.B. be very particular and tel me know whether Hanes has paid you or not.
  Wm Mc

It pleases me to hear from the children that they are going to School and learning fast.

You said nothing about recieving a set of knifes and Forks from me. I sent by Edmundson the miller.[34]

May 29, 1864
Rutland

Dear Brother,

    I sit down this plesant Sabath morning to write you an answer to your kind and afectionate letter of the 20th. It was a welcom letter Dear Brother as it was the only one I ever recieved from you and in my lonly condition it done me good. It showed me my Brother had not forgot me and my little fatherless children. May god in his kindness and love watch over and keep you safe from harm. I did not get to talk with you half as much as I wanted to but your time was so short and so many others wanted to see and talk with you that there was no chance to say much. But I will live in hope that you may Return safe again to your home and friends. Lelia and Thomy has come and brought me your Photograph whitch I thank you very much for. I think it looks very mutch like you did when you was at home. Sister Mary was here and stayed last night with me. She has just gone home and your children have gone with her. She got a Photograph. She was so glad. She huried home to show it to mother. It was very kind of you to offer to help me but do not rob yourself or your own family. If it was not for my kind friends my little ones would want for bread but with the blessing of god there will be some way for me to get along in very helpless condition. I hope to have better helth soon so that I can do more for my self and family. Asher has got home but I have not seen him. Mart and Ema Jane was to your house yesterday. He was helping to plant corn for Samaria. They have gone to take dinner with Asher today. Mary is going to send you a letter by John Ota.[35] He starts back tomorow.

    I dont know that I have any thing more to write but that the friends are all well. Your family is well this morning. I hope this will find you in the best of health. Write to me as often as can and I will answer. No more at present.

    From afectionate Sister J S Braley to William McKnight Lt.

Sunday May 29th 1864

Dearest Brother,

I embrace the presant time to address you a few fines in answer to your kind letter of May the 18th which I received last evening. Mother also received one of the 8th which had been mifsent and forwarded. We were very happy to hear of your good health. We are all well with the exception of myself and I am gaining slowly. I was very sick for a few days after you left. I have sick spells yet every few days but I should not complain while I am no worse. I walked down to Jannetts last evening and came up this morning. It was as mutch as a bargon to get home again. Jannett and Family are well and getting along as well as could be expected. Leila and Tommy came up this morning to spend the day and to bring that Photograph for which I thank you very mutch. It is just what I so wished for but hated to ask you to spend money to have it taken. We think it looks very naturel. Ma sat down and had a good cry over it.

The children started home a few minutes ago quite delighted with a little rabbit that Father caught for them. I intended to have writen to you this morning but Frank McKnight and family have been here all day so that I did not have a chance and I have no time to write more at presant as we want to send this with Mr Oty that is going to start back in the morning.[36] So I hope you will escuse a short and poorly ritten letter for I can hardly write any cince I have been sick. Will Halliday and Asher Entsminger came home yesterday. Ma I suppose has told you all the news. Hopeing to hear from you soon I end with my undying love for you. I remain your affectionate sister.

Mary McKnight

May 31, 1864
Langsville Ohio

Dearest Husband,

I embrace the present opportunity to address you a few lines in answer to your kinde and affectionate letters of the 19th & 23rd that I received last Satturday and was very glad to hear that you felt better but am sorry that you have to say alone. I will be alone in a few days. Please come and stay with me will you or not let me know in your next. Thoes Potograps cant be beat. O they are so pretty. I have one of them whare we can see it all the time and o dear it is to bad to have you away when we want you at home so bad and never kneeded you any worse. One of my eyes is sore and the lite of the paper is very disagreeble. We are doing the best we can dear but that is a poore do.

My pets can croll and I wish that you could see them. They dont look like they did when you was at home but they they can cry and half the children is at school. It is a beautiful day every thing seems to say gay and happy but poore me and I am almost sick not in boddy but mind. Later in the day I fel some better. We have our lot planted to corn for your health. The remedy you spoke of is an excellent cure and will help you if you will give it a fair trial. Write soon and let me know how you are getting along. Well I beleave I told you all that wil do any good and will write often as I can this leaves us well and hope it may find you in the best of health. Oh let me hear from you often. If you dont get a letter for every one you write so be a good man and I will do the best I can untill then.

Hoping this Ware will son close or let the poore soldiers return to their family. So let us be patient hoping thare is a better day in store for us.

The little ones is bothering me so & I make a grate many blunders but you will excuse me I Guess. I wish you knew how proud I feel abot some things. Well you can have an idea of what it may be. Well I will close hoping it wil not be long until you will say you have the proper cure or remedy. May our heavenly Father save and protect is the prayer of yours one that is never cold but is warm harted and true. From Molly as you call but I sign my Name differen from that with respect.

Mrs. McKnight to her man Lt Wm McKnight.
Good day. Come soon. That lock of hair is nice I guess it is some of yours you did not say.[37]
O how I wish you could see my Pets.

———

June 3, 1864
Head Quarters General Court Martial
Nicholasville, Ky

Beloved Wife,

I take the present opportunity to let you know that I am wel at present and hope this may find you all enjoying the Same Blessing. I have been kept on this court as a member for the last ten Days so that I have very little time to write on account of this and Company duties together. But

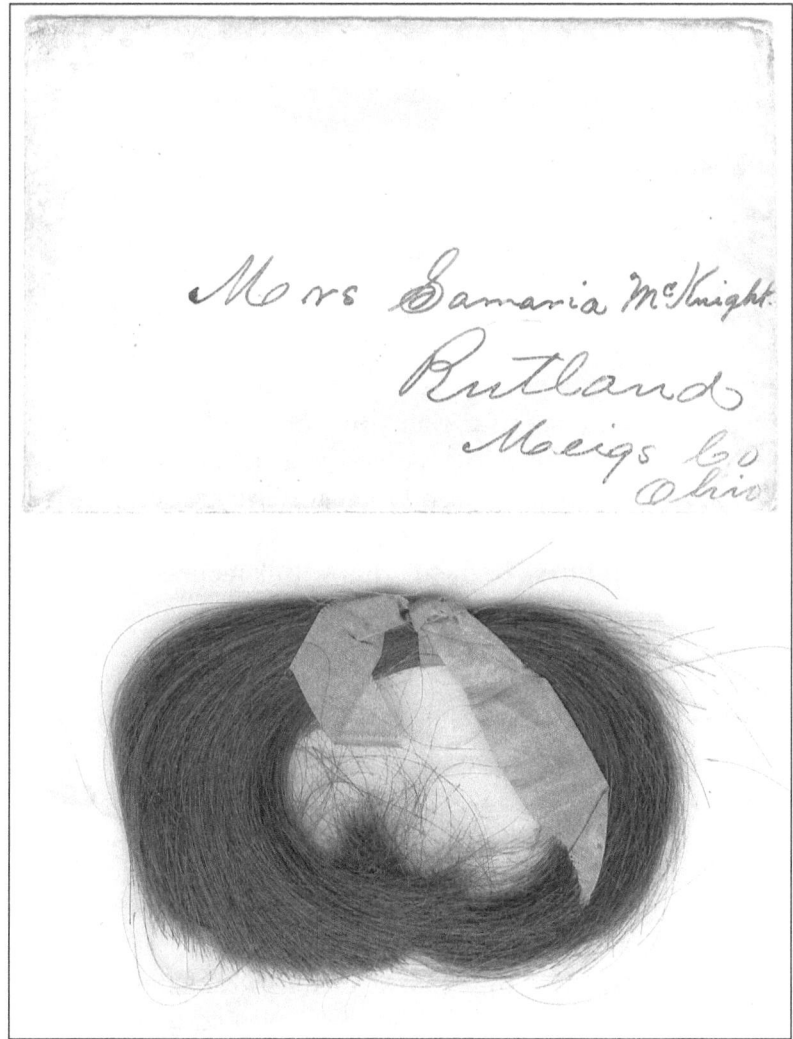

Lock of William McKnight's hair sent to Samaria. *Courtesy of Terry Hauger.*

we expect to get through today. I recd a letter from you a few days ago and was glad to hear that you was all wel but I am looking for another evry day. I recd one from Sister Jannet and Mary and from my ever dear good mother. The Boys are all wel and in fine spirits. My papers have gone to Lexington and in few days we wil get them. We wil be able to be mustered out and in again and Recieved our pay. It is now eleven months past since I recd any pay and when I get it I wil be able to send you some that wil do you some good.

I am anxious to know how Sam Hains settled with you. I have not time write any more at present and hope you wil excuse me for the present. Hopeing to hear from you soon. I close with my love for you all forever.

Yours truly until Death.

Wm McKnight

2nd Lt Comdg Co K 7th OVC

June 5, 1864
Nicholasville, Ky

Beloved Wife,

I once more seat myself to answer your very kind and welcome letter of the 31st May which came to hand yesterday and its contents was devoured with avidity. I was very glad to hear from you and that you was all wel except your Eye which I hope ere this is as wel as ever and all the rest in good health. I have been sufering with lameness in my back for ten days past so sometimes it is with dificulty that I can get my breath and sleep is out of the question at times. The sorest place is on each side of my back between the small and shoulder blades. I have no idels what it is or what causes it. I took a little ride today out a couple of miles with the Orderly and got a good dinner and a fine dish of Strawberries & cream & Sugar. O it was such a treat as only poor Soldiers know how to appreciate yes and besides I brought a nice boquet of Roses which I have before me on my writing desk to remind me of the loved ones at home and I feel much better and wonder if Mollies Roses are in bloom and if the little ones are picking Strawberris at home. I imagine that I can see them. What sweet thoughts of such a sweet family. O if I could only be there with them but God has been pleased to seperate us for some purpose and I hope for the better. I can only say thy wil not mine be done. Go say you are doing the best you can but it is a very poor doo what do you mean is it that you are suffering or is it that you cant get along with so much. I expect the latter, you must take things as easy as you can. Do what you can what you cant dont fret one bit about. I think you have got along first rate if you have got all that big field of corn planted. I say bully for you Molly. I would like to see your pets crawl and crow and help you take care of them for it seems to me that you have more than your share of trouble in this world but I hope it wil not always be so no not if I can help it. I have not had time lately to write being on this court martial but we expect to get through tomorrow. I am glad you think so wel of those Photographs, and that mother Recd hers or Mary I should have said and Jannett. I recd letters from them all last week but have not had time to answer them yet. The taps have blown for lights to be put out and all become quiet and my back hurts me so it seems that I cant sit any longer. O yes there is one thing I want to know what you are so proud about. I wil wait patiently for an answer. Sweet dreams for you tonight love. If I owned this whole State I would give it to be with you and this war at an end so that we might never more be seperated. I never did want to be with you so bad in my life. Evry day maks you seem nearer and dearer to me. You are probably in your soft bed of feather & I must return to mine of Barrel Stoves. I think it a first rate bed but Assure I would a little rather be in yours with it wouldnt spite me very much if you was in it. Ten oclock good night love but give me a kiss before you go. O do dont be so distant. No one wil know any thing about it. Wel if you want its no use talking so again I wish you good night and sweet dreams.

Monday May 6th, I again resume my pen to finish my letter before I go to Town.[38] I slept tolerable wel last night and feel better this morning. It is a butiful One. My Roses are stil fresh and butiful emblematic of the love I have for you but unlike them a days sunshine does not dim the lusture nor change my devotion to you although like the Rose and the parent stem we are seperated but it does not follow that we should allow our plighted vows to and love to fade upon our Hearts. Wel Molly I excuse you for not writing any oftener knowing that you have a very poor chance to write but it the greatest pleasure to me to me to read your letters. They are my only solace here, O such good kind letters. Hopeing to hear from you soon and that this may find you in fine spirits I close. My love to all and prayers for your welfare. May God fill you all with health and the comforts of life and restore me to you is my prayer.

Yours unconditionaly.
Wm McKnight To Samaria McKnight

The letter dated June 5, 1864, is the last known correspondence from McKnight before his death on June 12. However, McKnight in his diary entered remarks for the six days prior to his death at Cynthiana. They are as follows:

June 6
John Morgan reported in the State.
June 7
Clothing Drawn and ishued.
June 8, 1864
Drew from Lt. Col. Miner
44 Cav Saddles
43 Cav Bridles
43 Saddle Girths
43 Prs. And Straps
43 Horse Brushes
5 Saddle Blankets
June 9
Laid sick all forenoon. Started with the Regmt towards Clays Ferry 14½ miles after Rebels reported in that directions returned to Nicholasville got into camp 12 midnight.[39]
June 10
Started 8 A.M. for Lex. Cannon heard in that direction. Rebels Reported in the Town arrived at at Lex. 3 P.M. Rebels had gone we were 5 ms behind Halted and Fed and got Dinner. Slept 2 hours started out after Morgan in the direction of Paris took the george Town Road had an exciting chase.[40]
June 11
Moved out on George Town Road fel in with Squad. Rebels 40 / 6 miles out charged them Drove them 2 ms and returned to paris 11:30 a.m. went into camp.

June 14, 1864
Maysville Ky

Mrs. McKnight,

I will rite you a few lines to let you know that your Husband is Mortly Wounded. He was wounded at Cyntheanna Ky on the 11th of this month.[41] I left three men to attend him and I have not herd from him sinse he is Wounded in the Right Lung.

I will write to you again as soon as I her from him.
Your friend.
Wm. P. Hartley[42]
Ordly Sergeng of Co K 7th OVC[43]

June 20, 1864
On Bord express carrs Near cyntheanna[44]

Dear Sister,

You will have learned Before this that your Dear Husband is dead. I have met the colonel of the 7 he says Williams boddy has Bin sent Home. I have maid every enquiries along the Road But have not yet found it. I am going on to Cintheyana to learn the particulars and the Colonel wants me to go to Nicolesvill to get Williams effects.[45] Dear sister I have done the Best I could I could not git out any soner. I got a dispatch on Saturday from a man in cinthey that Brother William was dead and sent home. I hope you Received him Before this time. It may Be several days Before I git Home. There is a Bridge Burned here the cars cant go any farther on this Road.

I close you will here from me soon I hope. No more at presant.

But Remains your Deapley effecter Brother John McKnight.

June 21, 1864
Cynthiana, Ky

Sister Dear,

I have bin to the house of the man here that Nursed William and have found out the particulars about him. It is not nessesary for me to write them. I will Bring them to you. I start Home in about one hour you will git this Before I arrive. I have no dout that Mr. Wells has arived with your Dear Husbands Remains long Before this time.[46] He left here on Thursday June 16th at 2 oclock. I have paid all the expence of his Buriel case and his transportation. The case was 61.85 sixty one Dollar Eightyfive cents. Mr. McClintock furnished Mr. Wells with fifteen Dollars $15.00.[47] I paid the lady that took care of him fifteen Dollars. Do not Check any money to any one till I see you. I have paid all Expences. I have nothing more to write at presant

But Remain your efectionate Brother John McKnight.

Epilogue

Immediately following McKnight's death and the fighting at Cynthiana, the Seventh Ohio Volunteer Cavalry pursued a retreating John Hunt Morgan through rugged terrain in eastern Kentucky. Morgan eventually escaped, but the Seventh was able to release several hundred of General Hobson's men, who had been captured just days before by Morgan.[1] On July 4, 1864, the Seventh departed Nicholasville, Kentucky, to join General Sherman on the Atlanta Campaign (see appendix D). From late July until early September, the Seventh participated in the siege of the "Gate City," and from there the regiment left for Decatur, Georgia; there it remained until early November, when it saw fierce action at the battle of Franklin, Tennessee. During this time, the Seventh "subsisted chiefly upon the country, which was gathered in by foraging parties."[2] On Christmas Day 1864, the Seventh engaged the Rebels near Pulaski, Tennessee, driving the enemy "from the place in haste and disorder, capturing from him three pieces of artillery, [and] an ammunition-train."[3] By early 1865, the Seventh had constructed winter quarters in Gravelly Springs, Alabama, which was "something new for the 7th being the first time in her history that she went into winter quarters."[4]

By late spring of 1865, the Rebels had retreated from Plantersville, Alabama, to Selma, which was heavily fortified "with palisades of pine timber set in the ground and sharp at the upper end. The approach to Selma was through open ground with no protection whatever to our men."[5] Despite the fortifications, Selma fell quickly; Captain Rankin declared it to be "one of the most important places" in the Confederacy, for situated "in the midst of their iron regions, was . . . a solid machine shop, where a large portion of their ordnance was made."[6] From Selma, the Seventh departed for Montgomery, Alabama, where the Confederates "surrendered without a fight, after they had burnt a large amount of cotton."[7] Following Montgomery's capture, the Seventh turned its focus to Andersonville Prison, arriving "only in time to see the train moving out with a mass of skeletons caused by starvation. Some eighty-four of our men which beggared all description, not being able to be removed, were left in the prison pen."[8]

In April 1865, the Seventh received a telegram from General Grant to cease hostilities. Confederate General Robert E. Lee had "surrendered, Richmond had fallen, Johnston was surrounded, with Sherman in his rear and Sheridan in front, and would have to surrender or be captured."[9] The Seventh then moved to Macon, Georgia, and from there to Atlanta, "where it was engaged till the 15th of May in scouting Northern Georgia, to prevent the escape of Jeff. Davis."[10] Following Confederate president Jefferson Davis's capture, the Seventh was in charge of overseeing his removal to Augusta, Georgia. From that point, the Seventh marched to Chattanooga and then on to Nashville, "where it laid down its arms and was honorably mustered out of service, on the 4th day of July, 1865."[11]

With the surrender of Confederate forces, "Ohioans anxiously awaited the return of the surviving Union soldiers."[12] The Seventh Ohio Volunteer Cavalry began the war with 1,204 men and lost 364 soldiers during the conflict. For Company K, the majority of its members (70 men) mustered out of the service in July 1865. However, 13 soldiers from Company K did not return: 8 were killed in action or died in camp, while 5 of the men captured at Rogersville, Tennessee, in November 1863 died in prison (Duston Harper, Royall Hoyt, and Orrellence Williams perished at Andersonville, and Isaac Nelson and Henry Shiner died at Richmond) (see appendix E).[13]

Following the war, Samaria McKnight turned her attention to family matters. Widowed at twenty-six years of age, she was responsible for raising six children under the age of nine. Samaria's extensive family network—the Braleys, Entsmingers, Hallidays, McKnights, McMasters, and Rathburns—provided assistance. Samaria never remarried. In addition to her government pension, she earned income as a seamstress and kept a brief record book of her dealings.[14] Samaria, for example, charged "Jasper and Eddie" 10 cents for shirts on May 1; later, on September 25, a bonnet for "Ester" also cost 10 cents. Another entry, from June 27, 1872, documents "sewing I done for Doctor Browns family": "2 pars of pants" cost $2, to "finish 1 for the little girl [was] 50 cts," and "to make 2

EPILOGUE

Samaria and the McKnight girls. *Top left to front:* Mattie, Myrtha, Lettie, Samaria, and Leila. *Courtesy of Ruth Hayth.*

dresses and 2 overskirts for the big girls [cost] $5."

Two of William and Samaria's children eventually moved west, while four stayed in Ohio. Leila McKnight, the eldest, married Henry Kennedy. Henry and Leila lived in Aurora, Illinois, for many years. After Henry's death, Leila moved to Oakland, California, where she died while residing with her son, whose name is not known. Thomas, the second child, was William and Samaria's only son. According to newspaper clippings, "Tommie" moved to Iowa as a young man. In 1883, Thomas started work for the Western Wheeled Scraper Company in Mount Pleasant, Iowa. The company relocated to Aurora, Illinois, in 1891. At that time, Thomas was appointed superintendent and master mechanic of the new plant. Thomas married Evalyn Harrison of Mount Pleasant, Iowa, on September 20, 1900, and died suddenly in 1917 in Washington, D.C., during a business trip regarding a "big order for dump cars for use in France."[15]

Even though Leila and Thomas moved west, Samaria frequently mentions them in her diary. On April 2, 1885, Samaria writes that it has been "3 years today that I saw my boy," although on September 30, 1888, Samaria mentions that the "children were all at home."[16] In 1893, Samaria and her second daughter, Lettie, ventured west to Illinois and spent nearly two months (October 5–November 29) with Leila and Thomas. During that time, Samaria (along with Leila, Lettie, and Thomas) attended the 1893 World's Fair in Chicago and visited Lincoln Park and Lake Michigan.

Lettie, who never married, cared for Samaria until her death in 1905. The final letter in the collection from Thomas McKnight to P. W. Jones discusses Lettie's condition at the time of Samaria's death.

Epilogue

February 1, 1905
Langsville, Ohio

P.W. Jones
U.S. Pension Agent
Columbus Ohio
Dear Sir,

My Mother Samaria McKnight late widow of Wm McKnight died Jan 28th 1905.

I suppose according to law the estate will be entitled to two months of pension that is due her. We dont think it necessary to have administration as the five children are all of age as you can readily see. There is no debts hanging over the little home as I have borne expenses outside of her limited allowance from the U.S. Government. We are all agreed that the balance due on last voucher (Roll no 286) be paid to Lettie S. McKnight daughter of the late Samaria McKnight. Lettie has worn her own life almost out in caring for Mother in her declining years and is deserving pay for the hardship she has endured in watching over her.

There is no doubt that if application for nurse service had been made several years ago it would have been granted (and justly too).

Please write me here instructions and requirements in the matter above or forward to. The sister refered to is 45 yrs of age and helpless never married but completely broken in health working & taking care of Mother. If she is entitled to anything from the Government please inform me also.

Awaiting an early reply.
I am yours truly.
T.R. McKnight

Lettie stayed in the McKnight home in Langsville until her death in 1931. According to family records, Mary McKnight was briefly married to Ira Grimes but died soon thereafter (in 1878), the only child who did not outlive Samaria. Martha (Mattie), one of the "Fourth of July presents," married Fred Tuckerman on March 5, 1883. They lived in several southeastern Ohio communities. Mattie died May 12, 1932. Myrtha married Joseph Powell in 1882 and passed away in Toledo, Ohio, in 1922.

A newspaper clipping indicates that Samaria never left Meigs County and died "from the effects of the grip[pe]" (influenza) on January 28,

EPILOGUE

Flood of Langsville, Ohio, 1908. McKnight's house is left of center, with a large tree in front. *Courtesy of Susan Hayes.*

1905. The same article notes that "she was left a widow when her children were small, but raised them to be honest, loving christians as only a good mother can do." William and Samaria McKnight, along with Samaria's parents and their daughters Lettie, Mary, Mattie, and Myrtha, are buried just east of Langsville in Miles Cemetery off State Route 124.

Appendix A
Ohio Civil War Troop Statistics

Ohio Organizations Furnished in the Civil War

Organizations	Number
Cavalry Regiments	13
Cavalry Battalions	5
Cavalry Companies	10
Heavy Artillery Regiments	2
Heavy Artillery Battalions	0
Heavy Artillery Companies	0
Light Artillery Regiments	0
Light Artillery Battalions	42
Engineer Regiments	0
Engineer Companies	0
Sharp Shooters Regiments	0
Sharp Shooters Battalions	0
Sharp Shooters Companies	10
Infantry Regiments	227
Infantry Battalions	1
Infantry Companies	5
Total	315

Number of Ohio Troops in the Civil War

Category	Number
Furnished White Troops	304,814
Furnished Sailors and Marines	3,274
Furnished Colored Troops	5,092
Furnished Indian Nations	0
Total	313,180

APPENDIX A

Cause of Death and Number of Ohio Troops Killed

Cause of Death	Number Killed
Number of troops killed and mortally wounded	11,588
Died of disease	19,365
Died as prisoner	2,356
Died from accidents	1,168
Died from causes except battle	998
Total	35,475*

* = Includes 957 officers.
Source: Dyer 1959a.

Appendix B
List of Officers, Seventh Regiment Ohio Volunteer Cavalry

Rank	Name	Date of Rank	Remarks
Colonel	Israel Garrard	9-18-1862	Mustered out with regiment.
Lt. Colonel	George G. Miner	9-18-1862	On detached duty.
Major	Wm. Reany	9-20-1862	Mustered out July 4, 1865.
"	Augustus Norton	12-28-1862	Resigned Jan. 30, 1864.
"	James McIntyre	7-01-1863	Resigned March 26, 1864.
"	Wm. T. Simpson	3-28-1864	Resigned Aug. 26, 1864.
"	John Leaper	7-13-1864	Disch. as Capt. Oct. 25, 64. Rein. 5-5-1865.
"	Solomon L. Green	10-12-1864	Mustered out with regiment.
Surgeon	Isaac Train	10-09-1862	Mustered out with regiment.
Asst. Surgeon	R. H. Tullis	11-06-1862	Died at Marietta, Ga.
"	P. G. Barrett	6-09-1863	Honorably discharged 10-26-1864.
"	John Kraps	1-04-1865	Mustered out with regiment.
Captain	James McIntyre	8-25-1862	Promoted to Major.
"	Wm. T. Simpson	8-25-1862	Promoted to Major.
"	A. D. Ells	8-27-1862	Resigned 6-28-1863.
"	John Leaper	8-27-1862	Promoted to Major.
"	Allen S. Brownfield	8-28-1862	Resigned 6-3-1863.
"	John D. Kinney	9-01-1862	Resigned 12-13-1862.
"	Augustus Norton	9-02-1862	Promoted to Major.
"	Joel P. Higley	9-03-1862	Killed at Blue Springs, 9-10-1863.
"	Wm. H. Lewis	9-05-1862	Honorably discharged 8-17-1863.
"	James C. Campbell	9-12-1862	Resigned 1-27-1864.
"	Solomon L. Green	9-20-1862	Promoted to Major.
"	Eben Lindsay	11-01-1862	Resigned 12-25-1863.
"	John A. Ashbury	12-13-1862	Mustered out with regiment.
"	Nehemiah Warren	5-25-1863	Resigned 7-20-1864.
"	Lester G. Moore	6-03-1863	Resigned as 1st Lieut., 6-3-1863.
"	Joseph R. Copeland	6-03-1863	Honorably discharged 5-15-1865.
"	Richard C. Rankin	1-01-1863	Mustered out 7-4-1865.
"	James C. Shaw	4-02-1864	Mustered out with regiment.
"	Theodore F. Allen	4-02-1864	Must. out 7-4-65; brv't. Maj., Lt. Col. . . .
"	Albert A. Carr	4-02-1864	Resigned 8-26-1864.
"	Wm. R. Jackson	4-02-1864	Mustered out with regiment.
"	Joseph B. Santmyer	4-02-1864	Mustered out with regiment.
"	Andrew Hall	4-02-1864	Mustered out with regiment
"	John McColgin	5-25-1864	Died 3-22-1865.
"	Wm. D. Ketterman	10-12-1864	Lost on Steamer Sultana.
"	Oliver H. Eylar	10-12-1864	Mustered out with regiment.

APPENDIX B

"	Martin Shuler	10-12-1864	Mustered out with regiment.
"	George D. Womeldorff	6-16-1865	Mustered out with regiment.
"	Alfred N. Rich	6-16-1865	Must. out with reg. as 1st Lieut. and R.Q.M.
"	Wm. T. Burton	7-05-1865	Mustered out with regiment as 1st Lieut.
1st Lieutenant	Theodore F. Allen	8-28-1862	Promoted to Captain.
"	John McColgin	10-13-1862	Promoted to Captain.
"	Wm. R. Jackson	9-15-1862	Promoted to Captain.
"	Lester G. Moore	8-25-1862	Promoted to Captain.
"	James C. Shaw	8-27-1862	Promoted to Captain.
"	Roswell C. Nichols	9-01-1862	Resigned 2-23-1864.
"	Wm. L. Tripp	9-02-1862	Resigned 12-25-1863
"	Joseph R. Copeland	9-02-1862	Promoted to Captain.
"	Nehemiah Warren	9-02-1862	Promoted to Captain.
"	John Geyer	9-03-1862	Resigned 11-28-1863.
"	Albert A. Carr	9-12-1862	Promoted to Captain.
"	Richard C. Rankin	9-15-1862	Promoted to Captain.
"	Daniel Sayer	9-25-1862	Resigned 6-28-1863.
"	Joseph B. Santmyer	10-01-1862	Promoted to Captain.
"	Andrew Hall	10-01-1862	Promoted to Captain.
"	Peter Long	5-25-1863	Resigned 1-30-1864.
"	Samuel D. Murphy	6-03-1863	Died 7-16-1864.
"	Martin Shuler	6-28-1863	Promoted to Captain.
"	Oliver H. Eylar	6-03-1863	Promoted to Captain.
"	Wm. D. Ketterman	1-01-1864	Promoted to Captain.
"	John J. Smith	4-02-1864	Resigned as 2nd Lieut. 10-20-1863.
"	George D. Womeldorff	4-02-1864	Promoted to Captain.
"	Alfred N. Rich	4-02-1864	Promoted to Captain.
"	Wm. T. Burton	4-02-1864	Promoted to Captain.
"	Benj. Trago	4-02-1864	Mustered out with regiment.
"	David W. Fisher	4-02-1864	Mustered out with regiment.
"	Samuel Dryden	4-02-1864	Mustered out with regiment as R.C.S.
"	Charles F. Smith	4-02-1864	Discharged 7-14-1865.
"	Charles D. Mitchell	4-19-1864	Mustered out with regiment as Adjutant.
"	Eugene Little	4-19-1864	Mustered out with regiment.
"	John V. Srofe	4-19-1864	Mustered out with regiment.
"	Andrew J. Hardy	5-25-1864	Mustered out with regiment.
"	Thomas J. Williams	10-12-1864	Declined to accept.
"	Benj. F. Powers	10-12-1864	Killed, 1865.
"	Wm. Boggs	10-12-1864	Mustered out with regiment.
"	Philip Blazer	10-12-1864	Mustered out with regiment.
"	Wm. T. Archer	5-18-1865	Mustered out with regiment.
"	W. W. Manning	5-18-1865	Mustered out with regiment as 2nd Lieut.
"	Benj. R. Derstine	6-16-1865	Mustered out with regiment as 2nd Lieut.
"	Newton McLeod	6-16-1865	Mustered out with regiment as 2nd Lieut.
2nd Lieutenant	Martin Shuler	8-25-1862	Promoted to 1st Lieut.
"	Samuel B. Johnston	8-25-1862	Resigned 2-29-1864.
"	Samuel D. Murphy	8-25-1862	Promoted to 1st Lieut.
2nd Lieutenant	George D. Womeldorff	8-27-1862	Promoted to 1st Lieut.

"	John J. Smith	9-02-1862	Resigned 10-20-1863.
"	Peter Long	9-02-1862	Promoted to 1st Lieut.
"	Alfred N. Rich	9-02-1862	Promoted to 1st Lieut.
"	Thomas Bunker	9-03-1862	Resigned 6-23-1863.
"	Oliver H. Eylar	9-04-1862	Promoted to 1st Lieut.
"	Wm. T. Burton	9-05-1862	Promoted to 1st Lieut.
"	Wm. Ketterman	9-15-1862	Promoted to 1st Lieut.
"	Benj. Trago	9-01-1862	Promoted to 1st Lieut.
"	Homer Chase	5-25-1862	Resigned 1-20-1864.
"	David W. Fisher	6-03-1863	Promoted to 1st Lieut.
"	Samuel Dryden	6-03-1863	Promoted to 1st Lieut.
"	Chas. F. Smith	6-28-1863	Promoted to 1st Lieut.
"	Andrew J. Hardy	4-19-1864	Promoted to 1st Lieut.
"	Wm. McKnight	4-19-1864	Killed at Cynthiana, June 1864.
"	Thomas J. Williams	4-19-1864	Mustered out with regiment.
"	Benj. F. Powers	4-19-1864	Promoted to 1st Lieut.
"	Wm. Boggs	4-19-1864	Promoted to 1st Lieut.
"	Philip Blazer	4-19-1864	Promoted to 1st Lieut.
"	Wm. S. Archer	4-19-1864	Promoted to 1st Lieut.
"	W. W. Manning	4-19-1864	Promoted to 1st Lieut.
"	Benj. W. Derstine	9-26-1864	Promoted to 1st Lieut.
"	Newton McLead	3-18-1865	Mustered out with regiment as 1st Sergeant.
"	Homer E. Ware	3-18-1865	Mustered out with regiment.
"	Wilson Barber	3-18-1865	Mustered out with regiment as 1st Sergeant.
"	James McGee	3-18-1865	Mustered out with regiment as 1st Sergeant.
"	Samuel C. Tappan	3-18-1865	Mustered out with regiment.
"	Wm. H. Vane	3-16-1865	Mustered out with regiment as 1st Sergeant.
"	Grassen M. Cole	3-16-1865	Mustered out with regiment as 1st Sergeant.
"	Thomas H. Nutt	3-16-1865	Mustered out with regiment as 1st Sergeant.

Source: Reid 1895b.

Appendix C
Major Engagements Listed for the Seventh Ohio Volunteer Cavalry

Location	Date
Carter's Station, Tennessee	December 30, 1862
Mount Sterling, Kentucky	March 24, 1863
Dutton Hill, Kentucky	March 30, 1863
Monticello, Kentucky	May 1, 1863
Rocky Gap, Kentucky	June 9, 1863
Buffington Island, Ohio	July 19, 1863
Cumberland Gap, Tennessee	September 9, 1863
Carter's Station, Tennessee	September 22, 1863
Zollicoffer, Tennessee	September 24, 1863
Blue Springs, Tennessee	October 10, 1863
Rogersville, Tennessee	November 6, 1863
Siege of Knoxville, Tennessee	November 17 to December 4, 1863
Bean Station, Tennessee	December 14, 1863
Blain's Cross Roads, Tennessee	December 16, 1863
New Market, Tennessee	December 23, 1863
Dandridge, Tennessee	January 16–17, 1864
Fair Garden, Tennessee	January 27, 1864
Cynthiana, Kentucky	June 11, 1864
Siege of Atlanta, Georgia	July 28 to September 2, 1864
Franklin, Tennessee	November 30, 1864
Nashville, Tennessee	December 15–16, 1864
Pulaski, Tennessee	December 25, 1864
Plantersville, Alabama	April 1, 1865
Selma, Alabama	April 2, 1865

Source: Roster Commission 1891.

Appendix D
Official Roster, Company K, Seventh Ohio Volunteer Cavalry

Name	Rank	Age	Date of Entering the Service	Period of Service	Remarks
Higley, Joel	Captain	37	9-3-1862	3 yrs.	Killed Oct. 10, 1863, in action at Blue Springs, Tenn.
Shaw, James	"	35	8-27-1862	3 yrs.	Promoted from 1st Lieutenant Co. L April 2, 1864; mustered out with company July 1, 1865.
Geyer, John	1st Lieut.	...	9-3-1862	3 yrs.	Discharged Aug. 27, 1863, on Surgeon's certificate of disability.
Hardey, Andrew	"	22	8-30-1862	3 yrs.	Transferred from 1st Lieutenant Co. H Sept. 9, 1864; mustered out with company July 1, 1865.
Brunker, Thomas	2nd Lieut.	26	9-3-1862	3 yrs.	Resigned June 23, 1863.
McKnight, William	"	29	9-12-1862	3 yrs.	Appointed 1st Sergeant Nov. 8, 1863; promoted to 2nd Lieutenant April 19, 1864; killed June 12, 1864, at Cynthiana, Ky.
Barber, Wilson	"	33	9-16-1862	3 yrs.	Promoted from Regiment Company Sergeant March 18, 1865; mustered out with company July 1, 1865.
Hartley, William	1st Sergt.	24	9-12-1862	3 yrs.	Appointed Corporal March 8, 1862; Sergeant —; 1st Sergeant April 19, 1864.
Barrett, John	"	26	9-12-1862	3 yrs.	Appointed Sergeant Nov. 8, 1862; 1st Sergeant Aug. 31, 1864; mustered out with company July 1, 1865.
Carr, Hiram	Q.M.S.	36	9-12-1862	3 yrs.	Appointed Nov. 8, 1862; mustered out July 24, 1865, at Chattanooga, Tenn., by order of War Department.
Poston, Eliphalet	"	24	9-12-1862	3 yrs.	Appointed Feb. 28, 1865; mustered out with company July 1, 1865.

APPENDIX D

Name	Rank	Age	Date of Entering the Service	Period of Service	Remarks
McCann, Patrick	Com. Ser.	...	9-12-1862	3 yrs.	Appointed Sergeant Nov. 8, 1862; Company Sergeant —; mustered out with Company July 1, 1865.
Kennedy, John	Sergt.	24	9-12-1862	3 yrs.	Appointed Nov. 8, 1862; wounded Aug. 27, 1864, in action near Atlanta, Ga.; mustered out June 13, 1865, at Gallipolis, Ohio, by order of War Department.
Wiseman, John	"	22	9-12-1862	3 yrs.	Appointed Nov. 8, 1862; discharged April 30, 1864, on Surgeon's certificate of disability.
Dennison, James	"	34	9-12-1862	3 yrs.	Appointed Corporal Nov. 8, 1862; Sergeant —; mustered out with company July 1, 1865.
Hoyt, Alonzo	"	24	9-12-1862	3 yrs.	Appointed Corporal Nov. 8, 1862; Sergeant —; mustered out with company July 1, 1865.
McBride, Joseph	"	21	9-12-1862	3 yrs.	Appointed Corporal Nov. 8, 1862; Sergeant —; mustered out with company July 1, 1865.
Skinner, William	"	20	9-12-1862	3 yrs.	Appointed Saddler Nov. 8, 1862; Sergeant —; mustered out with company July 1, 1865.
Austin, Alonzo	Corporal	25	9-12-1862	3 yrs.	Appointed Wagoner Nov. 8, 1862; Corporal —; mustered out with company July 1, 1865.
Caldwell, Hamilton	"	22	9-12-1862	3 yrs.	Appointed Nov. 8, 1862; mustered out with company July 1, 1865.
Little, Levi	"	36	9-12-1862	3 yrs.	Appointed —; killed Oct. 10, 1863, in action at Blue Springs, Tenn.
Barstow, Zachariah	"	23	9-12-1862	3 yrs.	Appointed —; mustered out with company July 1, 1865.
Treadwell, John	"	23	9-12-1862	3 yrs.	Appointed —; mustered out with company July 1, 1865.

Official Roster, Company K, Seventh Ohio Volunteer Cavalry

Name	Rank	Age	Date of Entering the Service	Period of Service	Remarks
Davis, John	"	22	9-12-1862	3 yrs.	Appointed —; mustered out with company July 1, 1865.
Edmundson, Jesse	"	18	9-12-1862	3 yrs.	Appointed —; mustered out with company July 1, 1865.
Hartley, Thomas	"	19	9-12-1862	3 yrs.	Appointed —; mustered out with company July 1, 1865.
Conkle, William	"	27	9-12-1862	3 yrs.	Appointed —; mustered out with company July 1, 1865.
Nelson, Urias	Farrier	27	9-12-1862	3 yrs.	Appointed Nov. 8, 1862; mustered out with company July 1, 1865.
Vonschrelly, Daniel	"	36	9-12-1862	3 yrs.	Appointed Nov. 8, 1862; mustered out with company July 1, 1865.
Fountain, Lorenzo	Saddler	18	9-12-1862	3 yrs.	Mustered out with company July 1, 1865.
Morris, John	Wagoner	18	9-12-1862	3 yrs.	Mustered out with company July 1, 1865.
Burns, William	"	29	9-12-1862	3 yrs.	Appointed Nov. 8, 1862.
Andrews, Elisha	Private	23	9-12-1862	3 yrs.	Mustered out with company July 1, 1865.
Andrews, Robert	"	27	9-12-1862	3 yrs.	Mustered out with company July 1, 1865.
Babel, John	"	30	9-12-1862	3 yrs.	Discharged May 8, 1865, on Surgeon's certificate of disability.
Bahr, Abraham	"	18	9-12-1862	3 yrs.	Mustered out with company July 1, 1865.
Baily, James	"	18	9-12-1862	3 yrs.	. . .
Barton, James	"	21	9-12-1862	3 yrs.	Discharged Dec. 16, 1864, on Surgeon's certificate of disability.
Batchel, Peter	"	25	9-12-1862	3 yrs.	Mustered out with company July 1, 1865.
Brown, John	Private	35	9-12-1862	3 yrs.	Mustered out with company July 1, 1865.
Campbell, Alba	"	27	9-12-1862	3 yrs.	Mustered out with company July 1, 1865.
Chapder, Robert	"	18	9-12-1862	3 yrs.	Captured Nov. 12, 1863, at Rogersville, Tenn.; mustered out to date July 1, 1865, by order of War Department.

APPENDIX D

Name	Rank	Age	Date of Entering the Service	Period of Service	Remarks
Clark, Allen	Private	18	9-12-1862	3 yrs.	Mustered out with company July 1, 1865.
Colter, Warren	"	26	9-12-1862	3 yrs.	Died Jan. 2, 1864, at Knoxville, Tenn.
Cooper, William	"	24	9-12-1862	3 yrs.	. . .
Curtis, William	"	26	9-12-1862	3 yrs.	Captured Aug. 11, 1864, near Atlanta, Ga.; discharged May 12, 1865, on Surgeon's certificate of disability.
Deans, Andrew	"	18	9-12-1862	3 yrs.	Mustered out with company July 1, 1865.
Dillworth, Wesley	"	26	9-12-1862	3 yrs.	. . .
Dyke, Amos	"	28	9-12-1862	3 yrs.	Captured Aug. 11, 1864, near Atlanta, Ga.; mustered out June 20, 1865, at Camp Chase, Ohio, by order of War Department.
Elshire, James	"	28	9-12-1862	3 yrs.	Mustered out with company July 1, 1865.
Entsminger, Asher	"	18	9-12-1862	3 yrs.	Mustered out with company July 1, 1865.
Folden, William	"	18	10-21-1864	1 yr.	Accidentally wounded Dec. 15, 1864; mustered out with company July 1, 1865.
Foose, John	"	24	9-12-1862	3 yrs.	Captured Nov. 6, 1863, at Rogersville, Tenn.; mustered out with company July 1, 1865.
Fugate, Marion	"	24	9-12-1862	3 yrs.	Died June 6, 1863, at Stanford, Ky.
Garlow, Adam	"	22	10-4-1862	3 yrs.	Mustered out with company July 1, 1865.
Haley, James	"	35	9-12-1862	3 yrs.	Transferred to Veteran Reserve Corps Dec. 3, 1864; discharged from same Feb. 19, 1865, on Surgeon's certificate of disability.
Halliday, William	"	24	9-12-1862	3 yrs.	Mustered out with company July 1, 1865.
Harper, Duston	"	18	9-12-1862	3 yrs.	Captured Nov. 6, 1863, at Rogersville, Tenn.; died May 17, 1864, at Andersonville, Ga.

Official Roster, Company K, Seventh Ohio Volunteer Cavalry

Name	Rank	Age	Date of Entering the Service	Period of Service	Remarks
Harper, Temple	Private	43	9-12-1862	3 yrs.	Mustered out with company July 1, 1865.
Hartley, William	"	24	9-12-1862	3 yrs.	. . .
Hetzer, Columbus	"	30	9-12-1862	3 yrs.	Mustered out with company July 1, 1865.
Hoyt, Royall	"	18	9-12-1862	3 yrs.	Captured Nov. 6, 1863, at Rogersville, Tenn.; died Sep. 18, 1864, at Andersonville, Ga.
Jenkins, Morgan	"	18	9-12-1862	3 yrs.	Mustered out with company July 1, 1865.
Johnson, Joseph	"	24	9-12-1862	3 yrs.	Mustered out with company July 1, 1865.
Johnson, William	"	21	9-12-1862	3 yrs.	Captured Nov. 6, 1863, at Rogersville, Tenn.; mustered out with company July 1, 1865.
Jones, John	"	18	9-12-1862	3 yrs.	Mustered out with company July 1, 1865.
Jordan, Elijah	"	24	9-12-1862	3 yrs.	Accidentally wounded Aug. 22, 1864; mustered out May 3, 1865, at Camp Dennison, Ohio, by order of War Department.
Lewellyn, Samuel	"	43	9-12-1862	3 yrs.	Transferred to Veteran Reserve Corps, from which discharged May 24, 1865, on Surgeon's certificate of disability.
Lewellyn, Watkins	"	19	9-12-1862	3 yrs.	Mustered out with company July 1, 1865.
Lewis, Charles	"	18	9-12-1862	3 yrs.	Mustered out with company July 1, 1865.
McBride, Andrew	"	22	9-12-1862	3 yrs.	Mustered out with company July 1, 1865.
McCasky, Joseph	"	22	9-12-1862	3 yrs.	. . .
McMaster, Joshua	"	22	9-12-1862	3 yrs.	Mustered out with company July 1, 1865.
Meaner, Isaac	"	34	9-12-1862	3 yrs.	Died May 30, 1863, at Stanford, Ky.
Myers, Jonas	"	21	9-12-1862	3 yrs.	. . .
Midkiff, Evan	"	33	9-12-1862	3 yrs.	Mustered out with company July 1, 1865.

APPENDIX D

Name	Rank	Age	Date of Entering the Service	Period of Service	Remarks
Miller, William	Private	18	9-12-1862	3 yrs.	Mustered out with company July 1, 1865.
Morgan, David	"	25	9-12-1862	3 yrs.	Mustered out with company July 1, 1865.
Nelson, Edward	"	...	10-10-1862	3 yrs.	Discharged Dec. 1, 1862, on Surgeon's certificate of disability.
Nelson, Isaac	"	21	12-1-1862	3 yrs.	Never mustered into service; captured Nov. 6, 1863, at Rogersville, Tenn.; died April 1, 1864, in prison at Richmond, Va.
Nelson, Martin	"	...	9-12-1862	3 yrs.	Mustered out with company July 1, 1865.
Nelson, Wesley	"	31	9-12-1862	3 yrs.	Mustered out with company July 1, 1865.
Oty, John	"	28	9-12-1862	3 yrs.	Mustered out with company July 1, 1865.
Piles, Charles	"	24	9-12-1862	3 yrs.	Mustered out with company July 1, 1865.
Rannells, John	"	21	9-12-1862	3 yrs.	Mustered out with company July 1, 1865.
Rathburn, Elijah	"	18	10-21-1864	1 yr.	Mustered out with company July 1, 1865.
Rawlings, Richard	"	18	9-12-1862	3 yrs.	Mustered out June 1, 1865, at Louisville, Ky., by order of War Department.
Robison, John	"	21	9-12-1862	3 yrs.	Mustered out with company July 1, 1865.
Rumfield, Hiram	"	18	9-12-1862	3 yrs.	Mustered out with company July 1, 1865.
Rupe, William	"	19	9-12-1862	3 yrs.	Mustered out June 1, 1865, at Louisville, Ky., by order of War Department.
Sausbury, Franklin	"	26	9-12-1862	3 yrs.	Mustered out with company July 1, 1865.
Savage, Benjamin	"	29	9-12-1862	3 yrs.	Mustered out with company July 1, 1865.
Scott, Ezekiel	"	21	9-12-1862	3 yrs.	Mustered out with company July 1, 1865.
Shiner, Henry	"	24	9-12-1862	3 yrs.	Captured Nov. 6, 1863, at Rogersville, Tenn.; died Feb. 23, 1864, at Richmond, Va.

Official Roster, Company K, Seventh Ohio Volunteer Cavalry

Name	Rank	Age	Date of Entering the Service	Period of Service	Remarks
Shiner, Silvester	Private	27	9-12-1862	3 yrs.	Mustered out with company July 1, 1865.
Sisson, Levi	"	24	9-12-1862	3 yrs.	Mustered out with company July 1, 1865.
Sisson, John	"	18	9-12-1862	3 yrs.	Died March 7, 1863, at Harrodsburg, Ky.
Smart, William	"	20	9-12-1862	3 yrs.	Mustered out with company July 1, 1865.
Smith, James	"	22	9-12-1862	3 yrs.	Mustered out with company July 1, 1865.
Spiers, George	Private	29	9-12-1862	3 yrs.	Discharged May 24, 1864, on Surgeon's certificate of disability.
Spiers, William	"	22	9-12-1862	3 yrs.	Mustered out with company July 1, 1865.
Stobart, James	"	21	9-12-1862	3 yrs.	Captured Aug. 1, 1864, near Atlanta, Ga.; confined in Andersonville Prison, from which he enlisted in 10th Regiment East Tennessee Confederate Infantry; captured by Union forces Dec. 28, 1864, at Egypt Station, Mississippi; confined in Alton, Ill., Military Prison, until June 27, 1865, on which date he took oath of allegiance to the United States Government.
Thompson, Joseph	"	38	9-12-1862	3 yrs.	. . .
Walker, William	"	18	9-12-1862	3 yrs.	Returned to duty May 10, 1864, from Brown General Hospital, Louisville, Ky.; no final record found.
Watkins, Francis	"	19	9-12-1862	3 yrs.	Mustered out with company July 1, 1865.
Wells, Everett	"	18	9-12-1862	3 yrs.	Mustered out with company July 1, 1865.
Williams, Orrellence	"	22	9-12-1862	3 yrs.	Captured Nov. 6, 1863, at Rogersville, Tenn.; died Nov. 2, 1864, in Andersonville Prison, Ga.
Wilson, Burrell	"	18	9-12-1862	3 yrs.	Mustered out with company July 1, 1865.

Wiseman, Zachariah	"	41	9-12-1862	3 yrs.	Died April 20, 1863, at Lexington, Ky.
Wright, Guyan	"	18	9-12-1862	3 yrs.	Mustered out with company July 1, 1865.

Source: Roster Commission 1891.

Appendix E
William McKnight's Poem to Samaria, April 4, 1852

to Semary, April 4th, 1852

1

    Semary dear i lov you
    i love you as my life
    and with my heart and hand
    i would make you my wife

2

    But unto the ob jections
    my mother she does make
    our vows and our promises
    i fear they will break

3

    But my dear i love you
    I love you just as well
    i love to kiss those sugar lips
    That to me stories tell

4

    I know you think the time is long
    since I have been to see
    but often when I am alone
    I often think of thee

5

    Often how often I have kisst
    as often you have kisst me

but soon I think that time will come
when you and ile be free

6

I made this made this little rime myself
i hope you will accept it
i stole a little time away
where no one did expect

7

I am sorry that I cannot come
and see you as I might
but live in hopes my dearest dear
so I bid you a good night

William McKnight
your sincere lover

Notes

Preface

1. Matt Hauger is William McKnight's great-great-great-grandson.
2. Ruth Hayth is William McKnight's great-great-granddaughter.

Acknowledgments

1. Susan Hayes and Mary Johnston are both William McKnight's great-great-granddaughters, and Lois Mohler is a great-great-great-granddaughter to McKnight.

Introduction

1. Historian Chandra Manning in *What This Cruel War Was Over* (2007, 9) contends, "Civil War soldiers' letters and diaries offer unparalleled insight into the thoughts of ordinary Americans during a defining time in the nation's history."
2. Linderman 1987, 94. "Letters from home have been [of] crucial importance in sustaining morale in all literate armies" (McPherson 1997, 133).
3. Carroll 2001, 22; Woodworth 1996, 60.
4. Linderman 1987, 94.
5. Woodworth 1996, 60.
6. Gallagher et al. 2003, 149.
7. Linderman 1987, 7.
8. War letters "passed between those on the front lines and the loved ones back home have often provided the clearest views of armed conflict. Whether scribbled in a foxhole or composed at a kitchen counter, each serves as a reminder of the mark war leaves on every human swept into its path" (Carroll 2005, 78).
9. Early in the war, McKnight's letters were written on quality stationery and stamped with Union emblems. As the war continued, paper became scarce, as evidenced by the fact that McKnight often wrote on all the available space. On one occasion, McKnight wrote to Samaria on the back of orders he received from Captain Santmyer. Another letter was written on a sheet from an East Tennessee and Virginia Railroad ledger book.

10. Civil War letters, including McKnight's, were not censored; as a result, they are "extraordinarily candid and revealing about every facet of a soldier's life, from his opinion of officers and of political leaders to the boredom of life in the winter quarters and the terror of battle" (Burgess 1995, xi).

11. In addition to the letters, the McKnight collection contains three diaries written between 1863 and 1864. While the letters are in good condition, the diaries, which are in Ruth Hayth's possession, are not in good condition, and large portions are illegible.

12. William McKnight to Samaria McKnight, November 18, 1862.

13. William McKnight to Samaria McKnight, November 26, 1862.

14. William McKnight to Samaria McKnight, June 5, 1864.

15. Carroll 2005, 84.

16. William McKnight to Samaria McKnight, January 9, 1863.

17. William McKnight to Samaria McKnight, January 12, 1863.

18. Thomas McKnight to William McKnight, 1864.

19. Some soldiers were "motivated by a sense of duty and honor bound together in their understanding of manhood. Many volunteered for ideological reasons, leaving their homes to defend the Union, liberty, and their revolutionary inheritance" (Dee 2006, 94).

20. William McKnight to Samaria McKnight, November 14, 1862; William McKnight to Samaria McKnight, December 15, 1862.

21. William McKnight to Samaria McKnight, March 24, 1863.

22. William McKnight to Samaria McKnight, March 9, 1864.

23. "After the war, federal officials estimated that more than eighteen thousand Ohio soldiers deserted from the army—a figure that seems to underestimate the actual number of deserters" (Dee 2006, 129). Desertions from the Ohio army "averaged 44 men to each thousand, much lower than in some other states, Connecticut, for example, where the rate of desertion was 117 per thousand" (Harper 1961b, 10).

24. William McKnight to Samaria McKnight, January 24, 1863.

25. William McKnight to Samaria McKnight, March 24, 1863.

26. Linderman 1987, 102. Ohio troops "infused a religious zeal into the contest. They held their soldiers to be soldiers in a holy war; they truly believed that through battle, and siege, and reverse, God was waiting, in His own time, to give them the victory" (Reid 1895a, 15). Northern soldiers may have become more religious during the war (Sheehan-Dean 2007).

27. William McKnight to Samaria McKnight, May 2, 1863.

28. William McKnight to Samaria McKnight, May 4, 1863.

29. William McKnight to Samaria McKnight, May 7, 1863; William McKnight to Samaria McKnight, June 2, 1863.

30. William McKnight to Samaria McKnight, June 15, 1863; William McKnight to Samaria McKnight, March 18, 1864.

31. "Meeting of the Military Service," an article in the *Pomeroy Weekly Telegraph* on November 1, 1861, states that Joel P. Higley was a member of the Rutland Township committee to organize troops.

32. William McKnight to Samaria McKnight, March 28, 1864.

33. William McKnight to Samaria McKnight, January 12, 1863.

34. William McKnight to Samaria McKnight, May 15, 1863.

35. Higley and McKnight were both from Rutland Township in Meigs County (United States Bureau of the Census 1864).

36. Roster Commission 1891.

37. William McKnight to Samaria McKnight, October 21, 1863.

38. Rankin 1881, 10.

39. Entry dated October 10, 1863.

40. William McKnight to Samaria McKnight, March 28, 1864.

41. McClintock 1996, 464. Since the Colonial era, local, state, and federal authorities had supported widows and children who had lost "their male breadwinners as a result of military service" (ibid., 458). In July 1862, the "federal government expanded the scope of who qualified for benefits and increased the compensation rates. This was due in part to high casualty rates, diminishing support for the war, and the sheer number of troops involved" (ibid.). Following the war, many pension acts were politically motivated. Several bills appealed to the "soldier vote," and members of Congress were concerned with "finding solutions to the problems of widowhood and old-age dependency in order to guarantee the enlistment of future citizen soldiers" (ibid., 465).

42. Ibid., 458.

43. Samaria McKnight, widow's application for an increase of pension, 1873; certificate of increase of widows' pension, no. 60875, dated 1874, issued in Columbus, Ohio.

44. Connors and Dickson 2005; Hayth, unpublished "McKnight Family Ancestor Chart," 2005.

45. Hayth, unpublished "McKnight Family Ancestor Chart," 2005.

46. Cynthia Braley died on March 6, 1848, and Ruel Braley soon remarried, marrying Jane Entsminger, on May 25, 1848. Like his first wife, Jane Entsminger was born in Rutland, Ohio. Born in 1825, she died on August 21, 1889. Ruel and Jane Braley had eight children, giving him a total of seventeen. Samaria's eight siblings and eight half-siblings are as follows: James (b. December 10, 1828); Emarillia (b. November 22, 1831); Alexander (b. January 17, 1834); Ellanor (b. January 17, 1834); Emma Jane (b. September 9, 1836); Hartwell (b. May 27, 1840); Reuel (b. May 24, 1842); Sarapta (b. December 10, 1843);

Mary (b. April 4, 1849); Horton (b. March 4, 1851); Rosetta (b. January 24, 1853); Addison (b. June 19, 1855); Lawrence (b. March 12, 1857); Reuel Nash (b. April 12, 1859); Nathan (b. January 17, 1861); and McClellan (b. October 8, 1863). Susan Hayes, "Braley Genealogy: The Descendants of Roger Braley," unpublished document, 2009.

47. Edwards 1987, 88.
48. Samaria McKnight, widow's application for an increase of pension, 1873.
49. William McKnight to Samaria McKnight, July 11, 1863.
50. Ibid.
51. Holcomb 2004.
52. United States Bureau of the Census 1864.
53. Dee 2006.
54. Coles 1962, 3; Starr 1961, 168.
55. Dee 2006; Harper 1961b; Klement 1977.
56. Coles 1962, 15.
57. Dee 2006, 55.
58. Ibid.
59. Murdock 1963, 4.
60. Downer 1961; Reid 1895b has the number drafted at 8,750.
61. Murdock 1963, 4.
62. Of Ohio's contribution to the war, 35,475 lost their lives—nearly 11.3 percent (Dyer 1959a). Ohio troops constituted over 10 percent of the Union men killed in action, and nearly 30,000 more "came out of the war experience totally or partially disabled" (Downer 1961, 23).
63. Wheeler 1998, vii; Harper 1961b, 9.
64. Harper 1961b, 53–57. See Keifer 2004 for the number of Ohioans who achieved the rank of general (p. 229).
65. Harper 1961b, 52.
66. Downer 1961, 5.
67. Reid 1895a, 16.
68. Jones 1962; Weisenburger 1963.
69. Harding 1967; Tucker 1962; United States Bureau of the Census 1864.
70. Becker 1964, 6.
71. Ibid., 18.
72. Ibid., 22.
73. Rankin 1881, 1.
74. Roster Commission 1891; most Union cavalry units "had about 1,200 men" (Nofi 1992, 173).
75. Roster Commission 1891; Rankin 1881.
76. Nofi 1992, 172.
77. Roster Commission 1891.

78. The Seventh lost twenty-six men in the Sultana disaster in late April 1865. The overloaded steamer was taking former prisoners of war back home and exploded just north of Memphis, Tennessee, killing and wounding hundreds of passengers (Elliott 1962).

79. William McKnight to Samaria McKnight, March 29, 1863.

80. William McKnight to Samaria McKnight, April 4, 1863.

81. William McKnight to Samaria McKnight, September 14, 1863.

82. William McKnight to Samaria McKnight, April 4, 1863.

83. William McKnight to Samaria McKnight and family, January 1, 1863.

84. Meigs County was "known before 1787 as a part of the Northwest Territory," and "it became a part of the Ohio Company's lands when that association bought its immense Ohio tract from the general government. . . . The Meigs County land is a part of what was the Ohio Company's first purchase" (Lewis 1928, 558).

85. Howe 1908, 2:213.

86. United States Bureau of the Census 1864.

87. Ervin 1949, 170.

88. Ibid.

89. Ibid., 171.

90. Reid 1895a, 77.

91. Ervin 1949, 195.

92. Ashley 1987.

93. Gallagher et al. 2003, 80. "In both armies, eighteen-year-olds constituted the single largest age group the first year of the war" (Linderman 1987, 26).

94. Roster Commission 1891.

95 Horwitz 2001, 197.

96. Rankin 1881, 16. Henry Damon offered a Confederate veteran's perspective on Cynthiana: "19th of June, 1864, I became an inmate of Rock Island prison, having been captured June 12th, at Cynthiana, in the last battle fought by Morgan on Kentucky soil. . . . We were so completely outnumbered, that it was hardly a battle. The enemy approached us in front, and flanked us right and left. In a few minutes the fight became a rout, and our men were flying in every direction" (Damon 1990, 395).

97. *War of the Rebellion: A Compilation of the Official Records of the Union and Confederate Armies (OR),* series 1, vol. 39, part 1, p. 20. Hereafter cited as OR.

98. Rankin 1881, 16. Israel Garrard noted in the official record (OR, series 1, vol. 39, part 1, p. 47) that "during the chase Lieutenant McKnight, Company K, Seventh Ohio Volunteer Cavalry, a brave and experienced officer, was mortally wounded."

99. William Hartley to Samaria McKnight, June 14, 1864.

100. Samaria McKnight, widow's application for an increase of pension, 1873.

101. Bowles 1933.
102. Ibid.
103. Hoeflich 1972. Donna Tuckerman Russell was William's great-granddaughter; her grandmother was Martha McKnight Tuckerman—one of the twins born on July 4, 1863 (Hayth 2005).
104. Lewis 1928, 585.
105. Ibid., 586.
106. Horwitz 2001, 197.
107. Ibid..
108. October 2003 interviews with Mary Johnston and Ruth Hayth.
109. Hayth 1987, 331.
110. Johnston 2001, 117.
111. William McKnight to Samaria McKnight, July 11, 1863.
112. William McKnight to Samaria McKnight, August 4, 1863.
112. Thomas 1985, 99.
114. The official records (OR, series 1, vol. 39, part 1, p. 27) indicate that both President Abraham Lincoln and Secretary of War Edwin Stanton issued brief congratulations to those who fought at Cynthiana. President Lincoln on June 14, 1864, wrote the following to Brigadier-General Burbridge: "Have just received your dispatch of action at Cynthiana. Please accept my congratulations and thanks for yourself and command." Stanton added, "Please accept for your gallant command the thanks of this Department for the brave and successful operations of the last six days in Kentucky, achievements of valor, energy, and success that will be regarded with admiration by all loyal people of the United States."
115. William McKnight to Samaria McKnight, May 10, 1864.

Chapter 1: Preparing for War (September 1862–January 1, 1863)

1. This letter was undated; however, it was written prior to the company's muster date of September 12, 1862.
2. Athens, Ohio, is the seat of government for Athens County and just north of Meigs County (Hammond 1993).
3. Ripley, Ohio, sits on the Ohio River in southern Brown County (Hammond 1993). "Although a northern city by geography, Cincinnati was a border community and felt the tug and pull of both contending forces" (Tucker 1962, 4).
4. Company K was mustered in by Captain C. O. Howard at Camp Pomeroy, Ohio, and was ultimately mustered out of service with the company by Captain James Neill in Nashville, Tennessee, on July 1, 1865 (Roster Commission 1891). McKnight's military papers identify C. O. Howard as the mustering agent.
5. Second Lieutenant Thomas Brunker was also from Meigs County, Ohio. Brunker mustered in on September 3, 1862, and resigned on June 23, 1863.

McKnight also mentions Brunker's resignation; McKnight ultimately serves Company K as second lieutenant after Brunker's departure (Roster Commission 1891). The McKnight collection also contains two short letters from Thomas Brunker to Samaria in regard to a debt from December 1863.

6. William Rosecrans, who later became a major general, selected the site for Camp Dennison near the Little Miami River just north of Cincinnati (Starr 1961). Camp Dennison, "the Union's largest military hospital in Ohio during the war[,] . . . was originally organized at the request of Governor William Dennison[,] who served in that office from January 9, 1860 to January 13, 1862" (Horwitz 2001, 127).

7. Gallipolis is the seat of government for Gallia County in southeastern Ohio (Hammond 1993). Gallipolis played a pivotal role in the war because of its location on the Ohio River near the mouth of the Kanawha River (Harper 1961a). It served as a base of operations; thousands of Ohio troops—and many more from what would become West Virginia—came through Gallipolis along with a variety of war supplies.

8. McKnight is likely speaking of the Kanawha River (in West Virginia), which empties into the Ohio River just north of Gallipolis, Ohio.

9. Mary Lee Marchi, the director of the Gallia County, Ohio, Historical Society, stated in correspondence with the authors (dated January 24, 2006) that "one of the first sights that visitors to Gallipolis would see in the first half of the 19th century was the two-story American House Hotel that stood on the river side of the First and Court corner. The hotel was built in 1816 for Claudius Menager, who had operated a tavern on that spot as early as 1800." Throughout the early 1800s, the hotel changed hands and names on numerous occasions; by the 1850s, the "name had been changed back to the American House" (Marchi pers. comm. 2006).

10. Rutland is located in Meigs County, Ohio (Hammond 1993). Pomeroy, Ohio, is the seat of government for Meigs County and is located on the Ohio River not far from McKnight's hometown of Langsville (Hammond 1993).

11. McKnight never writes about slavery or slaves and only uses the term *Negro* twice: in this letter and again on May 4, 1863. See Wesley 1962 for a detailed account of African Americans in Ohio during the war. John Geyer was Company K's first lieutenant, mustering in on September 3, 1862, and leaving with a certificate of disability on August 27, 1863 (Roster Commission 1891).

12. Both Union and Confederate cavalry units used a tremendous number of horses. During the war, "about 284,000 horses were furnished to never more than 60,000 [Union] men in the field, which was an average of almost five horses per man" (Herr and Wallace 1953, 118–19).

13. Piketon is in Pike County, Ohio (Hammond 1993).

14. Locust Grove is in Adams County, Ohio (Hammond 1993).

15. Middleport is just south of Pomeroy in Meigs County on the Ohio River (Hammond 1993).

16. The "Harry Spires" McKnight mentions is most likely William H. Spiers, who mustered in as a private in Company K on September 12, 1862 (Roster Commission 1891).

17. Centerville is in western Gallia County, Ohio. Jackson is the seat of government for Jackson County, Ohio (Hammond 1993).

18. McKnight frequently uses "inst" in his letters. *Inst* is a Latin abbreviation (*instante mense*) that means "this month."

19. McKnight frequently refers to "Theop" or "Theops" in his letters. Theops is most likely Theopolis Wilson, who served as a blacksmith apprentice under McKnight and is listed in the 1860 census as part of the McKnight household (National Archives and Records Service 1963a). Private Theopolis J. Wilson joined Company A of the Eighteenth Regiment of Ohio Infantry on September 25, 1861, and was later transferred to Company D (Roster Commission 1886a).

20. "[A] soldier's day started with the sound of bugle and drum" (Coggins 1983, 20).

21. S. M. Grannis originally published "Do They Miss Me at Home?" in 1852, and the tune was popular during the Civil War. The North and South each had its own variation. The South's version—written by J. W. Naff, a member of the Third Louisiana Regiment—was titled "Do They Miss Me in the Trenches?" Grannis's version follows:

Do they miss me at home do they miss me
Twould be an assurance most dear
To know at this moment some loved one
Were saying I wish he were here
To feel that the group at the fireside
Were thinking of me as I roam
O yes twould be joy beyond measure
To know that they miss me at home

22. Patrick McCann was appointed Company K's sergeant on November 8, 1862, and was mustered out with the company on July 1, 1865 (Roster Commission 1891).

23. Lexington, in north-central Kentucky, is the seat of government for Fayette County (Hammond 1993).

24. The 1860 Meigs County census records contain a listing of William Sanders, son of M. and Ann Sanders, age sixteen at the time (National Archives and Records Service 1963a).

25. Private Marion Rathburn joined Company I of the Seventh on September 18, 1862, and died at Lexington, Kentucky, on April 12, 1863 (Roster

Commission 1891). As a second lieutenant, McKnight received $105.50 per month (Nofi 1992, 381).

26. McKnight's blacksmith shop was located in Langsville, Ohio (National Archives and Records Service 1963a).

27. Maysville, on the Ohio River in northern Kentucky, is the Mason County seat of government (Hammond 1993).

28. This letter should be dated New Year's Day 1863, not 1862.

29. Joseph McCasky and Jonas Myers both joined Company K on September 12, 1862 (Roster Commission 1891).

30. See Coggins 1983 for a complete description of Civil War tents.

Chapter 2: Life as a Soldier and Divided Kentucky (January 8, 1863–July 8, 1863)

1. Harrison and Klotter 1997, 187.
2. Ibid., 190.
3. Ibid.
4. "Nearly 80,000 Kentuckians fought in the Union armies—more than three times the number of Kentuckians who took up arms for the Confederacy" (Brown 2000, ii).
5. Prichard 1981, 119. In the years just prior to the war, "Kentucky had changed from a Southern to a border state. Twelve railroads connected Kentucky to the North, two to the South, altering older patterns of river trade. Patterns of immigration had changed Kentucky from a largely homogeneous Southern state to one of mixed population" (Simon 2000, 5).
6. Harrison and Klotter 1997, 182. These divisions were not confined to Kentucky's leading families: "family ties were rent asunder; father against son, and brother against brother. When they passed on the streets men looked askance at each other and said little" (Coleman 1968, 1).
7. Camp Ella Bishop, located in Lexington, was named after a young woman of the area. See Coleman 1968 (p. 31) for a detailed discussion of the naming of the camp: the "raiders lost no time in tearing down the Fitch [Union] flag and, after walking over it, proceeded to drag it through the streets of the city. The desecration of the Union flag by the Confederate raiders so infuriated Miss Ella Bishop, a young lady of seventeen, that she rushed after the soldiers, wrestled the flag from them and, wrapping it around her body, made off with it, saying 'she would give it up only with her life.' Shortly afterwards Brigadier-General G. Clay Smith arrived in town with several companies of Union troops and made his headquarters at the camp, which was named Camp Ella Bishop in honor of the courageous Lexington girl."
8. Eagle Creek flows into the Kentucky River near the convergence of Carroll, Henry, and Owen counties, Kentucky (DeLorme 2005).

9. Aberdeen is in Adams County in south-central Ohio, adjacent to the Ohio River (Hammond 1993).

10. "Many soldiers awaited their first battle impatiently; they felt eager to prove their courage and to defeat the enemy"; indeed, to "judge from their correspondence early in the war, most soldiers were 'spoiling for a fight'" (Mitchell 1988, 75).

11. Washington is in present-day Mason County, Kentucky (Hammond 1993).

12. Mays Lick is also in Mason County, Kentucky (Hammond 1993).

13. Coleman (1968, 11) describes a similar situation in which two men were wounded "as they passed one of the camps in a buggy shouting: 'Hooray for Jeff Davis.'" Jefferson Davis was president of the Confederate States of America; according to Faust (1986, 200), "few in the South truly loved him, but many revered the man who made himself the symbol of the lost cause, remaining proud, defiant and unrepentant to the end."

14. McKnight uses "Sesesh" interchangeably with "Confederates" and "Rebels."

15. Many soldiers cited "'duty' as having prompted them to enlist and 'honor' as having held them to soldiering through their terms of enlistment" (Linderman 1987, 16).

16. General Robert S. Granger, originally from New York and a West Point graduate, was a Mexican War veteran. Granger commanded the "District of Central Kentucky, Department of Ohio" from November 17, 1862, through January 25, 1863 (Sifakis 1988, 159). Previously, Granger had "been captain of the Third U.S. Cavalry and colonel of the Second Michigan Cavalry" (Rowell 1971).

17. Captain David Miles mustered in to Company F of the Eighteenth Ohio Infantry on September 25, 1861, and mustered out on November 9, 1864 (Roster Commission 1886a).

18. Rankin 1881 and Reid 1895b both support McKnight's version of this battle. Rankin (1881, 3) wrote that "they captured many prisoners, with their equipments. The number captured during their stay, would more than equal the entire command under Capt. Rankin." Reid (1895b) observed that companies A, B, C, and D of the Seventh left Winchester, Kentucky, to join General Samuel P. Carter on what was later known as the first raid into eastern Tennessee. The excursion was successful; however, the exhausted troops lost approximately one-half of their horses and went without rations for a period of time.

19. A paternal relationship often existed between officers and soldiers: "one of the highest compliments a soldier could pay an officer was to say he was "'like a father' to his men" (Mitchell 1993, 52). Moreover, "perhaps the best way to understand small-unit cohesion is to think of the company as a substitute family" (ibid., 158).

20. Winchester, Kentucky, is due east of Lexington and is Clark County's seat of government (Hammond 1993). Danville, south of Lexington, is Boyle County's seat of government (ibid.).

21. McKnight rarely complains about food and on several occasions provides details on the quality and quantity of the rations. McKnight seems to contradict Gallagher and colleagues' (2003, 83) contention that "men on both sides complained bitterly about the quality and quantity of their rations. Foraging and packages of food from home helped supplement rations, but many men complained of hunger." However, Gallagher and colleagues (ibid.) concede that "Union soldiers tended to be somewhat better fed than their Confederate counterparts."

22. Captain Joel Higley is mentioned frequently in McKnight's letters. Higley, also from Meigs County, was from one of the most prominent families in the area. In 1860, Joel and his wife, Mary, had three children (Electa, age 10; Ranson, 8; and Samuel, 4). Higley's great-grandfather, also named Joel Higley, arrived in Meigs County in 1803 from Granby, Connecticut (Larkin 1982). Brewster Higley IV, also from Meigs County and a relative of Joel Higley's, began a medical practice in Pomeroy, Ohio, and later moved to Kansas; in 1872, he penned the words to "Home on the Range," which became the state song of Kansas in 1947.

23. Harrison and Klotter (1997, 120) describe Clay as one of the nation's leading political figures for three decades and state that "his ability to 'drink, carouse, swear and gamble with the best of them' endeared him to many persons"; however, they observe that "it alienated others, who saw a lack of character and sound judgment."

24. John Hunt Morgan was born in Alabama in 1825 and later moved with his family to Kentucky. Despite the fact that Kentucky remained neutral during the war, Morgan joined the Confederacy and ultimately achieved the rank of brigadier general. Morgan is most famous for his raid across Indiana and Ohio in July 1863, when he went against Braxton Bragg's instructions not to cross the Ohio River (Horwitz 2001). Similar to McKnight's death, the details of Morgan's demise remain contested. Horwitz (2001) offers three different versions of his death in September 1864 in Greeneville, Tennessee; Thomas (1985, 110) similarly concludes that "events surrounding the death of Morgan are confused." In April 1868, John Hunt Morgan's body was returned to Lexington, Kentucky, where he is buried in the Morgan family plot in the Lexington Cemetery.

25. "[To] suppress desertion the extreme penalty of death was at times applied, especially after 1863; but this meant no more than the selection of a few men as public examples out of many thousands equally guilty. The commoner method was to make public appeals to deserters, promising pardon in case of voluntary return with dire threats to those who failed to return" (Randall and Donald 1969, 330).

26. Duty and honor were strong callings, and soldiers often "volunteered not simply as individual Americans, but as representatives of their families" (Mitchell 1988, 17).

27. Three "Ben Rutherfords" are listed in the official rosters—Captain Ben Rutherford of the 195th Ohio Infantry, First Lieutenant Ben Rutherford of the 141st Ohio Infantry, and Second Lieutenant Ben Rutherford of the 18th Independent Battery, Ohio Light Artillery (Roster Commission 1889a; 1889b).

28. See Raitz et al. 2008 for a brief overview of early Kentucky turnpikes and trails, many of which were utilized in the Civil War.

29. Rankin (1881, 1) observed, in referring to one "Major Malcolm McDowell," that as "soon as recruiting was fairly under way, Major McDowell was retired and resumed his original duties as Paymaster."

30. Leslie Combs served in the War of 1812 and again in the 1830s in the war for Texas independence; he also served several terms in the Kentucky House of Representatives and was president of the Lexington-Danville Railroad. The previous clerk of the Kentucky Court of Appeals died, and the Democrats selected Clinton McClarty to run against the elderly Leslie Combs, who won by more than 23,000 votes. Combs, described as a "staunch Unionist," was "clerk of the state court of appeals" between 1860 and 1866 (Kleber 1992, 219).

31. This is a reference to Tecumseh and some of the events of the War of 1812. The Shawnees, led by Tecumseh, fought a mounted militia led by William Harrison, who was later elected president of the United States. Harrison's "mounted frontiersmen put on a charge that routed Tecumseh and his men. But the horsemen were again fighting with knives, as they did in the only mounted charge of the War of 1812, when Richard M. Johnson, later Vice-President of the United States, commanded a thousand Kentucky horsemen at the Battle of the Thames, between Lakes Erie and Huron" (Wormser 1966, 38). Tecumseh was killed in the battle, which "just about ended the land, or British-and-Indian phase of the war" (Wormser 1966, 39).

32. "Newly enlisted soldiers would speak of this first experience of battle ever after as having 'seen the elephant.' It was the half humorous way they described the shocking brutality of combat" (Bennett 2006, 346). See McPherson 1997 for several accounts of "seeing the elephant."

33. Henry Clay was born in Hanover County, Virginia, on April 12, 1777 (Van Deusen 1937). A three-time presidential candidate, Clay served several terms in both the U.S. House of Representatives and the U.S. Senate. Referred to as Kentucky's most famous senator, Clay is best known for his attempts to forge a compromise between the North and South on the issue of slavery, which resulted in the Compromise of 1850 (Remini 1991). Clay died on June 29, 1852, and was buried in present-day Lexington National Cemetery. The limestone monument, erected in 1857, is 120 feet tall and would have been a focal point for the community then as it is today.

34. Many of the buildings at "Transylvania University, the oldest college in the West . . . were forcibly seized by the Union authorities who converted the buildings into military prisons and hospitals" (Coleman 1968, 16). "Dr. Robert Peter, of Transylvania University" was the "senior surgeon in charge of all military hospitals in Lexington" (ibid., 19). By the end of 1862, the "hospitals of the city were filled with sick and wounded soldiers" (ibid., 33).

35. Franklin Sausbury was a member of Company K. Sausbury joined on September 12, 1862, and mustered out with the company on July 1, 1865 (Roster Commission 1891).

36. McKnight often provides a detailed description of the landscape, which supports Gallagher and colleagues' (2003, 81) statement that "once in the service, volunteers confronted a strange new world. Few had previously traveled far from home."

37. Leading Creek is a small stream in Meigs County, Ohio. Today, as in McKnight's time, the creek runs along Langville's south side, not far from where McKnight's blacksmith shop once stood (Meigs County Pioneer and Historical Society, Inc. 1982). "In 1863, [Leading Creek] was a deep and wide body of water with a dam and a mill beside it" (Horwitz 2001, 196).

38. Camp Dick Robinson was approximately fifteen miles south of Lexington, Kentucky (Daviess 1924). In August 1861, the *Lexington Observer and Reporter* "noted the establishment of a military camp on the Dick Robinson farm near the Dix River, scarcely more than twenty-five miles south of Lexington. The very presence of such a camp in the Bluegrass so near the city infuriated many Confederate sympathizers, including John Hunt Morgan" (Thomas 1985, 13).

39. According to a later newspaper account, Higley's Sugar Camp was owned by J. B. Higley, who was listed as a farmer and thirty-seven years old in the 1860 census. J. B. Higley was also from Rutland Township in Meigs County (National Archives and Records Service 1963a).

40. Springs as described by McKnight are typical of karst topography. The upland South is "dotted with numerous solution-depression features where the relatively soluble limestone has dissolved into shallow sinkholes. Surface waters flow only a short distance before entering one of the sinkholes" (Hudson 2002, 121).

41. Braxton Bragg, who was a general and military advisor to Jefferson Davis, was deemed an "able administrator" but a "mediocre (at best) army field commander" (Current 1993, 206). Woodworth (1995, iii) penned a stronger indictment: "Bragg is beyond controversy. Since disgruntled subordinates turned their considerable political and public relations influence on him less than six months after his accession to command of the Confederate Army of Tennessee, it has been an article of faith among students of the war that Bragg was a perfectly atrocious general in every way."

42. "Mrs. Entsminger" is Emma Jane Entsminger, Samaria's sister. Emma Entsminger is listed on pension records as being present at the birth of several of the McKnight children (Samaria McKnight, widow's application for an increase of pension, 1873).

43. Harrodsburg, Kentucky, is southwest of Lexington and is the seat of government for Mercer County (Hammond 1993).

44. Crab Orchard was the site of at least six skirmishes in 1862 and 1863 (Dyer 1959b).

45. Crab Orchard, Kentucky, is in Lincoln County, forty-five miles straight south of Lexington (Hammond 1993).

46. Israel Garrard was appointed colonel of the Seventh Ohio Volunteer Cavalry in September 1862. From the time of his appointment to the war's end, Garrard was "absent from the field but eight days, and then his command was in camp recruiting" (Reid 1895a, 943). Garrard was promoted to brigadier general on June 20, 1865, and mustered out with the regiment on July 4 of that year (Roster Commission 1891). Although born in Cincinnati, Garrard retired to Minnesota after the war.

47. "Yellow woman" is most likely a term referring to a former black or mulatto slave.

48. In his diary, McKnight notes on February 9, 1863, that they "had a fight with Clukes men near hazel Green on Reed River. Whiped the Rebs took 25 Prisoners & 30 horses & Equipment killed 2 Rebs."

49. "Mineral springs abound in Mercer and Boyle counties. There is scarcely a neighborhood or large farm that has not some medical spring.... Harrodsburg has a number of springs" (Daviess 1924, 6). Additionally, DeLorme's *Kentucky Atlas and Gazetteer* (2005) records a "White Sulphur Spring"; however, it is located in Caldwell County in western Kentucky.

50. Stanford is the seat of government for Lincoln County, Kentucky (Hammond 1993).

51. The Cumberland River flows in a similar fashion to the Tennessee River. With its headwaters in eastern Kentucky, the Cumberland flows southwest into Tennessee, past Nashville, where it turns northwest. The Cumberland is somewhat parallel to the Tennessee in western Kentucky and empties into the Ohio River in Livingston County just upstream from Paducah (Hammond 1993).

52. McKnight was referring to King Solomon, who describes the cedars of Lebanon in 1 Kings 4:33 (International Bible Society 1984).

53. "Disease claimed the lives of two soldiers for every one killed in action. ... Measles, mumps, whooping cough and chicken pox ravaged units in the early months of the war. Men from isolated rural backgrounds lacked the immunities of urban dwellers and suffered most cruelly" (Gallagher et al. 2003, 83). Linderman (1987, 115) agrees and adds that "Union battle deaths—those

killed in combat or mortally wounded—numbered 110,000, but twice as many, 224,580, died of disease, and in the Confederate forces the ratio must also have approximated two to one."

54. The Mammoth Cave system was known by early pioneers from the late 1700s and is today the longest known cave system in the world—more than 360 underground miles have been recorded (Tarbuck and Lutgens 1992).

55. Morgan Jenkins joined Company K on September 12, 1862, and mustered out with the company on July 1, 1865 (Roster Commission 1891).

56. "Many defenseless residents in Virginia's debatable land between the shifting armies would have been at the mercy of the roving bands of deserters, turned bushwhackers, who had been left in the wake of both armies" (Randall and Donald 1969, 517). Although "bushwhacking is usually a term for a backwoodsman in American folklore, it was applied to Confederate guerrillas, implying private plunder as well" (Boatner 1988, 109).

57. Nicholasville, Kentucky, is the seat of government for Jessamine County, which is adjacent to Fayette County and Lexington (Hammond 1993).

58. From February 18 through March 5, 1863, the Seventh was involved in "operations in Central Kentucky against Clukes forces" (Colonel Roy Cluke commanded the Eighth Kentucky Cavalry), which included a skirmish at Slate Creek near Mount Sterling (Dyer 1959b, 734). "About this time (late February 1863), the Rebel Col. Cluke invaded Eastern Kentucky, and the Seventh was ordered out to assist in driving him from the state" (Rankin 1881, 93).

59. Both the North and the South granted furloughs, and both "specified that furloughs be granted by a commander actually quartered with the soldiers' company or regiment. . . . Furlough papers warned the soldier to rejoin his unit by the date specified or be considered a deserter" (Faust 1986, 294).

60. Colonel Benjamin P. Runkle of the Forty-fifth Ohio Volunteer Infantry entered the service on June 1, 1861, and was discharged on July 21, 1864 (Roster Commission 1887a). The Forty-fifth Ohio was organized at Camp Chase, Ohio, on August 19, 1862, and mustered out on June 12, 1865 (Keifer 2004; Roster Commission 1887a).

61. McKnight is most likely speaking of Lieutenant Colonel George Miner. According to the official roster, Lieutenant Colonel Miner achieved that rank on September 18, 1862, and remained in the service after the war (Reid 1895b).

62. Richmond is the seat of government for Madison County, Kentucky (Hammond 1993).

63. Mount Vernon, Kentucky, is south of Richmond and is Rockcastle County's seat of government (Hammond 1993).

64. Bighill is located in extreme southeastern Madison County, Kentucky (DeLorme 2005); "several sharp skirmishes occurred in the area" (Cromie 1965, 103).

65. This is a reference to Colonel Leonidas Metcalfe of the Seventh Kentucky. Metcalfe's regiment was defeated by General Kirby Smith's force under Colonel John S. Scott at Bighill near Berea (Morsberger and Morsberger 1980). "[The] notorious Metcalfe came thundering down the road, crying 'Charge, and shoot down the rebels.' Metcalfe's federals, on a very dark night, had no idea that they were riding into a prepared line of battle. When the Confederates opened fire, the Union cavalry charge was instantly brought to a halt" (McDonough 1994, 128). By the "close of that memorable Saturday, August 30, 1862, the battle of Richmond had been fought, [and] the Confederates had achieved one of the most complete and decisive victories of the war" (Peter 1882, 459). Metcalfe's defeat essentially opened the way for the two-month Confederate occupation of Lexington and General Kirby Smith's arrival in the city "with bands playing and [Confederate] colors flying" (Peter 1882, 459).

66. *Historic Madison County and Richmond, Kentucky* does not list any seminaries in Richmond; however, there is a discussion of "The Madison Female Institute," which was located in Richmond (Dorris 1934, 29).

67. The Kentucky River's headwaters begin in southeastern Kentucky's Cumberland Plateau. The Kentucky River flows in a northwestern direction and joins the Ohio River midway between Louisville and Cincinnati (Hammond 1993).

68. Americans entered the Civil War "with no experience in dealing with large numbers of battle casualties and few examples to follow. While the Union medical department eventually built a well supplied, remarkably efficient ambulance corps, supported by the United States Sanitary Commission, the Confederate soldiers' plight grew more difficult with each year of the war" (Faust 1986, 9).

69. The Lincoln administration initially opposed prisoner exchanges on the grounds that Confederates were viewed as traitors. By July 1862, however, the overwhelming number of prisoners had changed attitudes and policies. For the next year (July 1862–July 1863), prisoners were exchanged or released based on terms agreed upon by the North and South. Northern leaders stopped the exchanges primarily for military reasons—the North held a substantially higher number of prisoners and felt that holding them instead of releasing them would speed the end of the war. In Ohio, "more than 36,000 prisoners were confined in Ohio military prisons in the Civil War" (Shriver and Breen 1964, 7). Most of these prisoners were held either at Camp Chase or on Johnson's Island. Camp Chase held approximately 26,000 prisoners between July 1861 and July 1865, with a "maximum of 9,045" on January 31, 1865 (ibid., 6). Johnson's Island, which was reserved primarily for Southern officers, contained just shy of 9,000 prisoners during the war, with a "high enrollment of 3,209 prisoners on December 31, 1864" (ibid.).

70. "[The] treatment of prisoners of war, under military jurisdiction in both North and South, seemed sure to harden enmity. More than 30,000 Federal

soldiers died in Confederate prisons or camps (a mortality rate of 15.5 percent) and almost 26,000 Southerners in Northern facilities (a 12 percent mortality)" (Linderman 1987, 236).

71. By 1863, "every horse soldier on either side was armed with a breech-loading carbine; the Union had issued them, and the Confederacy had captured its share. The carbine could fire faster than the infantry rifle, but it had a much shorter range of accuracy" (Wormser 1966, 198).

72. Both Union and Confederate forces possessed a variety of twelve-pound artillery pieces. However, McKnight uses the term *mountain howitzers*—light artillery pieces for easy transport used in rough terrain. "[The] average mountain artillery battery consisted of six howitzers," and the "evidence suggests that they were used by both combatants, primarily in the high country of the western theater and in western Virginia" (Miller 2001, 262). The "12-pounder mountain howitzer was a lightweight piece designed to be easily disassembled and transported on muleback. It could be reassembled and one round fired in one minute" (Coggins 1983, 75).

73. Hazel Green is southeast of Lexington in Wolfe County, Kentucky (Hammond 1993).

74. Campton, Kentucky, is Wolfe County's seat of government (Hammond 1993).

75. The Red River is just north of Campton and flows into the Kentucky River northeast of Richmond (DeLorme 2005).

76. At the beginning of the war, Ohio officials bought two thousand Enfield rifles and paid $22.50 for each (Coles 1962).

77. This is a reference to Captain Lester Moore of Company D of the Seventh (Roster Commission 1891).

78. McKnight uses the term *carbine*—a short rifle. The infantry rifle, or "long Enfield, was too unwieldy on horseback" (Wormser 1966, 272).

79. See Miller 2001 for a complete discussion of Enfield and Springfield weapons. According to Wormser (1966, 272), "Enfield and Springfield [rifles] at that time were still muzzle loaders." The "time taken to load through the muzzle, and to ram home the load with a rod kept a soldier cool. . . . Having gone through all that trouble, he was not going to shoot wildly, but to take his time, aim, and make every bullet count" (ibid.).

80. The Forty-fourth Ohio Volunteer Infantry served three years, first in West Virginia and later in Kentucky (Keifer 2004). The Fourteenth Kentucky Cavalry was organized at Mount Sterling, Kentucky, and mustered in on November 6, 1862; serving primarily in Kentucky, the unit lost eighty men during the war (Dyer 1959c).

81. The "principal incentive that volunteers shared was their love for the Union. To them, the Union meant both the ideals of liberty and democracy

that they believed unique to the United States, and the government that would uphold those ideals" (Mitchell 1993, 154).

82. Evans 1962 identifies two rail lines in this area—the Maysville and Lexington and the Louisville, Frankfort, and Lexington railroads.

83. Mount Sterling, Kentucky, is approximately thirty miles east of Lexington and is the seat of government for Montgomery County (Hammond 1993).

84. General Quincy Adams Gillmore commanded the First Kentucky Cavalry—the so-called Wild Riders. Q. A. Gillmore was a brigadier general in the "District of Central Kentucky" (Dyer 1959a, 528). Kentucky was "divided into three military districts," and the "Central [was] under Brigadier General Q.A. Gillmore, with headquarters at Lexington," for a time; General Gillmore, "who had applied for leave of absence after his defeat of Pegram, was relieved by General Willcox, and did not return to the Department" (Woodbury 1867, 264).

85. The official roster lists all of these men; therefore, none of them is likely to have actually deserted (Roster Commission 1891). They may left for a short time without permission and then returned to duty.

86. McKnight is describing part of the operations against General Pegram (Dyer 1959b).

87. McKnight never uses foul language. In this letter McKnight writes "d—d" instead of "damned," and on August 4, 1863, and December 26, 1863, McKnight replaces "hell" with "h—l."

88. McKnight misdated this letter—it should be 1863 instead of 1862.

89. Hundreds of prisoners were taken in the engagement at Dutton Hill, and the Rebels abandoned their "train and two hundred fifty beef cattle that [the Rebels were] attempting to drive South" (Reid 1895b, 798).

90. Sergeant William McMaster joined Company A of the Seventh on August 6, 1861, and mustered out on September 6, 1864 (Roster Commission 1891).

91. Vicksburg, in western Mississippi, is the seat of government for Warren County (Hammond 1993). During the war, controlling Vicksburg meant controlling the Mississippi River and much of the Mississippi Valley (Wormser 1966).

92. Murfreesboro, in central Tennessee, is Rutherford County's seat of government (Hammond 1993). The battle of Stone's River was fought near Murfreesboro from December 31, 1862, through January 2, 1863. In this battle, both "armies suffered high casualties. . . . Although the Union victory was not decisive, it gave a psychological boost to a war-weary North" (Current 1993, 1096).

93. McKnight apparently misdated this letter—it should be 1863 instead of 1862.

94. Somerset, in southern Kentucky, is the seat of government for Pulaski County (Hammond 1993). McKnight is referring to Colonel John Scott of the First Louisiana Cavalry. An earlier plan for the "Confederate invasion of

Kentucky in 1862" included Scott's cavalry (Rowell 1971, 73). "Colonel John S. Scott's First Louisiana Cavalry was the advance unit of Major General E. Kirby Smith's wing of Braxton Bragg's Confederate Army of Tennessee. Twenty thousand strong, Smith's army was marching toward Lexington from Knoxville. Once in Lexington, they could threaten Louisville and Cincinnati. General Bragg would soon march with a larger army from Chattanooga toward Louisville. The plan called for the armies to join for an attack on Louisville" (Rowell 1971, 83). See Wheeler 1991 for a discussion of Scott's activities in Kentucky. McKnight notes an "Ashbys Cavalry," which is a reference to Colonel H. M. Ashby of the Second Tennessee Cavalry (CSA).

95. Augustus Norton mustered in on December 28, 1862, and resigned his commission on January 30, 1864 (Reid 1895b). Rankin (1881, 4) also mentioned Norton's conduct in this battle: "In this fight [the battle of Dutton Hill, Kentucky] we captured four hundred prisoners and four pieces of artillery. The enemy fell back in great disorder. Among the trophies captured, the Seventh claims three battle flags; one being captured by Lieut. Copeland, who greatly distinguished himself on that occasion for coolness and bravery. Major Norton also deserves mention for the gallant style in which he led his battalion in the charge." McKnight makes reference to the Confederates as "Butternut Devils," noting in a later letter that they were "clothed generaly in Butternut." *Butternut* was also a derogatory term used to describe lower-class citizens. The "lower classes of the cities had their counterpart in the 'Butternut Democracy' of the rural regions, made up mainly of Southerners who crossed into Ohio, Indiana, Illinois, or Iowa to pre-empt the poorer soils of those states. Their homesteads were often below average in size and quality. They were often illiterate and uncultured, according to New England standards" (Klement 1960, 33). Butternuts have also been described as "pro-Confederate residents of southern Illinois, Indiana, and Ohio" who denounced the war and predicted that it was "bound to end in failure" (Woodworth 2005, 296).

96. McKnight correctly notes that the Seventh led the charge ordered by General Gillmore, who stated that at "this juncture I ordered Runkle on the left, and a portion of Garrard's Cavalry, in the center, under Major Norton, to storm the hill" (OR, series 1, vol. 23, part 1, pp. 169–70).

97. There were no military prisons in Jackson or Jackson County, Ohio, during the Civil War (Howe 1908). Most likely, prisoners were headed to Jackson to board a train destined for Camp Chase in Columbus. Camp Chase was Ohio's largest military camp and became the burial site for 2,134 Confederate prisoners (Harper 1961b). See Pickenpaugh 2007 and Sanders 2005 for detailed discussions of the Camp Chase military prison.

98. McKnight is most likely referring to the Big Sandy River in eastern Kentucky (Hammond 1993).

99. Colonel Frank Wolford commanded the First Kentucky Cavalry Volunteers. The First Kentucky Cavalry was organized at Liberty, Burkeville, and Monticello, Kentucky, during October 1861 and mustered out on September 20, 1865; the regiment lost a total of 344 men (Dyer 1959c).

100. Daviess (1924, 6), in discussing limestone and its use in central Kentucky, stated that "if Mercer and Boyle [counties] have not precious metals or coal; we have material of which kings' palaces might be built and furnished; and of commoner material an abundance to extend and keep up for ages, turnpikes, those indispensible fedders of railroads and the unvalued but invaluable tributaries to social intercourse, the crowning charm of life."

101. The 1860 and 1870 Meigs County census records list several Stanburys (National Archives and Records Service 1963a; 1963b).

102. McKnight mentions songs on several occasions. "Soldiers in both armies loved to sing," and "sentimental tunes exerted a powerful attraction for lonely men far from loved ones" (Gallagher et al. 2003, 82–83). The McKnight collection contained one song, titled "Jim Fisk." McKnight provides these words for the chorus: "Dont show any favor to friend or to foe, the beger or prince at his door, the big millionare you must hang up also, but never go back on the poor."

103. McKnight's niece Emma was the daughter of Elliot and Janett Braley.

104. The bugle was first used in the American Revolution; by the Civil War, it had become essential for military communication. "Boots and Saddles" was adopted in 1841 as the signal for cavalrymen to put on their riding boots and saddles. Additionally, much of what the cavalry did on a daily basis and in battle was dictated by different bugle calls (Wormser 1966).

105. The gap in the letters from mid-April to early May is explained by McKnight's diary, which chronicles his trip home from April 16, 1863, to May 2, 1863. McKnight's entry for April 16 states, "received leave of absence." On his return, McKnight notes on April 29 that he took the "steamer St. Patrick" from Pomeroy, Ohio, to Cincinnati on April 29–30 and finally arrived back in camp near Stanford, Kentucky, on May 2.

106. Zachariah Wiseman was from Meigs County, Ohio, and enlisted on September 12, 1862, at the age of forty-one. The official roster places his death near Lexington, Kentucky, on April 20, 1863 (Roster Commission 1891). Wiseman is buried at Camp Nelson National Cemetery just south of Lexington.

107. Cincinnati is on the Ohio River in southwestern Ohio, just across the river from Boone, Campbell, and Kenton counties, Kentucky (Hammond 1993). McKnight mentions his uncle John McKay on several occasions. McKay resided in Cincinnati, and McKnight usually stayed with him on the way home and back to his unit, often taking steamers up and down the Ohio River.

108. Monticello, located in southern Kentucky, is Wayne County's seat of government (Hammond 1993).

109. The official roster states that James Smith of Company L under Captain Leaper was "killed May 1, 1863 in action at Monticello, Kentucky" (Roster Commission 1891). However, Smith was not listed as a bugler for the company.

110. According to the census, William and Lenox McMaster were both from Meigs County, Ohio (National Archives and Records Service 1963a; 1963b).

111. McKnight is most likely referring to what Dee (2006, 76) calls the "negro question." Given Ohio's proximity to the South, many feared that free blacks would overrun the state. "Because they feared an exodus of former slaves into the state, white Ohioans visualized an Africanization of their race" (Jackson 1980, 250). Laborers "feared the possible competition of free Negro labor" (Becker 1961, 235); indeed, the *Cincinnati Enquirer* warned its readers that "slaves were going to swarm into Cincinnati and supplant white labor" (Harding 1967, 238).

112. John Foose joined Company K on September 12, 1862, and was captured on November 6, 1863, near Rogersville, Tennessee (Roster Commission 1891). Urias Nelson (1995, 27), who was Company K's farrier, commented, "I made inquiries at the Pomeroy reunion last fall in reference to comrade John Foose and was told that he was in Illinois preaching. I always thought that John would make a good clown but not a preacher."

113. Quartermaster Sergeant George Ross joined Company E of the Seventh on September 3, 1862. At his own request, he returned to the rank of private; he later mustered out on July 4, 1865 (Roster Commission 1891).

114. West Virginia did not become a state until June 20, 1863, "two years after Virginia, of which it had been part, seceded from the Union" (Hudson 2002, 106). "Slavery was uncommon in the Appalachian Plateau and the Ohio Valley, but the Ridge and Valley portion of West Virginia had many slave owners. The people living in the counties that were to become West Virginia were divided about 60–40 in favor of the Union at the time of statehood" (ibid.). "Western Virginians had long resented eastern Virginians' dominance in political affairs. When Virginia seceded, public opinion in the state's western counties favored the Union. . . . Unionism culminated in the proclamation of the state of West Virginia, composed of fifty counties, in May 1862. West Virginia was admitted to the Union as the thirty-fifth state in April the following year" (Dee 2006, 54).

115. Blue Lick is southwest of Stanford, Kentucky, in Lincoln County (DeLorme 2005). The Licking River flows from central eastern Kentucky in a northwesterly direction all the way to the Ohio River at Cincinnati (DeLorme 2005).

116. Much of what was called New Mexico during the Civil War had been ceded to the United States from Mexico during the Treaty of Guadalupe Hidalgo in 1848 and from Texas in 1850. The vast area extended west from present-day Texas to California and from the United States–Mexico border north into

present-day Nevada and Utah; it includes the majority of today's Arizona and New Mexico. During the Civil War, many pro-Southerners were found in the area, and on August 1, 1861, the land south of the 34th parallel became the "Confederate Territory of Arizona" (Wexler 1995, 161).

117. Charles Lewis entered Company K on September 12, 1862, and mustered out with the company on July 1, 1865 (Roster Commission 1891).

118. Franklin Sausbury and Benjamin F. Savage joined Company K on September 12, 1862, and mustered out with the company on July 1, 1865 (Roster Commission 1891). Ben Savage was later reported to have had "in his possession a small flag made from the lining of a hat owned and worn by the Rebel General [Nathan] Forrest" (Meigs County Pioneer and Historical Society, Inc. 1982, 36).

119. Although the Confederate and Union armies both had a problem with desertion, it "did not cripple the Union war effort"; however, "bounty-jumping—enlisting in order to receive a bounty and then deserting, sometimes in order to enlist again—emerge[d] as a profession" in the North (Mitchell 1988, 182).

120. The Roster Commission (1891) lists two buglers from Company D: Leonidas Archer and William Trees. No buglers are listed for Company L, although McKnight identifies James Smith as a bugler from Company L in a previous letter. John Leaper entered the service as a captain on September 27, 1862, and was promoted to major on July 13, 1864 (Reid 1895b).

121. See Woodbury 1867 for a complete roster of the Ninth Army Corps.

122. McKnight refers to a "General Carter" being in immediate command. Rankin (1881, 4) agrees that Carter was in command but refers to him as "Captain Carter": "Three companies, under Captain Green, joined two companies of the 2nd Ohio Cav., and one company of the 1st Kentucky, all under command of Captain Carter, of the 1st Kentucky."

123. Asher Entsminger, who was also from Meigs County, is mentioned frequently by McKnight. Entsminger joined Company K on September 12, 1862, and mustered out with the company on July 1, 1865 (Roster Commission 1891).

124. "Vehicles of home influence were many: letters, army chaplains, visiting relatives, hometown newspaper correspondents, relief workers, hospital volunteers—even strangers" (Linderman 1987, 93).

125. This is a reference to Ulysses S. Grant, who was born on April 27, 1822, near Point Pleasant, Ohio. Grant, a West Point graduate, was given a commission in the western theater after the Civil War began and later commanded all the armies of the United States. After the war, Grant went on to serve two terms as the president of the United States, winning the elections of 1868 and 1872 (Sutherland 2002). "Grant was not the sort of soldier who caused his men to cheer wildly and toss their caps in the air . . . [but] was obviously a

man of drive, one who, to the pleasure of Abraham Lincoln, fought and fought with what he had on hand, not forever crying for more men and equipment" (Katcher 1992, 272). His methods were effective: "[The] formal capitulation of the fortress [at Vicksburg] took place on July 4th. At noon the guns of Grant's army began to thunder the national salute from their ring of hills. Mingled with the roar of artillery the strains of 'The Star Spangled Banner' floated through the streets of the stricken town.... The capture of Vicksburg was the greatest victory ever gained by an American army from the founding of the Republic to the year 1863" (Woodward 1928, 300). After both Gettysburg and Grant's decisive victory at Vicksburg, "the Confederacy had no chance on any front to win its independence by a military decision" (Current, Williams, and Freidel 1961, 424).

126. Sergeant James Johnson joined Company A of the Seventh on August 28, 1862, and mustered out on May 15, 1865 (Roster Commission 1891).

127. There are no "Huffs" listed on the 1860 or 1870 census reports for Meigs County, Ohio (National Archives and Records Service 1963a; 1963b).

128. Between the lines, McKnight added, "He [McRaskey] als said he stoped and seen you and you was better. I could not believe a word he told."

129. Lieutenant Colonel George Miner joined the Seventh on September 18, 1862, and mustered out with the regiment on July 4, 1865 (Roster Commission 1891).

130. Private William Halliday entered Company K on September 12, 1862, and mustered out with the company on July 1, 1865 (Roster Commission 1891).

131. William McMaster "bought the mills in 1845.... Both of the McMaster sons served in the Second West Virginia Cavalry during the Civil War. Thomas was killed at the battle of Five Forks in Virginia. John L. became a lawyer and served as mayor of Indianapolis, Indiana in 1883. William McMaster continued to run the mill for the next forty years until his death in 1885" (Clark 1987, 19). A November 17, 1927, article in the *Democrat* of Pomeroy, Ohio, titled "Masonic Sign," states that Morgan "detailed men to burn McMasters mill in reprisal for the burning of the bridge and obstructing the crossing with fallen trees. Judge Ledlie, who was a Mason and a man of commanding presence, approached Gen. Morgan. A sign was probably given and recognized. A few low words were spoken when the General turned to his men and ordered them to depart and the mill was saved."

132. Hickman Bridge was "twenty-six miles beyond Lexington, Ky." (Poore 1882, 211) and was the site of Burnside's headquarters for many campaigns in Kentucky and Tennessee. "Camp Nelson developed an important function as a way station; its location at Hickman Bridge made it an invariable route for troops fanned out on either side of the Kentucky River" (Sears 2002, 2).

133. According to the official roster, Isaac Meaner joined Company K on September 12, 1862, and died on May 30, 1863, near Stanford, Kentucky (Roster Commission 1891).

134. "In a country veined with numerous streams and rivers, bridging trains played a very important part in the strategy and tactics of every campaign. Bridges were among the primary objectives. Permanent bridges were among the first victims of war. Even a small river could prove an insurmountable obstacle to an army if unaccompanied by sufficient portable bridging material [pontoon bridges] and an efficient corps trained in its use" (Coggins 1983, 104).

135. The Ninth Corps was said to have been "transferred so often from one department to another" that it was known as "Burnside's Geography Class" (Poore 1882, 213).

136. Ambrose E. Burnside was born near Liberty, Ohio, in 1824. Burnside attended West Point and during the Civil War held numerous positions. Rising to the rank of brigadier general, Burnside commanded several different divisions, including the Army of the Potomac (Poore 1882; Woodbury 1867). After the war, Burnside was elected governor of Rhode Island three times and in 1874 was elected to the U.S. Senate (Poore 1882).

137. Fishing Creek flows into the Cumberland River southwest of Somerset on the border of Pulaski and Wayne counties (DeLorme 2005).

138. McKnight is probably referring to Steubenville, Kentucky, which is located in Wayne County (Hammond 1993).

139. McKnight is most likely referring to an encounter with General Pegram's men near Monticello, Kentucky. "General Burnside complimented the regiment, in orders, for their service in this engagement, which he announced as the 'spirited cavalry engagement at Rocky Gap, Kentucky'" (Reid 1895b, 799).

140. See Ash 1995, Earle 2001, and Hart 1976 for discussions on cotton production in the mid-1800s.

141. James Haley was a member of Company K, joining on September 12, 1862, until his transfer to the Veteran Reserve Corps on December 3, 1864 (Roster Commission 1891).

142. Sergeant James Dennison, a member of Company K and a Meigs County native, mustered out with the company on July 1, 1865 (Roster Commission 1891).

143. There are no Rasters listed in the 1860 or 1870 census records for Meigs County (National Archives and Records Service 1963a; 1963b). Additionally, the Seventh did not contain anyone named Raster (Roster Commission 1891).

144. *Frenching,* a term used in this letter and again on September 14, 1863, is synonymous with desertion. In a discussion of desertion, Randall and Donald (1969, 330) note that the "sense of war weariness, the lack of confidence in commanders, and the discouragement of defeat tended to lower the morale of

the Union army and to increase desertion." One type of desertion is described as "taking French leave when on picket duty" (ibid.).

145. S. S. Hanes is recorded in the 1860 Meigs County, Ohio, census records. At the time, Hanes was thirty-one years old; his place of birth is listed as Pennsylvania (National Archives and Records Service 1963a). McKnight later mentions Hanes to Samaria on several occasions, questioning whether he had paid his debt.

146. George Spiers, a private in Company K, entered the service on September 12, 1862, and was discharged on May 24, 1864 (Roster Commission 1891).

147. See Nofi 1992, Miller 2001, and Coggins 1983 for discussions of artillery tools and forges.

148. Mill Springs is in northern Wayne County, Kentucky (Hammond 1993). McKnight is likely referring to Private Zachariah Wiseman. On the morning of January 19, 1862, the Confederates led by General George Crittenden attacked General George Thomas's troops near Mill Springs. In the confusion of Kentucky's "first sizable battle, [General] Zollicoffer rode into Union lines and was killed" (Harrison and Klotter 1997, 197). Fierce fighting resulted in 522 Confederate casualties and 262 Union casualties; the loss was a major setback for Confederate influence and morale in Kentucky. The "news of the Battle of Mill Springs created extraordinary excitement in both the North and the South. The Union had its first significant victory of the war. Eastern Kentucky was now firmly in Union hands and East Tennessee was open for Union invasion" (Nicholas 2000, 72). The "retreat of the Confederate troops from Kentucky allowed the pro-Union groups to consolidate their power and ensure that Kentucky would remain in the Union. This show of power . . . convinced most undecided Kentuckians that the South could not regain Kentucky or win the war. Kentucky would never be the source of manpower and support the South had hoped it would be" (Nicholas 2000, 72).

149. Confederate brigadier general John Pegram served in the eastern and western theaters and was ultimately killed in action on February 6, 1865, in the battle of Hatcher's Run (Current 1993). One of Burnside's orders was to capture General Pegram and take "steps to check the undercurrent of rebellious sentiment which had been flowing unchecked through the State [Kentucky]" (Poore 1882, 207).

150. The Second Ohio Volunteer Infantry was organized at Camp Dennison, Ohio, from July 17 to September 20, 1861, and served primarily in Tennessee (Keifer 2004; Roster Commission 1886a). Colonel Frank Wolford led the First Kentucky until his dismissal over critical comments regarding the use of black soldiers. President Lincoln first authorized the use of black troops in December 1862. This did not allow them to serve in Kentucky; however, two years later,

blacks were allowed to join the service. Harrison and Klotter (1997, 179) write that Colonel Wolford was so "enraged that he publicly attacked the president and the administration. At a Lexington banquet in March 1864 he remarked, 'What with Abe Lincoln on one side and Jeff Davis on the other, our poor distracted country reminds me of Christ crucified between two thieves.'" Soon thereafter, Wolford was dishonorably dismissed "for violation of the fifth section of the Rules and Articles of War, in using disrespectful words against the President of the United States, for disloyalty, and for conduct unbecoming an officer and a gentleman. E. D. Townsend Assistant Adjutant-General March 24, 1864" (OR, series 1, vol. 32, part 3, p. 147). Seymour (1963, 224) identifies a "Law's Howitzer Battery" and a "15th Indiana Battery" within the First Division of the cavalry corps—McKnight's Seventh Ohio was in the Second Division. However, McKnight is referring to Brigadier General John Wilder, who had been colonel of the Seventeenth Indiana Infantry, known as "Wilder's Mounted Infantry." The 103rd Ohio Volunteer Infantry was organized at large throughout the state in August and September 1862 and was led by Colonel John Casement, who was later promoted to brigadier general (Roster Commission 1888b).

151. Travis Mill is just south of the Kentucky state line in Pickett County, Tennessee (DeLorme 2004).

152. The Wolf River flows in a westerly fashion along the Kentucky-Tennessee border and joins the Obey River just before it empties into the Cumberland River in Clay County, Tennessee (DeLorme 2004).

153. Randall and Donald (1969, 313) note that it was "not until 1863 that the Federal government passed, one should not say an effective, but at least a definitely national conscription law."

154. There was no formal draft in the summer of 1863. The earlier Enrollment Act in March 1863 had stipulated that "following each call for troops, district quotas would be determined by the size of the enrollment. If the quota was not filled with[in] a specified time, the draft would occur" (Murdock 1963, 5). The "certain class of men" is a reference to those whom many viewed as unpatriotic in their willingness to volunteer and serve.

155. Woodbury (1867, 291) described a "Colonel W.P. Sanders" as a "very brave and skillful cavalry officer." Rankin observed that in this engagement he had "received orders from Col. Sanders to send 50 of his men out on . . . [his] right to skirmish, and to support the artillery with the remainder of his command, which was one section of Battery D, First Ohio" (Rankin 1881, 6).

156. From July 2 to July 26, 1863, elements of the Seventh were involved in "operations against Morgan's Raid in Kentucky, Indiana, and Ohio" (Dyer 1959b, 735).

157. Lebanon, Kentucky, is southwest of Lexington and is the seat of government for Marion County (Hammond 1993).

Chapter 3: The Fourth of July Presents and John Hunt Morgan's Raid (July 11, 1863–August 20, 1863)

1. Harrison and Klotter 1997, 202.
2. Dee 2006, 131.
3. Abbott 1962, 31.
4. Ramage 1986, 181.
5. Harper 1961b; Reid 1895a.
6. Martha (Mattie) and Myrtha were born on July 4, 1863.
7. McKnight's "Jim Town" is most likely Jamestown, Kentucky, in Russell County (Hammond 1993).
8. Morgan has been judged to have been "dreaming of glory"; with a "gambler's love of risk he had merely used pretense of a Kentucky raid to deceive Bragg into allowing him to depart on the most daring and dramatic cavalry raid of all—a bold thrust across the Ohio River into the free states" (Woodworth 1998, 169). He "took more than the authorized number of troops, leaving the right wing helplessly weak, and set off for the North with nary a backward glance. When Bragg less than a week later exercised his recall option in the face of Rosecrans' advance, Morgan had already ridden himself and a fifth of Bragg's total cavalry strength right out of the campaign" (ibid.).
9. The "sutler was a civilian, a sort of peripatetic P.X. One was allowed to each regiment, and was appointed either by the governor of the state from which the regiment came or by regimental or brigade officers" (Coggins 1983, 124). Sutlers justified their high prices by arguing that "in case of enemy raid or sudden retreat" they were a prime target "for the ragged and always half-starved enemy" (ibid.).
10. Clinton is just south of Akron, Ohio, in Summit County (Hammond 1993).
11. Nearly one year prior to Morgan's foray into Meigs County, General Albert Gallatin Jenkins had led some 350 cavalrymen across the Ohio River at Portland in eastern Meigs County. Jenkins and his men crossed near Buffington Island and raided Racine, Ohio (also in Meigs County), taking horses and killing one individual (Harper 1961b, 22).
12. Many inconsistencies exist in regard to McKnight's whereabouts during Morgan's raid through Meigs County, Ohio (see the introduction to this volume). Horwitz (2001, 197) contends that "when Captain McKnight entered Langsville as part of the pursuing Union force, he stopped for ten minutes to visit his wife and infant daughters and check how they fared during the Confederate occupation." McKnight's letters, however, clearly indicate that he was not part of the force pursuing Morgan.
13. See Ramage 1986 and Thomas 1985 for complete discussions of Morgan's incursion into Ohio and his capture in northern Ohio.

NOTES TO PAGES 114–116

14. This undated letter appears to have been written in late July or early August 1863, after Morgan's Raid and the birth of the twins. Unlike almost every other McKnight letter, this one was not dated and did not have any opening remarks that provided a location.

15. George Washington Harris was the author of *Sut Lovingood's Yarns*. "Mark Twain in later years, like many other American humorists, learned much from the riotous and incorrigible Sut Lovingood, the greatest practical joker in all history and surely one of the keenest of all backwoods philosophers. More than one distinguished critic, in fact, is ready to argue that Tom Sawyer and Huck Finn might never have taken shape in Mark Twain's imagination if Harris had not earlier created his gangling, long-legged, fluently satirical yarnteller of the East Tennessee Knobs" (Davidson 1946, 248).

16. Ohio had a significant number of citizens who opposed the war. Called Copperheads, they were led by Clement Vallandigham (Harper 1961b). Ohioans realized that the war would not be a quick affair; with this realization came frustration and disillusionment, resulting in "a cry for peace even at the price of disunion" (Zornow 1961, 21). Peace Democrats nominated Vallandigham to run against John Brough for governor in 1863, which led one Unionist to declare that Vallandigham was supported by a "secret organization instituted by the secessionists" (ibid., 26). Peace Democrats rallied under the slogan The Final Months (April 1, 1864–June 21, 1864) "the Constitution as it is, the Union as it was, and the Negroes where they are" (Roseboom 1952, 42). Roseboom discusses the Peace Democrats and notes that "soldier[s'] hostility toward Copperheads was bitter and unrelenting" (ibid., 33).

17. "Even men who had been strict teetotalers when they entered the service often succumbed after sometime in the army; and soldiers became adept at circumventing the restrictions officially placed on the distribution of liquor" (Wagner, Gallagher, and Finkelman 2002, 469).

18. McKnight was troubled by the Confederate sympathizers in southern Ohio. Unionists referred to them as Butternuts, Copperheads, and Peace Democrats (Wagner, Gallagher, and Finkelman 2002). They were judged to be "domestic enemies . . . busy in attempting to thwart the plans of the government, to prevent enlistments of troops, and to give aid and comfort to the public enemy" (Woodbury 1867, 265). As a result, Burnside issued "General Order No. 38," which states that "the commanding general publishes for the information of all concerned, that hereafter all persons found within our lines who commit acts for the benefit of the enemies of our country, will be tried as spies or traitors, and, if convicted, will suffer death" (ibid.).

19. McKnight is possibly referring to Benjamin Rickey, who was a farmer from Meigs County and seventy-five years old at the time of this letter (United States Bureau of the Census 1864). The Meigs County Historical Society staff

were unable to find any other information on Rickey and did not find any mention of hangings in Meigs County during the war.

20. Camp Nelson was established in August 1861 and "served first for a recruiting station for white volunteers, and afterwards for the same purpose for blacks and making for that race a place of refuge throughout the war" (Daviess 1924, 96). "Camp Nelson was a major Union supply depot for the armies of the Ohio and Cumberland" (Richards 2003, 163). After the war, "Camp Nelson was one of 40 burial grounds listed by a joint resolution of the Senate and House of Representatives in 1866 to become National Cemetery sites" (National Cemetery Administration n.d.). Today, the house that served as the officers' quarters is the only remaining structure of the "300 that were part of the camp" (Richards 2003, 163). See Sears 2002 for a complete discussion of Camp Nelson.

21. McKnight is referring to a series of skirmishes on July 31 at Lancaster and Paint Lick Bridge and again at Lancaster on August 1, 1863 (Dyer 1959b, 736).

22. The so-called Bluegrass region of rolling meadows is "divided into roughly concentric Inner and Outer regions. . . . The Inner Bluegrass, which surrounds the city of Lexington, has a gently undulating surface; at the time it was settled, it had deep and fertile limestone soils" (Hudson 2002, 123). "Kentucky bluegrass is of European origin and probably was introduced when herds of cattle were brought to Kentucky from the East in the 1790s" (ibid., 124).

23. Problems "arose when the soldier thought that the people at home were not fair to his family or were grasping and picayune in money matters while he risked his life for the cause" (Mitchell 1988, 67).

24. The Ohio State Historical Society maintains a Web site that contains images of Civil War battle flags. The 7th OVC's flag is found at the following address: www.ohiohistory.org/etcetera/exhibits/fftc/relicroom/search.cfm.

25. See Poore 1882 for a complete discussion of Burnside's rifle.

26. Knoxville, Tennessee, is the seat of government for Knox County and is located in the eastern portion of the state (Hammond 1993).

27. McKnight as a first sergeant would have been paid $20.00 per month, and Geyer as a first lieutenant would have received $105.50 per month (Nofi 1992).

Chapter 4: Going for Dixie (August 25, 1863–March 28, 1864)

1. Guernsey and Alden 1866, 123.
2. OR, series 1, vol. 4, pp. 239–40.
3. Ibid., 251.
4. OR, series 1, vol. 31, part 1, p. 551.
5. OR, series 1, vol. 4, p. 552.

6. Ibid., 553–54.

7. Similar accounts describing the conditions in eastern Tennessee include that of Sarah Espy from Cherokee County, Alabama, who stated that "there is not a living thing on the place . . . except a few chickens. God help us, for we have almost nothing. My beautiful farm is in ruins. We had hogs enough for two years, but they are gone, and [our] corn too, and desolation all around" (Ash 1995, 92). A newspaper correspondent wrote, "Fallow fields were spread out before the vision. Fences had been absorbed in camp-fires; the click of the old mill wheel had ceased; broken windows and shattered frames stared from deserted homesteads. Ravage and desolation everywhere. There were no little children gamboling on cabin thresholds. Hardly a dog barked" (ibid., 106).

8. Williamsburg, the seat of government for Whitley County, Kentucky, is in the southeastern part of the state (Hammond 1993).

9. During the Civil War, Kentucky was not considered part of "Dixie." Instead, the "Lincoln administration regarded Delaware, Maryland, Kentucky, and Missouri as border states, critical because of their geographical positions and questionable in loyalty because of their strong ties to both South and North" (Faust 1986, 71).

10. An entry from September 9, 1863, in McKnight's diary mentions that they took the "Cumberland Gap with 2600 prisoners without firing a gun."

11. "Christians were particularly prone to attribute escape from death in battle to providential intervention, the result of prayer and devotion" (Mitchell 1988, 78).

12. The Angelico Mountains are located in extreme southeastern Tennessee, straddling the Georgia–North Carolina–Tennessee border (DeLorme 2004).

13. The New River and Brimstone Mountain are in Scott County, Tennessee (DeLorme 2004).

14. "Horses and mules connected with the army were tasked to their utmost, and many of them gave out exhausted by the severities of the march" (Woodbury 1867, 305).

15. Kingston, Tennessee, is approximately forty miles west of Knoxville and is Roane County's seat of government (Hammond 1993).

16. The Emory River joins the Clinch River just north of Kingston, Tennessee, in Roane County (McDonald and Muldowny 1982).

17. Lenoir City is just north of the Holston River in Loudon County, Tennessee (Hammond 1993).

18. Loudon, Tennessee, is southwest of Knoxville and is the seat of government for Loudon County (Hammond 1993).

19. A "considerable force of the enemy being at London, and some fighting going on, the regiment was ordered to that point, and on reaching there found the rebels gone and the bridge that spanned the Tennessee River, in flames" (Rankin 1881, 10).

20. The Holston River joins the Tennessee near Knoxville; the Clinch River joins the Tennessee in Roane County, due west of Knoxville (DeLorme 2004).

21. The importance of the Cumberland Gap is well documented. McKnight actually arrived at the Gap a few days before he wrote the September 14 letter. In his diary entry for September 10, 1863, McKnight notes that on September 10, he was "at 9 1/2 AM in Cumberland gap over looking the Celebrated and wonderful works afoot and nature overlooking the States of Ten, Ky, [and] Va."

22. Tazewell, just south of the Cumberland Gap, is the seat of government for Claiborne County, Tennessee (Hammond 1993).

23. McKnight is most likely referring to the Powell River instead of the Howell River. The Powell River skirts the southern edge of the Cumberland Gap and extends into southwestern Virginia (Hammond 1993).

24. See Reid 1895b for a similar account: on "September 3rd the regiment entered Knoxville, the metropolis of East Tennessee. On the 4th it marched from Knoxville via Tazewell to within two miles of Cumberland Gap, and, with other troops, invested that stronghold. A summons to surrender was made, but refused until the afternoon of the 9th of September, when preparations for carrying the place by assault having been made, the garrison, under General Frazier, consisting of two thousand six hundred men, with fifteen pieces of artillery, surrendered, and the River Regiment was detailed to receive the surrender, and occupy this 'gateway to East Tennessee'" (Reid 1895b, 800).

25. Daniel Boone's trail (the Wilderness Road) "followed an old path through Cumberland Gap, an easy entrance to the Plateau that the native people had long used for hunting and trade. . . . Thousands of settlers bound for the trans-Appalachian frontier took the Wilderness Road through Cumberland Gap in succeeding years and then were guided by either the Kentucky or the Cumberland River toward the better lands to the west" (Hudson 2002, 104–5).

26. "[In] August 1863 the Union finally began keeping detailed records of Confederate deserters who entered Union lines and swore the oath of allegiance. Now oath takers had names, ranks, units, physical descriptions, and, perhaps most importantly, clearly defined homes, if only by state and county. The Register of Confederate Deserters to the Union Army, 1863–1865, provides some insight into just how widespread oath swearing was among Confederate soldiers" (Weitz 2005, 130). Indeed, "Tennessee soldiers represent the largest number of deserters swearing the oath from any state. By the time the Union began keeping records, much of middle Tennessee from Clarksville to Chattanooga was in Union hands, and men who swore the oath could go home without fear of retribution or capture by Confederate military or civilian authority" (ibid.).

27. Eastern Tennessee was different from the rest of the Deep South in that the region opposed secession and "was a bitterly divided region both during and after the Civil War" (Fain 2004, xxv). It was deemed a "civil war within a

civil war" from 1861 to 1865 (Northen 2003, 6). See also Guernsey and Alden 1866 for a discussion of eastern Tennessee and secession.

28. Woodbury's account (1867, 308) supports McKnight's comments on their welcome in Tennessee: "gray-haired men, with tears streaming down their cheeks, women who had lost their all, children whose tender age had not escaped the cruelty of the rebel rule, came forth to greet the General and his officers at every turn, and to express their gratitude for the redemption which he had brought."

29. The October 1, 1863, letter from McKnight to Samaria was written on the back side of an order dated September 23, 1863. The original order was given to McKnight by Joseph P. Santmyer (its content follows McKnight's letter to Samaria in the text).

30. Morristown is the seat of government for Hamblen County in eastern Tennessee (Hammond 1993).

31. Captain Nehemiah Warren mustered into the service on September 2, 1862, and was promoted to captain on May 25, 1863. Warren resigned on July 20, 1864 (Reid 1895b).

32. Sergeant Alonzo Hoyt, of Company K, joined on September 12, 1862, and mustered out with the company on July 1, 1865 (Roster Commission 1891).

33. First Lieutenant Santmyer joined Company B of the Seventh on October 1, 1862. Santmyer was later promoted to captain and mustered out with the company on July 1, 1865 (Roster Commission 1891).

34. The East Tennessee and Virginia Railroad began operations in 1858 and ultimately merged with the East Tennessee and Georgia Railroad in 1869 to form the East Tennessee, Virginia, and Georgia Railroad. During the Civil War, the East Tennessee and Virginia Railroad was a vital connection between Atlanta and Richmond. As a result, both Union and Confederate forces destroyed much of the East Tennessee and Virginia line. During the war, "Confederate authorities did not take full charge of the road. Although they left its operation in the hands of the company officials, they had their supplies and troops given preference" (Smith 1930, 42).

35. Greeneville is in extreme eastern Tennessee in the Appalachian Mountains and is Greene County's seat of government (Hammond 1993).

36. McKnight's reference to "last Monday" (October 5, 1863) coincides with Dyer's (1959b, 863) date for the action at Blue Springs.

37. General Orlando Willcox served in both the eastern and western theaters and earned the Congressional Medal of Honor (Sifakis 1988, 454). Willcox retired from the military in 1887; eight years later, "Congress awarded him the Medal of Honor for his performance at First Bull Run" (Faust 1986, 828). Willcox died in Cobourg, Ontario, in 1907 and is buried in Arlington National Cemetery.

38. McKnight's letter dated October 21, 1863, was written on a "Transportation Bill" from the East Tennessee and Virginia Railroad.

39. Rogersville, Tennessee, the seat of government for Hawkins County, is in eastern Tennessee some sixty miles northeast of Knoxville (Hammond 1993).

40. Warren Coulter died near Knoxville, Tennessee, on January 2, 1864; Peter Batchel mustered out with the company on July 1, 1865 (Roster Commission 1891).

41. McKnight may have been referring to Blue Springs, although a local history (Smith 1986) does mention a "Lick Creek" in this vicinity.

42. A bivouac is a temporary shelter that soldiers put up in the field (Nofi 1992).

43. Blue Springs is east of Johnson City in Carter County, Tennessee (DeLorme 2004). See Beard 1997 for a complete description of the battle of Blue Springs.

44. The Tenth Ohio Volunteer Infantry was organized at Camp Dennison on June 4, 1861, and served three years under the leadership of Colonel William Lytle. Lytle, originally from Cincinnati, was later promoted to brigadier general (Roster Commission 1886a).

45. Corporal Alonzo Austin entered Company K on September 12, 1862, and mustered out with the company on July 1, 1865 (Roster Commission 1891).

46. McKnight is possibly referring to Colonel Archibald Campbell, who was the commander of the First Brigade, which included the Ninth Pennsylvania, Second Michigan, and First East Tennessee regiments (Rowell 1971). The "First Brigade was to work with Colonel Israel Garrard's Division of the Army of the Ohio Cavalry" (ibid., 160).

47. A rod is a unit of measurement and a surveying term. One rod is sixteen feet six inches in length, and one acre equals 160 square rods.

48. Soldiers "worked to construct Good Deaths for themselves and their comrades amid the conditions that made dying—and living—so terrible. As war continued inexorably onward and as death tolls mounted ever higher, soldiers on both sides reported how difficult it became to believe that the slaughter was purposeful and that their sacrifices had meaning" (Faust 2008, 30).

49. William M. Rupe mustered in on September 12, 1862, and left the service on June 2, 1865, at Louisville, Kentucky (Roster Commission 1891).

50. McKnight's description of Corporal Levi Little's death is supported by John Robinson, also of the Seventh: at the "battle of Blue Springs, Tennessee, Capt. Higley was killed, as was also Levi Little the same day. Little was from Danville, Ohio. We couldn't get him for two hours, and he bled to death. Robert Andrews [also a member of the Seventh] and myself waited on him till he died" (Robinson 1995, 20). McKnight in his diary entry for October 10, 1863, adds that "Levi Little was wounded died at 10 PM. Capt. Higley was instantly killed at the head of his Comd in the afternoon he lost nothing. Levi lost evything he had on him the Capt. things were all saved."

51. One historian has concluded, "Within the army itself, there was barely time to acknowledge individual deaths, let alone to show the proper respect to the dead" (Mitchell 1993, 145). Yet McKnight appears to have gone to great lengths to care for Higley and Little. A few months later, he returned to their graves with tombstones paid for by donations from others in the company.

52. Hiram Carr was appointed quartermaster sergeant on November 8, 1862, and mustered out on July 24, 1865, at Chattanooga, Tennessee (Roster Commission 1891). McKnight also refers to "Wm McBurns." McKnight is most likely referring to William M. Burns, a wagoner for Company K of the Seventh (Roster Commission 1891).

53. "Captain Joel P. Higley, of company K, . . . was killed while leading the second battalion" in the final charge in the battle of Blue Springs (Reid 1895b, 800).

54. Jonesborough is the seat of government for Washington County in the eastern tip of Tennessee (Hammond 1993).

55. Blountville is in extreme eastern Tennessee just a few miles south of the Virginia state line and is Sullivan County's seat of government (Hammond 1993).

56. Zollicoffer was in eastern Tennessee—an area that appears to have been flooded by a TVA project. Beard's (1997) map of eastern Tennessee shows Zollicoffer approximately halfway between Bristol and Jonesborough. The Holston River's north and south forks flow out of Virginia and join in eastern Tennessee. The Holston ultimately joins the Tennessee River (Hammond 1993).

57. Bristol, Tennessee, is in Sullivan County in the state's eastern tip and straddles the Tennessee-Virginia state line (Hammond 1993).

58. Rankin (1881, 11) assessed this engagement similarly: "[The Rebels] continued their retreat through Zollecoffer and Bristol. We followed and burnt the bridge at Zollecoffer, on our way and captured at Bristol two locomotives and fifty cars, which were all destroyed, besides a considerable amount of commensary stores."

59. Kingsport is in northwestern Sullivan County, Tennessee (Hammond 1993).

60. This is a reference to the Union's Second East Tennessee Mounted Infantry. Troops under General William Jones and Colonel Henry Giltner (CSA) "captured nearly the entire Second East Tennessee Mounted Infantry," and this battle "marks one of the first actions of the Knoxville campaign" (Sutherland 1996, 219).

61. Big Creek enters the Holston River just east of Rogersville in Hawkins County (DeLorme 2004). Brigadier General William Jones led the Confederate forces to victory at Big Creek, which is also referred to as the battle of Rogersville. "On the night of November 5, in a cold and chilling rain, Colonel Henry L. Giltner of the Fourth Kentucky Cavalry (C.S.A.), who also commanded the Second East Tennessee Cavalry Brigade, left Kingsport with about twelve hundred men,

heading towards Surgionville. Giltner's troops surprised the Union forces the next morning and routed them with no more than ten casualties on the Confederate side" (Fain 2004, 132). In this engagement, a "force of twenty-seven hundred men had attacked a much smaller force—twelve hundred Union cavalry—and captured most of them. Cavalry units under attack from a superior force would ordinarily have been able to retreat, but events conspired against the mounted Federals on this particular day. These circumstances included the effects of bad weather and the fact that most of the Union officers were alleged to have spent the evening before at a dance in a public house in Rogersville" (Fain 2004, 132).

62. Bulls Gap is in Hawkins County, Tennessee, due east of Morristown and south of Rogersville (DeLorme 2004).

63. Duston Harper was captured on November 6, 1863, at Rogersville, Tennessee, and died in Andersonville Prison on May 17, 1864 (Roster Commission 1891).

64. In addition to Duston Harper, four of these men mentioned by McKnight were also listed in official records as having been captured on November 6, 1863, near Rogersville and having later died in prison (Roster Commission 1891). Royal Hoyt and Orrellence Williams died in Andersonville Prison, and Isaac Nelson and Henry Shiner died in prison at Richmond, Virginia (Roster Commission 1891). Additionally, William Walker entered the service on September 12, 1862, and was later wounded and released from Brown General Hospital in Louisville, Kentucky. Walker returned to duty on May 10, 1864; however, no final records of his discharge are available (Roster Commission 1891).

65. Russellville, Tennessee, is northeast of Morristown in Hamblen County (Hammond 1993).

66. "It was a terrible defeat, such as is inevitable when one thousand men are left unaided to fight three thousand five hundred; but no discredit can attach to men who were fairly whipped from the field" (Reid 1895b, 801). See Fain 2004 and Sutherland 1996 for detailed discussions of the fighting near Rogersville in early November 1863. Confederates commanded by General William E. Jones and Colonel Henry Giltner captured almost the entire Second East Tennessee Mounted Infantry and approximately half of the Seventh Ohio Cavalry—some eight hundred men, nearly one thousand horses, four pieces of artillery, and thirty-two wagons in all.

67. The five officers captured were Allen, Carr, Copeland, McColgin, and Shaw. After their capture, Allen and Carr escaped the "following night" (Reid 1895b, 801). Rogersville was a major Confederate victory and one of the Union's biggest losses in eastern Tennessee. "Nothing of any great importance, however, took place until the 10th of November, when the attack came from another direction. A portion of the enemy's force, that had been threatening our left

flank from Virginia, came down upon our garrison at Rogersville under Colonel Garrard, and succeeded in driving it out and back to Morristown, with a loss of about five hundred prisoners, four pieces of artillery, and thirty-six wagons" (Woodbury 1867, 330). This defeat was not soon forgotten. In June 1864, during the battle in which McKnight was killed, chants and cries of "Rogersville!" were heard from the Union troops, who "killed, wounded, and captured a large number of the same enemy who had defeated them at Rogersville, Tennessee, November 6, 1863" (Reid 1895b, 802).

68. Robert Chapder joined Company K at the age of eighteen on September 12, 1862. Chapder was captured on November 12, 1863, at Rogersville, and he mustered out of the service with the company on July 1, 1865 (Roster Commission 1891). W. E. Lefavor was a member of Company B of the 116th Ohio Volunteer Infantry and recalls being captured with several men from the Seventh Ohio Cavalry. One of his fellow captives was the Seventh's Royal Hoyt, who is mentioned here by McKnight. According to Lefavor (1995, 98), "[In] the evening we marched into prison [Andersonville]. As we marched in Royal Hoyt looked back at the closing gates and said, 'Boys, I shall never go out of here alive,' and he never did." The official roster indicates that Hoyt died at Andersonville on September 18, 1864. Walt Whitman (1963, 100–101) described the prison conditions and noted that "the releas'd prisoners of war are now coming up from the southern prisons. I have seen a number of them. The sight is worse than any sight of battle-fields, or any collection of wounded, even the bloodiest. There was, (as a sample), one large boat load, of several hundreds, brought about the 25th, to Annapolis; and out of the whole number only three individuals were able to walk from the boat. The rest were carried ashore and laid down in one place or another. Can those be *men*—those little livid brown, ash streak'd, monkey-looking dwarfs?—are they really not mummied, dwindled corpses? They lay there, most of them, quite still, but with a horrible look in their eyes and skinny lips (often with not enough flesh on the lips to cover their teeth). Probably no more appalling sight was ever seen on earth."

69. The Seventh was taken by surprise and suffered a major defeat at Rogersville, Tennessee. Reid (1895b, 801) contended that as a result of the "surprise in camp," General Burnside had ordered that Colonel Garrard be censured, but after an investigation by Colonel Loring, inspector-general of the Army of the Ohio, Garrard was instead credited "for his management of the late affair at Rogersville."

70. Amos Dyke joined Company K on September 12, 1862 (Roster Commission 1891). Dyke was captured on August 11, 1864, near Atlanta, Georgia, and ultimately mustered out on June 20, 1865, at Camp Chase, Ohio (ibid.).

71. McKnight refers to himself here and in his letters of November 13 and December 11, 1863, as "captain," but the official roster and his pension records

indicate otherwise. McKnight also wrote in his diary (November 3, 1863) that he had been "appointed Capt of Co K OVC."

72. According to the Roster Commission (1891), William Lemon Johnson joined the Seventh on September 12, 1862, at the age of twenty-one. Johnson was captured on November 6, 1863, near Rogersville, Tennessee, and after his imprisonment at Andersonville, Georgia, mustered out with the rest of Company K on July 1, 1865.

73. "In this affair, the Seventh lost everything in the shape of books and papers, camp and garrison equipage, all the train and everything but what was carried away by the men on their horses" (Rankin 1881, 13). McKnight's concern and involvement with the supply train is typical of a staff officer: the "Union Army's supplies moved on wheels, whether railroad or wagon, and a train of wagons, miles long, snaking its way along the rough roads of 19th century America, was a familiar sight. Responsibility for the management of such trains, including assembling the wagons and mules, fell to staff officers" (Miller 2001, 268).

74. Captain James McIntire joined the Seventh on August 25, 1862, and was promoted to major on July 1, 1863. McIntire resigned on March 26, 1864 (Roster Commission 1891).

75. Bean Station is in northeastern Grainger County, Tennessee (Hammond 1993).

76. McKnight is describing the action at Morristown, Tennessee, and the skirmishes that led up to the battle of Bean's Station, which officially began on December 13, 1863, and continued until December 17, 1863 (Reid 1895b).

77. Carbines such as the Burnside percussion carbine "were well suited to cavalry operations. These were shorter and handier than rifles . . . and weighed considerably less. Rate of fire was high, as a majority, at least in the Federal service, were breechloaders, and many were repeaters" (Coggins 1983, 58). See Poore 1882 for a detailed account of the Burnside carbine.

78. McKnight is possibly referring to William Tease of the First Ohio Artillery's Battery F (Roster Commission 1889b).

79. "Ohio, Indiana, Illinois, Michigan, and Eastern Kentucky, with the prospective addition of East Tennessee" constituted the "command of the Department of the Ohio" (Woodbury 1867, 261). Burnside was ultimately relieved of his command of the Army of the Ohio by General John G. Foster and offered his resignation on December 16, 1863 (Poore 1882). Burnside moved to the eastern theater in the spring of 1864 (Faust 1986).

80. McKnight was not the only one to use this nickname for Burnside: "As had been the case when he was moving among them, in camp or on the march, when they [soldiers] met him in civil life there was always a cheer for 'Old Burney'" (Poore 1882, 276). The siege of Knoxville began on the "17th of

November, 1863 and several days were marked by assaults and counter-assaults between the opposing parties. The most desperate contest was early on Sunday morning, Nov. 29, when an assaulting column composed of three picked brigades moved against Fort Saunders. These men, veterans of Lee's, Jackson's, and Longstreet's forces, confident of promised victory, advanced into a rain of lead. Wires had been stretched from stump to stump in front of the works. Over these the advancing Confederates fell in confused heaps, with killed and wounded all about them. . . . General Longstreet lost, that day, upwards of one thousand men. General Burnside permitted him to remove his wounded and bury his dead, but there was no disposition to renew the attack" (Poore 1882, 219–20). See Poe 1991 for a complete account of Knoxville's defense.

81. McKnight's diary entry from December 16, 1863, states that they had "Skirmished all day the Rebs drove us 4 miles but without much loss. . . . Skirmished heavy falling back halted at Night stood in line of battle in cornfield all night rained."

82. New Market is in northern Jefferson County, Tennessee (Hammond 1993).

83. "Diarrhea and dysentery ran rampant throughout the war. Malnutrition, filthy camps . . . and tainted water from streams and ponds contributed to a woeful medical picture" (Gallagher et al. 2003, 83). Of all illnesses, diarrhea caused the most deaths (30,481) and had the greatest number of reported cases (1,325,714) (Wagner, Gallagher, and Finkelman 2002, 648).

84. Dyer (1959b, 869) notes this as the Hays Ferry battle near Dandridge.

85. A Private David Vires joined Company M on October 10, 1862 (Roster Commission 1891).

86. Woodbury 1867 likewise lists a Colonel Cameron.

87. The Second Michigan Cavalry was "organized at Detroit, Michigan, and mustered in October 2, 1861" (Dyer 1959c, 1269). The Second Michigan Cavalry, which mustered out on August 17, 1865, lost 342 men during the war (Dyer 1959c).

88. Company I was mustered into service on November 5, 1862, at Athens, Ohio, and mustered out on July 3, 1865, at Nashville (Roster Commission 1891).

89. McKnight is describing the December 24–28 "operations about Dandridge and Mossy Creek" (Dyer 1959b, 869).

90. James Longstreet was born on "January 8, 1821; he died January 2, 1904. The eighty-three years between these dates were richer and more varied in human experience than are most lifetimes" (Sanger 1952, 5). Longstreet rose to the rank of lieutenant general and fought in both eastern and western campaigns (Current 1993, 944). McKnight mentions the capture of Longstreet's courier in this letter; on January 9, 1864, McKnight writes that he had heard that Longstreet "had sent in a flag of truce." A similar account in Wormser 1966 highlights the many rumors that often spread through the

troops: General Sheridan's "signalmen had interpreted a heliograph message to Early from Longstreet; the two Confederate armies were to get together and 'crush Sheridan'" (Wormser 1966, 250). "There were rumors all over the field that Longstreet was about to join Early, as promised in the intercepted message; the intelligence Sheridan got from his captives denied this, and then Powell, cavalry commander watching the gap through which Longstreet would have to come, reconnoitered and sent word to Sheridan that the relieving Gray army was not present" (Wormser 1966, 253).

91. McKnight's "R Downing" most likely is Rodney Downing of Meigs County. Downing was born in Maine and came with his family to southeastern Ohio in 1815. Downing lived in two Meigs County communities, Rutland and Middleport, and "served as Meigs County Clerk of Court for twelve years" (Johnson 1979, 135). R. Downing is also the attorney listed on McKnight's pension requests filed by Samaria McKnight.

92. The mountain passes were important because "only three rivers—the Potomac, the James, and the Roanoke—cross the Blue Ridge Mountains, and no crossing is south of Roanoke, Virginia" (Hudson 2002, 111).

93. General John Foster was assigned to the Ohio command from December 9, 1863, through February 9, 1864 (Sifakis 1988).

94. This is a reference to Paducah, Kentucky, located in McCracken County near the confluence of the Ohio and Tennessee rivers (Hammond 1993).

95. See Miller 2004, Swanson 2004, and Evans 1962 for detailed Civil War maps. Additionally, Pearson 2005 provides an important discussion on the accuracy of Civil War maps.

96. McKnight clearly recognizes the importance of eastern Tennessee for the Union cause.

97. Governor Tod might have been reluctant to commission more officers after just losing the Republican nomination for governor to John Brough (Abbott 1962). David Tod, a native of Youngstown, was an attorney who had "made a fortune from the coal and iron resources of the Mahoning Valley"; he ultimately served as president of the Cleveland and Mahoning Railroad (Abbott 1962, 22).

98. Ironclads, submarines, gunboats, and torpedo boats were some of the many "types of vessels that played an integral role in the strategies employed by North and South" (Wagner, Gallagher, and Finkelman 2002, 521).

99. Maryville is the seat of government for Blount County in southeastern Tennessee, not far from the North Carolina state line (Hammond 1993).

100. Sergeant John Wiseman joined Company K on September 12, 1862, and was discharged on April 30, 1864 (Roster Commission 1891).

101. Urias Nelson offered a different version of Coulter's death. Nelson joined Company K on September 12, 1862, and later that year was commissioned as

the company's farrier. When the Seventh arrived at Knoxville, Nelson (1995, 26) recalled, "we went into camp near Ft. Saunders. I remember while there of a mule kicking a loaded carbine. It was discharged and killed Warren Coulter of our company."

102. Private Sam Foose joined Company M of the Seventh on October 10, 1862, and mustered out with the regiment on July 3, 1865 (Roster Commission 1891). In 1780, Virginia's capital was moved from Williamsburg to Richmond. Richmond not only has served as Virginia's state capital but also was the capital of the Confederate States of America: after Virginia, Arkansas, North Carolina, and Tennessee left the Union, the "Confederacy soon moved its capital from Montgomery to Richmond, Virginia" (Gallagher et al. 2003, 31). In March 1862, the "first permanent Confederate prisoner-of-war facilities were established" in Richmond (Swanson 2004, 36). By July 1862, some "10,000 Federal prisoners [were] in Confederate hands, 8,000 in Richmond alone"; by October 1863, "Confederate prisoner-of-war camps, most of which were in Richmond and other parts of Virginia, were overcrowded due to the breakdown of the Dix-Hill Cartel a few months earlier. This was particularly true of Belle Isle, in the middle of the James River" (Swanson 2004, 74).

103. Dandridge is the seat of government for Jefferson County, Tennessee, and is approximately thirty miles straight east of Knoxville (Hammond 1993).

104. Strawberry Plains is on the Holston River in western Jefferson County, Tennessee (Hammond 1993). Sevierville, Tennessee, approximately twenty miles southeast of Knoxville, is the seat of government for Sevier County (Hammond 1993). The Smoky Mountains, which stretch along the North Carolina–Tennessee border, include some of the highest peaks in eastern North America (Hudson 2002).

105. The Little River flows to the northwest and enters the Tennessee River near Knoxville (DeLorme 2004).

106. This is also mentioned in Rankin 1881. "[A] detachment of the brigade were sent into North Carolina to capture Thomas' Legion, which was made up mostly of Indians, (Thomas being formerly an Indian agent). The expedition was successful, they brought back 50 prisoners, but not without heavy loss on our own side" (Rankin 1881, 15).

107. Isaac Train was listed as the "Surgeon" for the regiment (Reid 1895b). McKnight in his diary entry for October 23, 1863, also mentions a "Doctor Tallis." R. H. Tullis was the 7th OVC's assistant surgeon, who mustered in on November 6, 1862, and died at Marietta, Georgia, on September 20, 1864 (Reid 1895b).

108. "One of the few serious issues raised against [General] Grant was his wartime Order No. 11. Grant had lashed out at the *sutlers* who frequented Union army camps. They were notorious for overcharging for inferior foodstuffs

and other goods the homesick young soldiers desperately craved. But instead of focusing on wrongdoers and their specific actions, Grant had banned Jewish peddlers from his camp. The reaction during the war was swift. President Lincoln immediately *countermanded* Grant's order, the only time he did so" (Bennett 2006, 411).

109. Covington is just across the Ohio River from Cincinnati in Kenton County, Kentucky (Hammond 1993).

110. Captain James Campbell joined the Seventh on September 12, 1862, and resigned on January 27, 1864 (Reid 1895b).

111. David Tod was born on February 21, 1805, in Youngstown, Ohio. Tod ran for governor and lost on two occasions in 1843 and 1845 before being named by President Polk as ambassador to Brazil from 1847 through 1851. After returning to Ohio, Tod served as the state's twenty-fifth governor, from 1862 to 1864 (Trester 1950; 1953).

112. Fort Sanders, straight west of Knoxville, was named in honor of General Sanders, a native of Kentucky who was killed in action at age twenty-eight (Poore 1882; Woodbury 1867). The death of General Sanders "cast a gloom over the entire command. It was felt that a most brilliant and promising name had been lost from the roll of the army. General Burnside felt his loss most keenly, and ordered that the earthwork, in front of which the engagement in which he fell had taken place, should be named Fort Sanders in honor of his memory" (Woodbury 1867, 341). Fort Higley was southwest of Knoxville (Poore 1882). According to Reid (1895b, 800), the death of Captain Higley of Company K at the battle of Blue Springs led General Burnside to name "one of the principal forts near Knoxville . . . in honor of this gallant officer, whose merits he well knew and appreciated."

113. "[The] Union government itself devoted far greater attention to the hospitalization and general care of the troops than in former wars; but the burden was too great for the government, and private initiative made a memorable contribution in the work of the United States Sanitary Commission. . . . The commission served as a valuable civilian auxiliary to the medical bureau of the war department in tending the wounded and ministering to the morale and comfort of the soldiers. It may be regarded as the forerunner of the Red Cross" (Randall and Donald 1969, 488–89). See Reid 1895a for a complete discussion of relief efforts in Ohio.

114. "Despite staggering battle casualties . . . the Civil War soldier remained at a far greater risk of death by disease than by a minie ball. It is estimated that two-thirds of the war's fatalities were attributed to diseases" (Wagner, Gallagher, and Finkelman 2002, 643).

115. The Clinch River flows out of western Virginia and joins the Tennessee River in Roane County, Tennessee (Hammond 1993).

116. "We had to subsist exclusively off of the country for forage and provisions for men and the horses, and the supply becoming exhausted our horses were reduced to skeletons and were no longer able to do duty" (Rankin 1881, 15).

117. William Simpson was appointed captain on August 25, 1862, and was promoted to major on March 28, 1864. Simpson resigned on August 26, 1864 (Reid 1895b).

118. On March 11, 1864, McKnight penned the following in his diary: "Working on Comp History to send to Gov. Brough." Governor John Brough was an Ohio native, born in Marietta in 1811. Before the war, Brough operated several successful newspapers. In 1863, Brough defeated Copperhead Clement Vallandigham for Ohio governor; however, Brough did not complete his first term, dying in August 1865 (Abbott 1962).

119. Clinton, northwest of Knoxville, is the seat of government for Anderson County, Tennessee (Hammond 1993).

120. Solomon Green joined the Seventh on September 20, 1862, and served as captain until his promotion to major on October 12, 1864 (Reid 1985b).

121. "[The] Christian Commission, a project of the Young Men's Christian Associations, which provided religious ministration (though this function was more regularly performed by army chaplains), distributed Bibles, offered various forms of diversion to relieve the ennui of camp life, supplied magazines, and sent soldiers' money home to families" (Randall and Donald 1969, 489).

122. Evans 1962 and Swanson 2004 locate Mossy Creek some thirty miles straight east of Knoxville. Another map of eastern Tennessee has Mossy Creek between Morristown and Strawberry Plains (Wilson and Snapp 1986). In present-day Jefferson County, this area is now inundated by the TVA's Douglas Lake.

123. Ulysses Grant (1956, 455) noted in an essay titled "We Will Hold the Town Till We Starve" that "Burnside was in about as desperate a condition as the Army of the Cumberland had been, only he was not yet besieged. He was a hundred miles from the nearest possible base, Big South Fork of the Cumberland River, and much farther from any railroad we had possession of. The roads back were over mountains, too, all supplies along the line had long since been exhausted. His animals, too, had been starved, and their carcasses lined the road from Cumberland Gap, and far back toward Lexington, Kentucky."

124. In his diary (March 17, 1864), McKnight lists the "Co Members [who donated] to erect a Slab over Capt. Higley Grave." McKnight gave $2.00; William Hartley, Urias Nelson, John Kennedy, Andrew McBride, Guyan Wright, William Miller, Jesse Edmundson, Asher Entsminger, Alonzo Austin, and Lorenzo Fountain each donated $1.00.

125. McKnight in his diary (March 24–26, 1864) also notes all the individuals who contributed to "erect Grave Stone over Little & Coulters." In addition to McKnight, nineteen soldiers gave $1.00 each, and another six each donated

50 cents to the cause. Members from Company K who donated $1.00 are as follows: William McKnight, Urias Nelson, William Skinner, James Smith, Adam Garlow, William Burns, Elisha Andrews, Lorenzo Fountain, Burrell Wilson, Martin Nelson, John Kennedy, Guyan Wright, Andrew McBride, Hiram Rumfield, Jesse Edmundson, Alonzo Austin, Columbus Hetzer, John Davis, William Smart, and William Miller. Those Company K members who gave 50 cents are as follows: Samuel Lewellyn, Everett Wells, Daniel Vonschrelly, Albert Campbell, and Abraham Bahr. Also listed as donating 50 cents is C. Henni; the only Henni found in the official roster for Ohio is Private John Henni of the Company D of the Sixty-seventh Ohio Volunteer Infantry (Roster Commission 1887b).

126. Allowing the men to elect their own officers was not common although the practice, "especially as to officers below the rank of colonel, was 'widespread,' and was 'recognized by both state and federal governments'" (Randall and Donald 1969, 326).

127. Both Sergeant John Wiseman and James Elshire joined Company K on September 12, 1862. Wiseman was discharged on April 30, 1864, and Elshire mustered out with the company on July 1, 1865 (Roster Commission 1891).

128. "During the first years of the war, both North and South scrambled to improvise general hospitals out of hotels, factories, warehouses, boarding schools and even prisons. The army often commandeered any large building available" (Wagner, Gallagher, and Finkelman 2002, 627). In particular, "college buildings proved almost irresistible to military commanders, who needed space for hospitals or for housing troops" (Harrison and Klotter 1997, 210).

129. The McKnight collection also contains a tombstone receipt from George Hagan of Knoxville, Tennessee, dated March 26, 1864. The note reads as follows: "Recieved twenty two Dollars in full for two sets of Tomb Stones from Lt. William McKnight to be set by the undersigned to the graves of Corporal Levi Little and Warren W. Coulter of Co K 7th O.V.C. situated at this place. Geo. W. Hagan & Bro."

130. The Knoxville National Cemetery was established by General Burnside after the siege of Knoxville. The cemetery is laid out essentially as McKnight describes it. Captain Joel P. Higley was apparently one of the first buried. Higley is buried in the first row in the cemetery's center—Section A, Site 12.

Chapter 5: The Final Months (April 1, 1864–June 21, 1864)

1. McKnight's sister Mary is likely referring to Salem Township in Meigs County, Ohio (Meigs County Pioneer and Historical Society, Inc. 1982).

2. The 1860 Meigs County census records include a James Sansbury, age twenty-seven, who was a neighbor of the McKnights in Rutland Township (National Archives and Records Service 1963a).

3. Hannah Jane Lyle was married to John McKnight and was thus William McKnight's sister-in-law.

4. Homer Lewis Love joined Company K of the Forty-ninth Ohio Volunteer Infantry on September 5, 1861, and was discharged with a certificate of disability on May 18, 1862 (Roster Commission 1887a).

5. Private Alexander Patterson of the Thirty-sixth Ohio Volunteer Infantry mustered in to Company K on August 10, 1861, and died May 9, 1864, of wounds received in the battle of Cloyd's Mountain, Virginia (Roster Commission 1886b). Private John Halliday joined Company H of the Twenty-sixth Ohio Volunteer Infantry on August 12, 1861, and was later promoted to first sergeant; he mustered out with the regiment on July 27, 1865 (Roster Commission 1886b). Private Alexander Washington Halliday was also a member of the Twenty-sixth Ohio Volunteer Infantry, joining Company H on August 12, 1861, and mustering out of service on July 27, 1865 (Roster Commission 1886b).

6. Two Wisemans served in Company K of the Seventh Ohio Volunteer Cavalry. Mary is most likely referring to John Wiseman, who was appointed sergeant on November 8, 1862, and was discharged on April 30, 1864. Zachariah Wiseman was also a member of Company K, but he died near Lexington, Kentucky, on April 20, 1863, well before this letter was written (Roster Commission 1891).

7. McKnight in his diary entry for April 2, 1864, shares his thoughts on Frankfort: "left Loisville 6:00 arived at Frankfort 12 . . . does not come up to my views of a great State Capital being rather an inferior one Horse Town. We arrived at Lexington 2 P.M. evrything appearing Pleasant and almost like a new world aliting from the Carrs we felt thankful that we had accomplished our long Jorney without accident haveing traveled 6 Days 431 Miles from Knoxville by rail took Cars for Paris late in the afternoon but being detained we did not get to go camped for the night."

8. Paris, Kentucky, is northeast of Lexington and is the seat of government for Bourbon County (Hammond 1993).

9. Chattanooga is in south-central Tennessee near the state boundaries of Alabama, Georgia, and Tennessee (Hammond 1993). McKnight added further detail to this event in his diary: "Tuesday [March] 29th 1864 4 p.m. Maj. General Wm T. Sherman came up on Special Train was Saluted by 1st Ill. Battery 13 Guns. Our Regmt Drew up in line along the R.R. and Cheered the General standing on the Platform of Rear Carr Salueted and smild gracously."

10. The First Illinois Light Artillery had thirteen different battery divisions—A through M. Several were in the vicinity of Chattanooga during this time (Dyer 1959c).

11. Athens, Alabama, is the seat of government for Limestone County (Hammond 1993). Missionary Ridge, located just east of Chattanooga, runs north–south, straddling the Georgia-Tennessee state boundary (Miller 2004).

12. Lookout Mountain is in northeastern Alabama, straddling the border between De Kalb and Cherokee counties (Hammond 1993).

13. This is a reference to Theopolis J. Wilson of the Eighteenth Ohio Volunteer Infantry.

14. This is a reference to Grant's defeat of Bragg at Lookout Mountain and Missionary Ridge (Buck 1908).

15. The battles at Lookout Mountain and Missionary Ridge took place in late November 1863. These Union victories opened the opportunity for Union forces to move into the heart of the Confederacy (Wagner, Gallagher, and Finkelman 2002).

16. This is apparently a reference to Lineville, Alabama, which is approximately sixty miles east of Birmingham in Clay County (Hammond 1993).

17. Bridgeport is on the Tennessee River in northeastern Jackson County, Alabama (Hammond 1993).

18. The Cumberland Tunnel was between Winchester and Tracy City in south-central Tennessee, not far from the Alabama state line (Evans 1962).

19. Stevenson, Alabama, is also near the Tennessee River in Jackson County (Hammond 1993).

20. This is likely a reference to stops along the Nashville and Chattanooga Railroad and the Louisville and Nashville Railroad (Evans 1962).

21. "Especially noteworthy is the fact that women in great numbers declined to flee despite rumors that the Northern soldiers intended to rape their way through the South"; like McKnight, "every observer in the occupied South was struck by the dearth of men" (Ash 1995, 19, 196). In regard to poverty, the "poor, in particular, were often left wholly destitute. In June 1863 a Pennsylvania soldier in northern Virginia spoke with a young woman, an overseer's wife, who 'gave me such a story of struggles to keep alive, to get enough to keep from starving, as made all the hard times I have ever seen seem like a life of luxury. I did pity her. On such as she, the poor whites of the South, the burden of this war is heaviest'" (Ash 1995, 177).

22. This is a reference to Elliot Braley, who was married to McKnight's sister Janett.

23. McKnight's diary provides a more detailed account of his second trip home. According to the diary, McKnight "started for Ohio" on April 25, 1864, in "Company with Wm. H. Skinner and Wm. H. Spires Sergt Barrett and A Campbell." On April 26, 1864, McKnight paid a fare of $3.45 for a train from Cincinnati to Athens, Ohio, and from there paid $2.95 for a stage to Meigs County, Ohio. On May 3, 1864, McKnight took a steamer to Cincinnati and ultimately arrived back in camp on May 6, 1864. During this trip, McKnight in his diary entry for May 3 mentions a "Lt. Wolmeldorf." George Womeldorf was first lieutenant in the Seventh and was promoted to captain on June 16, 1865 (Reid 1895b).

24. This undated letter from William McKnight's father mentions that "Susan" had been "seack on the boat." McKnight's letter dated May 4, 1864, discusses the same issue.

25. Langsville, Ohio, which is McKnight's hometown, is located in southwestern Meigs County (Hammond 1993).

26. Private John Babel joined Company K on September 12, 1862, and mustered out on May 8, 1865 (Roster Commission 1891).

27. Ellen Savage was not recorded in the 1860 Meigs county census records, and there were several Savage families. However, Ellen is likely to have been the infant daughter of Joseph and Mary Savage, who were in their thirties and had several small children. Joseph and Mary are listed in the census records following William and Samaria's entry for Rutland Township (National Archives and Records Service 1963a).

28. Farrier Dan Logan joined Company I of the Seventh on September 12, 1862, and mustered out with the company on July 3, 1865 (Roster Commission 1891).

29. This is most likely a reference to Clarksville, Virginia, which is in Mecklenburg County not far from the North Carolina state line (Hammond 1993).

30. Although the official rosters of Ohio soldiers during the Civil War (1886a; 1886b; 1887b; 1888a; 1888b; 1888c; 1889a; 1889b) contain fourteen John McKnights, none seems to correspond with McKnight's letter dated May 19, 1864, in regard to his discharge. William's comment that his brother "could not stand marching" indicates that John McKnight was in the infantry.

31. During this time, Grant was involved in the Wilderness Campaign in Virginia. The Wilderness Campaign began on "May 5, 1864 . . . [and] ended, properly speaking, six weeks later" (Woodward 1928, 320). By this time, Grant had been placed in charge of all Union armies (Goodwin 2005). "Grant was promoted to lieutenant general, a rank Congress last bestowed on George Washington" (Bennett 2006, 372–73).

32. This is likely a reference to Private Silvester Shiner, who mustered into Company K on September 12, 1862, and was discharged on July 1, 1865 (Roster Commission 1891). Henry Shiner was also in Company K, but he was captured at Rogersville, Tennessee, in November 1863.

33. See Reid 1895a for a complete discussion of Ohio's recruiting efforts; throughout 1864, several calls for troops were issued. Meigs County's quota for 1864 was 338 troops, but of that number, only 30 were drafted (Reid 1895a, 201).

34. Corporal Jesse Edmundson joined Company K on September 12, 1862, and mustered out with the company on July 1, 1865 (Roster Commission 1891).

35. John Oty was a member of Company K and served from September 12, 1862, until July 1, 1865 (Roster Commission 1891).

36. Private Francis McKnight joined Company H of the 140th Ohio Volunteer Infantry on May 2, 1864, and after one hundred days of service mustered out with the unit on September 3, 1864 (Roster Commission 1888c).

37. McKnight's descendants are in possession of a small envelope of hair addressed to "Mrs Samaria McKnight Rutland Meigs Co Ohio" that was enclosed in a letter dated May 31, 1864.

38. McKnight writes "May 6th" when actually it was June 6th, 1864.

39. Clay Ferry is on the Kentucky River in northern Madison County, approximately fifteen miles south of Lexington (DeLorme 2005).

40. Georgetown, Kentucky, is Scott County's seat of government and is located just north of Lexington (DeLorme 2005).

41. Cynthiana, Kentucky, is Harrison County's seat of government and is located approximately thirty miles north of Lexington (Hammond 1993).

42. William Hartley, also from Meigs County, joined Company K on September 12, 1862; he was appointed first sergeant on April 19, 1864 (Roster Commission 1891).

43. "Announcing, describing, and explaining" a soldier's death to the "people they left behind became part of an officer's duty" (Mitchell 1993, 84).

44. "Morgan's two famous Kentucky raids in 1862 and 1864 included significant engagements with Union forces at Cynthiana" (Richards 2003, 151). Confederate colonel Henry Giltner "lost hundreds of men from his brigade when Morgan was surprised near Cynthiana. Morgan tried to gloss over the defeat, but was roundly criticized in several quarters" (Sutherland 1996, 244–45).

45. This quest was not uncommon. "Desperate families both North and South traveled by the hundreds to battlefields to search in person for missing kin" (Faust 2008, 127).

46. This is most likely a reference to Herold Wells. Wells is listed in the 1860 Meigs County census as a "Cabinet Maker" from Massachusetts (National Archives and Records Service 1963a).

47. This is possibly a reference to John McClintock, a physician from Meigs County (National Archives and Records Service 1963a).

Epilogue

1. Reid 1895b.
2. Rankin 1881, 19.
3. Reid 1895b, 803.
4. Rankin 1881, 26. Gravelly Springs is northwest of Florence, Alabama, in Auderdale County near the Tennessee River (Hammond 1993).
5. Rankin 1881, 27.
6. Ibid.

7. Ibid., 28.
8. Ibid.
9. Ibid.
10. Reid 1895b, 803.
11. Ibid.
12. Dee 2006, 190.

13. James Stobart was also captured and sent to Andersonville Prison, where he joined the Tenth East Tennessee Confederate Infantry. Stobart was later captured again, this time by Union forces at Egypt Station, Mississippi. Stobart was released from the military prison in Alton, Illinois, after pledging allegiance to the U.S. government on June 27, 1865 (Roster Commission 1891).

14. Ruth Hayth has possession of Samaria's diaries, which contain brief lists of her services—item and amount charged.

15. Susan Hayes of Mount Vernon, Ohio, is Mattie McKnight Tuckerman's great-granddaughter. Mrs. Hayes has several uncited newspaper clippings that contain family information. One, dated 1917, is titled "T. R. McKnight Dies Suddenly," and another discusses Samaria's death in 1905.

16. Samaria's pocket diaries contain brief and spotty entries that chronologically span several years—most mention little more than daily weather conditions or mundane everyday chores.

References

Abbott, Richard. 1962. *Ohio's War Governors*. Columbus: Ohio State University Press, Ohio Civil War Centennial Commission.

Ash, Stephen. 1995. *When the Yankees Came*. Chapel Hill: University of North Carolina Press.

Ashley, June. 1987. *Veterans of the Civil War, Taken from* The Tribune Telegraph, *Pomeroy, Ohio, 1905*. Pomeroy, OH: Meigs County Genealogical Society.

Beard, William. 1997. *Blue Springs*. Strawberry Plains, TN: Strawberry Plains Press.

Becker, Carl. 1961. "The Genesis of a Copperhead." *Bulletin of the Historical and Philosophical Society of Ohio* 19 (4): 235–53.

———. 1964. "Entrepreneurial Invention and Innovation in the Miami Valley during the Civil War." *Bulletin of the Cincinnati Historical Society* 22: 4–28.

Bennett, William. 2006. *America: The Last Best Hope*. Nashville, TN: Nelson Current.

Boatner, Mark. 1988. *The Civil War Dictionary*. New York: McKay Company.

Bowles, J. F. 1933. "General Morgan Protected Widow of Brave Soldier Who Was Slain by Union Private." *Pomeroy Daily Sentinel,* January 8.

Brown, Kent. 2000. *The Civil War in Kentucky*. Mason City, IA: Savas Publishing Company.

Buck, Irving. 1908. *Cleburne and His Command*. New York: Neale Publishing Company.

Burgess, Lauren. 1995. *An Uncommon Soldier*. New York: Oxford University Press.

Carroll, Andrew. 2001. *War Letters*. New York: Washington Square Press.

———. 2005. "War Letters." *National Geographic* (November): 78–95.

Clark, Mary. 1987. "The Langsville Mill." In *Meigs County, Ohio,* vol. 2, ed. Meigs County Pioneer and Historical Society, 19. Salem, WV: Walsworth Publishing Company.

Coggins, Jack. 1983. *Arms and Equipment of the Civil War*. New York: Fairfax Press.

Coleman, J. Winston. 1968. *Lexington during the Civil War*. Lexington, KY: Henry Clay Press.

Coles, Harry. 1962. *Ohio Forms an Army*. Columbus: Ohio State University Press, Ohio Historical Society.

Connors, Sharon, and Velna Dickson. 2005. *Family of Samuel McKnight and Elizabeth {Halliday} McKnight*. Shediac, NB: Dupuis Printing.

Cromie, Alice. 1965. *A Tour Guide to the Civil War*. Chicago: Quadrangle Books.

Current, Richard. 1993. *Encyclopedia of the Confederacy*. New York: Simon and Schuster.

Current, Richard, T. Harry Williams, and Frank Freidel. 1961. *American History: A Survey*. New York: Alfred A. Knopf.

Damon, Henry. 1990. "A Florida Boy's Experience in Prison and in Escaping." In *Southern Historical Society Papers,* ed. J. William Jones, 395–402. Wilmington, NC: Broadfoot Publishing Company.

Davidson, Donald. 1946. *The Tennessee,* vol. 1. New York: Rinehart and Company.

Daviess, Maria. 1924. *History of Mercer and Boyle Counties*. Harrodburg, KY: Harrodsburg Herald.

Dee, Christine. 2006. *Ohio's War: The Civil War in Documents*. Athens: Ohio Univeristy Press.

DeLorme. 2004. *Tennessee Atlas and Gazetteer*. Yarmouth, ME: DeLorme.

———. 2005. *Kentucky Atlas and Gazetteer*. Yarmouth, ME: DeLorme.

Dorris, Jonathan. 1934. *Historic Madison County and Richmond, Kentucky*. Richmond: Richmond Daily Register Company.

Downer, Edward. 1961. *Ohio Troops in the Field*. Columbus: Ohio State University Press, Ohio Historical Society.

Dyer, Frederick. 1959a. *A Compendium of the War of the Rebellion,* vol. 1. New York: Thomas Yoseloff.

———. 1959b. *A Compendium of the War of the Rebellion,* vol. 2. New York: Thomas Yoseloff.

———. 1959c. *A Compendium of the War of the Rebellion,* vol. 3. New York: Thomas Yoseloff.

Earle, Carville. 2001. "Beyond the Appalachians, 1815–1860." In *North America: The Historical Geography of a Changing Continent,* ed. Thomas McIlwraith and Edward Muller, 165–88. Lanham, MD: Rowman and Littlefield.

Edwards, Marion. 1987. "Braley-Savage." In *Meigs County, Ohio,* vol. 2, ed. Meigs County Pioneer and Historical Society, 88. Salem, WV: Walsworth Publishing Company.

Elliott, James. 1962. *Transport to Disaster*. New York: Holt, Rinehart and Winston.

Ervin, Edgar. 1949. *Pioneer History of Meigs County, Ohio, to 1949.*

Evans, Clement. 1962. *Atlas to Accompany Confederate Military History*. New York: A. S. Barnes and Company.

Fain, John. 2004. *Sanctified Trial*. Knoxville: University of Tennessee Press.

Faust, Drew. 2008. *This Republic of Suffering: Death and the American Civil War*. New York: Alfred A. Knopf.

Faust, Patricia. 1986. *Historical Times Illustrated Encyclopedia of the Civil War*. New York: HarperPerennial.

Gallagher, Gary, Stephen Engle, Robert Krick, and Joseph Glatthaar. 2003. *The American Civil War.* Osceola, WI: Osprey Publishing.

Goodwin, Doris Kearns. 2005. *Team of Rivals.* New York: Simon and Schuster.

Grant, Ulysses. 1956. "We Will Hold the Town Till We Starve." In *Battles and Leaders of the Civil War,* ed. Ned Bradford, 445–72. New York: Appleton-Century-Crofts.

Guernsey, Alfred, and Henry Alden. 1866. *Harper's Pictorial History of the Great Rebellion in the United States.* New York: Harper and Brothers.

Hammond. 1993. *Hammond United States Atlas—Gemini Edition.* Maplewood, NJ: Hammond.

Harding, Leonard. 1967. "The Cincinnati Riots of 1862." *Bulletin of the Cincinnati Historical Society* 25 (4): 228–39.

Harper, Robert. 1961a. *Gallipolis, 1861–1865.* Columbus: Ohio State University Press, Ohio Civil War Centennial Commission.

———. 1961b. *Ohio Handbook of the Civil War.* Columbus: Ohio Historical Society, Ohio Civil War Centennial Commission.

Harrison, Lowell, and James Klotter. 1997. *New History of Kentucky.* Lexington: University Press of Kentucky.

Hart, John Fraser. 1976. *The South.* New York: D. Van Nostrand Company.

Hayth, Ruth. 1987. "The Tuckerman Family." In *Meigs County, Ohio,* vol. 2, ed. Meigs County Pioneer and Historical Society, 331–32. Salem, WV: Walsworth Publishing Company.

Herr, John, and Edward Wallace. 1953. *The Story of the U.S. Cavalry, 1775–1942.* Boston: Little, Brown and Company.

Hoeflich, Charlene. 1972. "Capt. McKnight Died This Day." *Pomeroy Daily Sentinel,* June 11.

Holcomb, Julie. 2004. *Southern Sons, Northern Soldiers.* Dekalb: Northern Illinois University Press.

Horwitz, Lester. 2001. *The Longest Raid of the Civil War.* Cincinnati, OH: Farmcourt Publishing.

Howe, Henry. 1908. *Historical Collections of Ohio in Two Volumes.* Cincinnati, OH: C. J. Krehbiel and Company.

Hudson, John. 2002. *Across This Land.* Baltimore, MD: Johns Hopkins University Press.

International Bible Society. 1984. *Holy Bible, New International Version.* Grand Rapids, MI: Zondervan Publishing.

Jackson, W. Sherman. 1980. "Emancipation, Negrophobia and Civil War Politics in Ohio, 1863–1865." *Journal of Negro History* 65 (3): 250–60.

Johnson, Martha. 1979. "Rodney F. Downing." In *Meigs County, Ohio,* vol. 1, ed. Meigs County Pioneer and Historical Society, 135. Dallas, TX: Taylor Publishing Company.

Johnston, Mary. 2001. "Raymond C. Johnston Family." In *Meigs County, Ohio*, vol. 3, ed. Meigs County Pioneer and Historical Society, 117–18. Waynesville, NC: County Heritage.

Jones, Robert. 1962. *Ohio Agriculture during the Civil War.* Columbus: Ohio State University Press, Ohio Historical Society.

Katcher, Philip. 1992. *The Civil War Source Book.* New York: Facts on File.

Keifer, Joseph. 2004. *Civil War Regiments from Ohio.* Pensacola, FL: eBooksOnDisk.com.

Kleber, John. 1992. *The Kentucky Encyclopedia.* Lexington: Kentucky Bicentennial Commission, University Press of Kentucky.

Klement, Frank. 1960. *Copperheads in the Middle West.* Chicago: University of Chicago Press.

———. 1977. "Sound and Fury: Civil War Dissent in the Cincinnati Area." *Cincinnati Historical Society Bulletin* 35: 98–114.

Larkin, Stillman. 1982. *The Pioneer History of Meigs County, Ohio.* Defiance, OH: Hubbard Company.

Lefavor, W. E. 1995. "No. 145." In *The Camp Fire,* vol. 1, ed. William Middleswarth and Margaret Daniels, 98. Pomeroy, OH: Meigs County Pioneer and Historical Society.

Lewis, Thomas. 1928. *History of Southeastern Ohio and the Muskingum Valley, 1788–1928.* Chicago: S. J. Clarke Publishing Company.

Linderman, Gerald. 1987. *Embattled Courage.* New York: Free Press.

Manning, Chandra. 2007. *What This Cruel War Was Over: Soldiers, Slavery, and The Civil War.* New York: Alfred A. Knopf.

McClintock, Megan. 1996. "Civil War Pensions and the Reconstruction of Union Families." *Journal of American History* 83 (2): 456–80.

McDonald, Michael, and John Muldowny. 1982. *TVA and the Dispossessed.* Knoxville: University of Tennessee Press.

McDonough, James. 1994. *War in Kentucky.* Knoxville: University of Tennessee Press.

McPherson, James. 1997. *For Cause and Comrades: Why Men Fought in the Civil War.* New York: Oxford University Press.

Meigs County Pioneer and Historical Society, Inc. 1982. *Meigs County, Ohio, from Hardesty's Historical and Geographical Encyclopedia, 1883.* Defiance, OH: Hubbard Company.

Miller, David. 2001. *The Illustrated Directory of Uniforms, Weapons, and Equipment of the Civil War.* Osceola, WI: MBI Publishing Company.

Miller, William. 2004. *Great Maps of the Civil War.* Nashville, TN: Rutledge Hill Press.

Mitchell, Reid. 1988. *Civil War Soldiers.* New York: Viking Penguin.

———. 1993. *The Vacant Chair.* New York: Oxford University Press.

Morsberger, Robert, and Katherine Morsberger. 1980. *Lew Wallace: Militant Romantic*. New York: McGraw-Hill.
Murdock, Eugene. 1963. *Ohio's Bounty System in the Civil War.* Columbus: Ohio State University Press, Ohio Historical Society.
National Archives and Records Service. 1963a. *Population Schedules of the Eighth Census, 1860*. Washington, DC: General Services Administration. Record Group 653, Microfilm Roll 1008.
———. 1963b. *Population Schedules of the Ninth Census, 1870*. Washington, DC: General Services Administration. Record Group 593, Microfilm Roll 1242.
National Cemetery Administration. N.d. *Camp Nelson National Cemetery*. Nicholasville, KY: National Cemetery Administration.
Nelson, Urias. 1995. "No. 42." In *The Camp Fire,* vol. 1, ed. William Middleswarth and Margaret Daniels, 26–27. Pomeroy, OH: Meigs County Pioneer and Historical Society.
Nicholas, Ron. 2000. "Mill Springs: The First Battle for Kentucky." In *The Civil War in Kentucky,* ed. Kent Brown, 47–78. Mason City, IA: Savas Publishing Company.
Nofi, Albert. 1992. *A Civil War Treasury*. Conshohocken, PA: Combined Books.
Northen, Charles. 2003. *All Right, Let Them Come*. Knoxville: University of Tennessee Press.
Pearson, Brooks. 2005. "Comparative Accuracy in Four Civil War Maps of the Shenandoah Valley: A GIS Analysis." *Professional Geographer* 57: 376–94.
Peter, Robert. 1882. *History of Fayette County, Kentucky*. Chicago: O. L. Baskin and Company.
Pickenpaugh, Roger. 2007. *Camp Chase and the Evolution of Union Prison Policy*. Tuscaloosa: University of Alabma Press.
Poe, Orlando. 1991. "The Defense of Knoxville." In *Battles and Leaders of the Civil War,* vol. 3, ed. Robert Johnson and Clarence Buel, 731–45. New York: Castle Books.
Poore, Ben. 1882. *The Life and Public Services of Ambrose E. Burnside, Soldier-Citizen-Statesman*. Providence, RI: J. A. and R. A. Reid.
Prichard, James. 1981. "Champion of the Union: George D. Prentice and the Secession Crisis in Kentucky." *Cincinnati Historical Society Bulletin* 39: 113–25.
Raitz, Karl, Nancy O'Malley, Dick Gilbreath, and Jeff Levy. 2008. *Kentucky's Frontier Trails: Warrior's Path, Boone's Trace, and Wilderness Road*. Lexington: University of Kentucky Press.
Ramage, James. 1986. *Rebel Raider: The Life of General John Hunt Morgan*. Lexington: University of Kentucky Press.
Randall, J. G., and David Donald. 1969. *The Civil War and Reconstruction*. Lexington, MA: D. C. Heath and Company.

REFERENCES

Rankin, R. C. 1881. *History of the Seventh Ohio Volunteer Cavalry.* Ripley, OH: J. C. Newcomb, Printer.

Reid, Whitlaw. 1895a. *Ohio in the War,* vol. 1. Cincinnati, OH: Robert Clarke Company.

———. 1895b. *Ohio in the War,* vol. 2. Cincinnati, OH: Robert Clarke Company.

Remini, Robert. 1991. *Henry Clay: Statesman for the Union.* New York: W. W. Norton.

Richards, Sarah. 2003. *Civil War Sites.* Guilford, CT: Globe Pequot Press.

Robinson, John. 1995. "No. 34." In *The Camp Fire,* vol. 1, ed. William Middleswarth and Margaret Daniels, 20. Pomeroy, OH: Meigs County Pioneer and Historical Society.

Roseboom, Eugene. 1952. "Southern Ohio and the Union in 1863." *Mississippi Valley Historical Review* 39 (1): 29–44.

Roster Commission. 1886a. *Official Roster of the Soldiers of the State of Ohio in the War of the Rebellion, 1861–1866,* vol. 2. Cincinnati, OH: Wilstach, Baldwin and Company.

———. 1886b. *Official Roster of the Soldiers of the State of Ohio in the War of the Rebellion, 1861–1866,* vol. 3. Cincinnati: Ohio Valley Publishing and Manufacturing Company.

———. 1887a. *Official Roster of the Soldiers of the State of Ohio in the War of the Rebellion, 1861–1866,* vol. 4. Akron, OH: Werner Printing and Lithography Company.

———. 1887b. *Official Roster of the Soldiers of the State of Ohio in the War of the Rebellion, 1861–1866,* vol. 5. Akron, OH: Werner Printing and Lithography Company.

———. 1888a. *Official Roster of the Soldiers of the State of Ohio in the War of the Rebellion, 1861–1866,* vol. 6. Akron, OH: Werner Printing and Lithography Company.

———. 1888b. *Official Roster of the Soldiers of the State of Ohio in the War of the Rebellion, 1861–1866,* vol. 7. Cincinnati: Ohio Valley Press.

———. 1888c. *Official Roster of the Soldiers of the State of Ohio in the War of the Rebellion, 1861–1866,* vol. 8. Cincinnati: Ohio Valley Press.

———. 1889a. *Official Roster of the Soldiers of the State of Ohio in the War of the Rebellion, 1861–1866,* vol. 9. Cincinnati: Ohio Valley Press.

———. 1889b. *Official Roster of the Soldiers of the State of Ohio in the War of the Rebellion, 1861–1866,* vol. 10. Cincinnati: Ohio Valley Company.

———. 1891. *Official Roster of the Soldiers of the State of Ohio in the War of the Rebellion, 1861–1866,* vol. 11. Akron, OH: Werner Printing and Lithography Company.

Rowell, John. 1971. *Yankee Cavalrymen.* Knoxville: University of Tennessee Press.

Sanders, Charles. 2005. *While in the Hands of the Enemy*. Baton Rouge: Louisiana State University Press.

Sanger, Donald. 1952. *James Longstreet*. Baton Rouge: Louisiana State University Press.

Sears, Richard. 2002. *Camp Nelson, Kentucky*. Lexington: University of Kentucky Press.

Seymour, Digby. 1963. *Divided Loyalties*. Knoxville: University of Tennessee Press.

Sheehan-Dean, Aaron. 2007. *Why Confederates Fought: Family and Nation in Civil War Virginia*. Chapel Hill: University of North Carolina Press.

Shriver, Phillip, and Donald Breen. 1964. *Ohio's Military Prisons in the Civil War*. Columbus: Ohio State University Press, Ohio Historical Society.

Sifakis, Stewart. 1988. *Who Was Who in the Union*. New York: Facts on File.

Simon, John. 2000. "Lincoln, Grant, and Kentucky in 1861." In *The Civil War in Kentucky*, ed. Kent Brown, 1–22. Mason City, IA: Savas Publishing Company.

Smith, David. 1986. "Military History." In *Broken Hearts, Broken Lives: Jefferson County, Tennessee, 1860–1868*, ed. Sandra Wilson and Dennis Snapp, 12–43. Jefferson City, TN: Jefferson Printing Company.

Smith, Ross. 1930. *Reminiscences of an Old Timer*. Johnson City, TN: privately published.

Starr, Stephen. 1961. "Camp Dennison, 1861–1865." *Bulletin of the Historical and Philosophical Society of Ohio* 19 (3): 166–90.

Sutherland, Daniel. 1996. *A Very Violent Rebel*. Knoxville: University of Tennessee Press.

Sutherland, Jonathan. 2002. *Commanders and Heroes of the American Civil War*. Shrewsbury, UK: Airlife Publishing.

Swanson, Mark. 2004. *Atlas of the Civil War*. Athens: University of Georgia Press.

Tarbuck, Edward, and Frederick Lutgens. 1992. *The Earth*. New York: Macmillan Publishing Company.

Thomas, Edison. 1985. *John Hunt Morgan and His Raiders*. Lexington: University of Kentucky Press.

Trester, Delmer. 1950. "The Political Career of David Tod." Ph.D. dissertation, Ohio State University, Columbus.

———. 1953. "David Tod and the Gubernatorial Campaign of 1844." *Ohio History* 62: 162–78.

Tucker, Louis. 1962. *Cincinnati during the Civil War*. Columbus: Ohio State University Press, Ohio Historical Society.

United States Bureau of the Census. 1864. *Eighth Census of the United States, 1860*. Washington, DC: Government Printing Office.

United States Bureau of the Census. 1872. *Ninth Census of the United States, 1870*. Washington, DC: Government Printing Office.

Van Deusen, Glyndon. 1937. *The Life of Henry Clay*. Boston: Little, Brown and Company.

Wagner, Margaret, Gary Gallagher, and Paul Finkelman. 2002. *Civil War Desk Reference*. New York: Simon and Schuster.

War of the Rebellion: A Compilation of the Official Records of the Union and Confederate Armies (OR). 1880–1901. 128 vols. Washington, DC: Government Printing Office.

Weisenburger, Francis. 1963. *Columbus during the Civil War*. Columbus: Ohio State University Press, Ohio Historical Society.

Weitz, Mark. 2005. *More Damning than Slaughter*. Lincoln: University of Nebraska Press.

Wesley, Charles. 1962. *Ohio Negroes in the Civil War*. Columbus: Ohio State University Press, Ohio Historical Society.

Wexler, Alan. 1995. *Atlas of Westward Expansion*. New York: Facts on File.

Wheeler, Joseph. 1991. "Bragg's Invasion of Kentucky." In *Battles and Leaders of the Civil War*, vol. 3, ed. Robert Johnson and Clarence Buel, 1–25. New York: Castle Books.

Wheeler, Kenneth. 1998. *For the Union*. Columbus: Ohio State University Press.

Whitman, Walt. 1963. "Releas'd Union Prisoners from South." In *Prose Works, 1892*. Vol. 1, *Specimen Days*, 100–101. Ed. Floyd Stovall. New York: New York University Press.

Woodbury, Augustus. 1867. *Major General Ambrose E. Burnside and the Ninth Army Corps*. Providence, RI: Sidney S. Rider and Brother.

Woodward, W. E. 1928. *Meet General Grant*. New York: Horace Liverlight.

Woodworth, Steven. 1995. *Leadership and Command in the American Civil War*. Campbell, CA: Savas Woodbury Publishers.

———. 1996. *The American Civil War*. Westport, CT: Greenwood Press.

———. 1998. *The Art of Command in the Civil War*. Lincoln: University of Nebraska Press.

———. 2005. *Nothing but Victory*. New York: Alfred A. Knopf.

Wormser, Richard. 1966. *The Yellowlegs*. New York: Doubleday and Company.

Zornow, William. 1961. "Clement L. Vallandigham and the Democratic Party in 1864." *Bulletin of the Historical and Philosophical Society of Ohio* 19: 21–37.

Index

American House Hotel, 21, 217n9
Andersonville Prison, 139, 141, 191, 245nn63–64, 246n68, 247n72, 258n13
Andrews, E., 4, 72
Andrews, Robert, 4, 72, 243n50
Angelico Mountains, 124, 240n12
Antietam, 9
Appomattox, 9
Arlington National Cemetery, 242n37
Ashby, H. M., 75, 229n94
Athens, OH, 216
Atlanta, GA, 191
Atlanta Campaign, 190
Austin, Alonzo, 243n45

Babel, John, 176, 256n26
Batchel, Peter, 131, 243n40
Bean Station, battle of, 122, 247
Becker, Carl, 10
Belle Isle, VA, 250n102
Benjamin, Judah Philip, 121
Big Creek, 136, 244n61
Big Hill, 64
Bighill, KY, 225n64
Bishop, Ella, 219n7. *See also* Camp Ella Bishop
bivouac, 132, 243n42
Bluegrass, 116, 239n22
Blue Springs, battle of, 5, 122, 132, 242n36, 243n41, 243n43, 243n50, 244n53
Boone, Daniel, 241n25
"Boots and Saddles," 78, 230n04
Bragg, Braxton, 52, 61, 108, 146, 148, 170, 221n24, 223n41, 229n94, 237n8, 255n14
Braley, Addison, 7
Braley, Alexander, 7
Braley, Cynthia, 6, 213n46
Braley, Elliott, 168, 173, 230n103, 255n22
Braley, Janett, 173, 183, 230n103
Braley, Ruel, 6, 213n46
bridges, 94, 233n132, 234n134
Brough, John, 249n97, 252n118
Brown, Sam, 169

Brunker, Thomas, 60, 83, 89–90, 99, 103, 129, 153, 216–17n5
Buffington Island, 139, 237n11
Burbridge, Stephen, 13
Burns, William, 4, 72, 244n52
Burnside, Ambrose, 11, 94, 108, 122, 124, 127, 144, 234n136, 234n139, 235n149, 238n18, 246n69, 247–48nn79–80, 251n112, 252n123, 253n130
Burnside's rifle, 118, 143, 239n25, 247n77
bushwhackers, 62, 127, 225n56
butternut(s), 75–76, 95, 229n95, 238n18

Camp Chase, 109, 225n60, 226n69, 229n97, 246n70
Camp Dennison, 20, 163, 217n6, 235n150, 243n44
Camp Dick Robinson, 52, 76, 81, 223n38
Camp Ella Bishop, 35, 39, 219n7. *See also* Bishop, Ella
Camp Nelson, 116, 153, 230n106, 233n132, 239n20
Camp Pomeroy, 216n4
Camp Riley, 18, 33
Campbell, James, 153, 251n110
Carpenter, Daniel, 122
Carr, Hiram, 134, 143, 151, 155, 244n52, 245n67
Carroll, Andrew, 3
Chancellorsville, battle of, 9
Chapder, Robert, 138, 246n68
Chattanooga, Tennessee, 169, 191
Chickamauga, battle of, 9
Christian Commission, 158–59, 252n121
Cincinnati, OH, 8, 10, 152–53, 171, 230n105, 230n107
Clay, Henry, 44, 50, 68, 221n23, 222n33
Cleveland, OH, 8
Clinch River, 125–26, 141, 156, 240n16, 241n20, 251n115
Cluke, Roy, 35, 224n48, 225n58
Columbus, OH, 8, 229n97
Combs, Leslie, 48, 222n30
Company K, 11, 18, 33, 39, 40, 191

267

confederacy, 127, 148–49
Copperheads, 116, 238n16. *See also* Vallandigham, Clement
cotton, 96
Coulter, Warren, 131, 151, 160, 243n40, 249n101, 252n125, 253n129
Covington, KY, 153, 162, 251n109
Crab Orchard, KY, 54–55, 63, 64, 74–76, 110, 118, 224n44
Crittenden, George, 235n148
Cumberland Gap, 122, 126–28, 147, 240n10, 241nn21–25, 252n123
Cumberland River, 60, 81, 116, 224n51, 252n123
Cynthiana, KY, 8, 13–14, 17, 168, 187–90, 215n96, 216n114, 257n41, 257n44

Damon, Henry, 215n96
Dandridge, TN, 151, 248n84
Davis, Jefferson, 38, 121, 191, 220n13, 236n150
Dayton, OH, 8
Dennison, James, 99, 234n142
Dennison, William, 8–9, 217n6
desertion, 4, 46, 72, 76, 131, 141, 153, 212n23, 221n25, 225n59, 232n119, 234–35n144, 241n26
diarrhea, 144, 146, 248n83
Dixie, 121, 123, 240n9
"Do They Miss Me at Home?" 27, 218n21. *See also* Grannis, S. M.
Downing, Rodney, 147, 249n91
draft, 9, 104, 181, 214n60, 236n154, 256n33. *See also* quota
Dutton Hill, battle of, 228n89, 229n95
duty, 4, 22, 47, 212n19, 220n15, 222n26. *See also* honor
Dyke, Amos, 138, 147, 149, 151, 246n70

east Tennessee, 121–22, 125, 139, 147–48, 165, 167, 172, 220n18, 235n148, 238n15, 240–42 passim, 247n79, 249n06
East Tennessee & Virginia Railroad, 131, 242n34, 243n38
Edmundson, Jesse, 182, 252n124, 256n34
Elshire, James, 162, 253n127
Enfield Rifle, 67, 69, 73, 140, 227n76
Entsminger, Asher, 123, 232n123

Entsminger, Emma, 7
Entsminger, Jane, 213n46
Entsminger, Martin, 7

faith, 4, 5, 79, 99, 147, 159
First Illinois Light Artillery, 254n10
First Kentucky Cavalry, 228n84, 230n99. *See also* Wolford, Frank
First Louisiana Cavalry. *See* Scott, John
Foose, John, 81, 136, 138, 143, 231n110
Foose, Sam, 151, 250n102
Forrest, Nathan Bedford, 232n118
Fort Higley, 154, 251n112
Fort Sanders, 154, 248n80, 251n112
Fort Sumter, 8
Forty-fourth Ohio Infantry, 227n80
Forty-fifth Ohio Infantry, 64, 225n60
Foster, John, 148, 247n79, 249n93
Fourth Kentucky Cavalry. *See* Giltner, Henry; Second East Tennessee Cavalry
Frankfort, KY, 254n7
Franklin, TN, battle of, 190
Fredricksburg, battle of, 9
French leave, 99, 125, 234–35n144
furlough, 8, 63, 70, 79, 225n59

Gallagher, Gary, 3
Gallipolis, OH, 10, 18, 217nn7–9
Garfield, James, 9
Garrard, Israel, 56, 122, 138, 142, 145, 162, 215n98, 224n46, 229n96, 243n46, 246n67, 246n69
General Order No. 38, 238n18
Gettysburg, 9, 16, 35, 233n125
Geyer, John, 217n11
Gillmore, Quincy Adams, 11, 70, 75, 228n84
Giltner, Henry, 244–45nn60–61, 245n66, 257n44. *See also* Fourth Kentucky Cavalry; Second East Tennessee Cavalry
Granger, Robert, 40, 220n16
Grannis, S. M., 218n21. *See also* "Do They Miss Me at Home?"
Grant, Ulysses S., 9, 16, 35–36, 88, 170, 180, 191, 232–33n125, 250–51n108, 252n123, 255n14, 256n31
Green, Solomon, 157, 252n120

Haley, James, 163, 234n141
Halliday, Alexander, 254n5
Halliday, John, 254n5

Halliday, Will, 8, 183
Hanes, S. S., 181, 235n145
Harper, Duston, 136, 138, 191, 245n63
Harrison, Benjamin, 9
Harrison, Evalyn, 192
Harrison, Lowell, 37, 108
Harrodsburg, KY, 224n49
Hartley, William, 14, 168, 188, 257n42
Hayes, Rutherford, 9
Hayes, Susan, 258n15
Hayth, Ruth, 14, 16, 258n14
Hickman Bridge, 91, 233n132
Higley, Brewster, 221n22. *See also* "Home on the Range"
Higley, Joel, 5, 17, 42, 60, 78, 85, 122, 132–34, 160, 165, 221n22, 243n50, 244n51, 244n53, 251n112, 252n124, 253n130
Higley, Mary, 147, 153, 221n22
Higley's Sugar Camp, 52, 223n39
Holston River, 126, 135–36, 156, 240n17, 241n20, 244n56
"Home on the Range," 221n22. *See also* Higley, Brewster
honor, 4, 221n22. *See also* duty
Horwitz, Lester, 13, 221n24, 237n12
Howard, C. O., 216n4
Hoyt, Alonzo, 129, 242n32
Hoyt, Royal, 129, 136, 138, 191, 245n64, 246n68

Jenkins, Morgan, 62, 225n55
"Jim Fisk," 230n102
Johnson, Donald, 139
Johnson, James, 8, 233n126
Johnson, William Lemon, 136–42, 247n72
Johnston, Mary, 14, 16
Jones, William, 244nn60–61, 245n66

Kanawha River, 20, 217n7
Kennedy, Henry, 192
Kentucky: landscape, 51–52, 59, 223n40; neutrality, 36–37, 219nn5–6; strategic locations, 36–37
Kentucky River, 66
Klotter, James, 37, 108
Knoxville National Cemetery, 165–66, 253n130
Knoxville, TN, 119, 144, 148, 151, 161, 165, 179, 239n26, 241n24, 247n80, 251n112

Langsville, OH, 6, 16, 108, 176, 183, 193–94, 217n10, 219n26, 237n12, 256n25
Leading Creek, 51, 223n37
Leaper, John, 80, 152, 231n109, 232n120
Lee, Robert E., 9, 16, 191
letters: Civil War, 1, 3, 87, 91, 211nn1–2, 211–12nn8–11; homesickness, 1, 179; loneliness, 18, 179; number of, 1
Lewis, Charles, 143, 232n117
Lexington, KY, 80, 166, 218n23, 219n7
Lexington National Cemetery, 222n33
Libby Prison, 141
likeness, 3, 4, 30, 41, 43, 93, 152, 173, 183
Lincoln, Abraham, 8, 36, 216n114, 235–36n150, 251n108
Linderman, Gerald, 3
Little, Levi, 122, 133–34, 147, 160, 243n50, 244n51, 252n125, 253n129
Logan, Dan, 177, 256n28
Longstreet, James, 122, 141, 146, 150, 152, 248–49n90
Lookout Mountain, 170, 255n12
Loundon, TN, 240; Loudon bridge, 125–26
Lyle, Hannah Jane, 254n3

Macon, Georgia, 191
Magoffin, Beriah, 37
Mammoth Cave, 60–61, 225n54
McBurns, William, 134, 244n52
McCann, Patrick, 150, 218n22
McCasky, Joseph, 153, 219n29
McClintock, Megan, 6, 213n41
McDowell, Malcolm, 222n29
McIntire, James, 142, 247n74
McKay, John, 79, 230n107
McKinley, William, 9
McKnight collection, 3
McKnight, Francis, 257n36
McKnight, Jane, 6
McKnight, John, 146, 157, 168, 180, 189
McKnight, Leila, 41, 151, 174, 182–83, 192
McKnight, Lettie, 41, 151, 192–93
McKnight, Martha, 8, 107, 111, 194, 237n6, 258n15
McKnight, Mary Lucy, 41, 193–94
McKnight, Myrtha, 8, 107, 111, 193–94, 237n6
McKnight, Samaria, 3, 5–7, 15, 168, 191, 193–94, 258n16

McKnight, Thomas (William's father), 4, 6, 167, 175
McKnight, Thomas (William's son), 48, 83, 151, 155, 174, 179, 182–83, 192
McKnight, William, 2, 6, 12, 17, 167–68, 189, 194, 215n98, 219n26, 238n18, 239n27, 246n71, 247n73, 255n23
McMaster, Lenox, 8, 231
McMaster, William, 8, 180, 228n90, 231n110, 233n131
Meaner, Isaac, 4, 92, 234n133
Meigs County, 6, 11–12, 16, 139, 193, 215n84, 217n10, 223n37, 237nn11–12, 238n19, 249n91, 255n23, 256n33
Metcalfe, Leonidas, 64, 226n65. *See also* Seventh Kentucky Cavalry
Middleport, OH, 18
Miles, David, 40, 220n17
Mill Springs, KY, 101, 235n148
Miner, George, 225n61, 233n129
Missionary Ridge, 9, 169, 254n11, 255nn14–15
Montgomery, Alabama, 191
Moore, Lester, 67, 227n77
Morgan, John Hunt, 14, 16, 45, 107–9, 112, 115, 168, 188, 190, 215n96, 221n24, 223n38, 233n131, 236n156, 237n8, 237–38nn11–14, 257n44
Mossy Creek, 158, 248n89, 252n122
Mount Sterling, KY, 69, 166, 225n58, 227n80, 228n83
Mount Vernon, KY, 225n63
mountain howitzer, 65, 227n72
Myers, Jonas, 219n29
Murfreesboro, TN, battle of, 9, 228n92

Nashville, Tennessee, 9, 11, 191
negroes, 80, 231n111, 238n16. *See also* slavery
Nelson, Isaac, 136, 138, 191, 245n64
Nelson, Urias, 231n112, 249n101
New Brunswick, Canada, 6
New Market, TN, 151, 248n82
New Mexico, 231n116
Nicholasville, KY, 225n57
Ninth Michigan, 143
Norton, Augustus, 75, 229n95

oath of allegiance, 127, 241n26
Ohio: agriculture, 10; in the war, 8, 214n62; manufacturing, 10

103rd Ohio Infantry, 130
116th Ohio Infantry, 246n68

Paducah, KY, 36, 148, 249n94
Paris, KY, 254nn7–8
Patterson, Alexander, 254n5
Pegram, John, 35, 101, 228n84, 228n86, 234n139, 235n149
pensions, 6
Peter, Robert, 223n34
photograph. *See* likeness
Pillow, Gideon, 36
Polk, Leonidas, 36
Pomeroy, OH, 6, 12, 233n131
poverty, 85, 102, 123, 172, 240n7, 255n21
Powell, Joseph, 193
Prichard, James, 37
prisoners of war, 226–27n70, 229n97
Pulaski, TN, 190

quota, 8. *See also* draft

Rankin, R.C., 3, 14, 190
Rathbun, Marion, 8, 218n25
rations, 44, 221n21
Rebels, 11, 17, 73, 75, 84, 91, 95, 115, 126–27, 130, 139, 190
Reid, Whitlaw, 3
Richmond, KY, 64, 225n62, 226nn65–66
Richmond, VA, 151, 250n102
Ripley, OH, 216n3
Robinson, John, 243n50
Rocky Gap, KY, 234n139
Rogersville, TN, battle of, 122, 135–37, 139, 142–43, 191, 231n112, 243n39, 244–46nn61–69, 247n72
roll call, 27
Rosecrans, William, 217n6, 237n8
Ross, George, 231n113
Runkle, Benjamin, 225n60, 229n96
Rupe, William, 133, 243n49
Rutland, OH, 217n10

Sanders, W. P., 105, 236n155
Sanders, William, 218n24
Santmyer, Joseph, 129, 211n9, 242n29
Sansbury, James, 168, 253n2
Sausbury, Franklin, 94, 223n35, 232n118
Savage, Benjamin, 232n117
Scott, John, 75, 226n65, 228n94
secessionist, 37–38, 220n14, 238n16

Second East Tennessee Cavalry, 122, 136–38, 244n60. *See also* Fourth Kentucky Cavalry; Giltner, Henry
Second Michigan Cavalry, 248n87
Second Tennessee Cavalry. *See* Ashby, H. M.
Second Ohio Infantry, 235n150
"seeing the elephant," 48, 222n32
Selma, Alabama, 190–91
Seminary Hospital Ward, 162, 253n128
Seventeenth Indiana Infantry, 236. *See also* John Wilder
Seventh Kentucky Cavalry, 226n65. *See also* Metcalfe, Leonidas
Seventh Ohio Volunteer Cavalry, 2, 10, 35, 72–73, 75, 122, 126, 136–37, 140–41, 145, 190–91, 215n98, 236n150, 239n24, 245n66, 246nn68–69, 247n73
Sherman, William, 9, 169, 190–91, 254n9
Shiloh, battle of, 9
Shiner, Henry, 136, 138, 191, 245n64, 256n32
Sidenstricker, Ellen, 7
Simpson, William, 156, 252n117
slavery, 217n11, 222n33, 231n114. *See also* negroes
Smith, G. Clay, 219n7
Smith, James, 80, 231n109
Smith, Kirby, 121, 226n65, 229n94
Smoky Mountains, 151, 250n104
Somerset, KY, 228n94
Spiers, George, 100, 235n146
Spires, Harry, 4, 25, 72, 132
Stanton, Edwin, 216n114
Stobart, James, 258n13
Sultana, 215n78
Sut Lovingood's Yarns, 114, 238n15
sutler, 110, 237n9, 250n108

Tazewell, TN, 241n22
Tecumseh, 222n31. *See also* Combs, Leslie
Tennessee River, 140, 148, 240n19
Tenth East Tennessee Confederate Infantry, 258n13

Tenth Ohio Volunteer Infantry, 132, 243n44
tents, 81
Thomas, George, 235n148
Tod, David, 10, 108, 149, 153, 249n97, 251n111
Train, Isaac, 152, 154, 250n107
Transylvania University, 223n34
Tuckerman, Fred, 193

United States Sanitary Commission, 154–55, 226n68, 251n113

Vallandigham, Clement, 238n16, 252n118. *See also* Copperheads
Vicksburg, MS, 4, 9, 16, 35, 74, 88, 150, 228n91, 233n125

Walker, William F., 136, 245n64
Walker, William T., 143
Warren, Nehemiah, 128, 242n31
Wells, Herold, 189, 257n46
West Virginia, 82, 217n7, 231n14
Whitman, Walt, 246n68
Wilder, John, 102, 236n150. *See also* Seventeenth Indiana Infantry
Wilderness Campaign, 256n31
Wilderness Road, 241n25
Willcox, Orlando, 130, 138, 228n84, 242n37
Williams, Orrellence, 136, 138, 151, 191, 245n64
Wilson, Theopolis, 74, 218n19, 255n13
Wiseman, John, 151, 160, 249n100, 253n127, 254n6
Wiseman, Zachariah, 78, 101, 147, 235n148, 254n6
Wolford, Frank, 77, 230n99, 235–36n150. *See also* First Kentucky Cavalry
Woodworth, Steven, 3

Zollicoffer, Felix, 36, 235n148
Zollicoffer, TN, 244n56